Leslie Fiedler
and
American Culture

Leslie Fiedler
and
American Culture

Edited by
Steven G. Kellman
and Irving Malin

DELAWARE

Newark: University of Delaware Press
London: Associated University Presses

Associated University Presses
440 Forsgate Drive
Cranbury, NJ 08512

Associated University Presses
16 Barter Street
London WC1A 2AH, England

Associated University Presses
P.O. Box 338, Port Credit
Mississauga, Ontario
Canada L5G 4L8

The paper used in this publication meets the requirements
of the American National Standard for Permanence of Paper
for Printed Library Materials Z39.48-1984.

Library of Congress Cataloging-in-Publication Data

Leslie Fiedler and American culture / edited by Steven G. Kellman and
Irving Malin.
    p.   cm.
    Includes index.
    ISBN 0-87413-689-X (alk. paper)
    1. Fiedler, Leslie A.—Criticism and interpretation.   2. National
characteristics, American—Historiography.   3. Criticism—United
States—History—20th century.   4. United States—Civilization—
Historiography.   5. Fiedler, Leslie A.—Views on culture.
6. Culture—Philosophy.   I. Kellman, Steven G., 1947–   .
II. Malin, Irving.
PS3556.I34Z76   1999
810.9—dc21   99-18961
                                                                  CIP

PRINTED IN THE UNITED STATES OF AMERICA

Contents

Introduction

By Steven G. Kellman

During a recent sojourn at the American Studies Center in Hyderabad, India, I was shown an extraordinary piece of furniture: what the devoted scholars who run the Center drolly call their Leslie Fiedler Chair. Hyderabad accomplishes much with limited resources, and during one of his two visits, the illustrious American critic donated an actual chair. Unlike the Samuel Clemens Chair that Fiedler has occupied for many years at SUNY Buffalo, the Leslie Fiedler Chair in Hyderabad is not intended to honor the sitter, merely provide a spot to put a butt. Yet it testifies to Fiedler's exalted standing worlds away from Newark, Missoula, and Buffalo, while it demonstrates that even learned folks still need a place to sit.

Even in his eighties, an aura of precocity lingers around Leslie Fiedler. Like *On Native Grounds*, the passionate, personal encounter with the literary tradition of the United States that Alfred Kazin published when he was only twenty-seven, Fiedler's *Love and Death in the American Novel* forever after altered the terms of the country's literary conversation. And it, too, seems a young man's book, the radiant thoughts of an author whose ardor has not yet been tempered by demands from a world oblivious to the whiteness of an imaginary whale. Yet Fiedler was already forty-three when, in 1960, he published the book that propelled him into the role of *enfant terrible* of American letters. It is true that *Love and Death*, as Emerson noted about the first edition of *Leaves of Grass*, "had a long foreground somewhere, for such a start"; its germination is already evident in the bravura essay "Come Back to the Raft Ag'in, Huck Honey!" first published back in 1948 in *Partisan Review*. But, just as Tolstoy endures in the image of the aging sage of Yasnaya Polanye, Fiedler seems destined to play the perpetual role of academic Peter Pan, the evergreen insurgent who never grew old, if not up. He even outlasted the Bolshevik Revolution, which occurred a few months after his birth, on March 8, 1917.

Fiedler's career—as critic, teacher, fiction writer, and lecturer—has been a series of provocations. Though Kenneth Rexroth once attacked him for "his membership in a small circle of extremely ethnocentric people—the self-styled New York Establishment," Fiedler has in fact performed the part of outrageous outlander, one who finds his secret self among Jews, freaks, Blackfeet, and other vanishing Americans. He has exerted an enormous influence on two or three generations of literary critics, but Fiedler, who redefines himself and his subject with each bold book, might well echo Thoreau's exemplary refusal to be exemplary: "I would not have anyone adopt *my* mode of living on any account; for, beside that before he has fairly learned it I may have found out another for myself, I desire that there may be as many different persons in the world as possible." When he departed Missoula, Montana, in 1965, after twenty-three years in an intellectual wilderness that encouraged the wildness in himself, it was to move to Buffalo, a town that only the postal service and a snooty California poet would identify as New York.

During a review of *A Fiedler Reader* (1977) and *Freaks* (1978), Alison Lurie, a novelist and specialist in children's literature, faulted Fiedler for childish failings: "overstatement, restlessness, and egotism." But many others have responded positively to the breadth, bravado, and intimacy found in Fiedler's writings. For them, he has been the gadfly that quickened the rasping nag of literary studies. Calling him "a redskin most at home in white clown makeup," Gore Vidal, a scourge of pallid pedantry, described Fiedler as "America's liveliest full-time professor and seducer of the *Zeitgeist*."

Fiedler's timing has always seemed precocious. While men of his age still wore hats, he was both stretching and relaxing the diction of literary discourse. He was challenging the canon when the proper reaction was still reverence. He was practicing cultural studies and gender studies without a license, reading American Indian literature and science fiction when to do so was raffish. Polyglot and polymath, Fiedler confounded categorical minds by writing about Edgar Rice Burroughs, Margaret Mitchell, and Olaf Stapledon with the same intensity he devoted to Dante, Donne, and Shakespeare. The seducer of the *Zeitgeist* was ahead of his time, but he also defined and clocked it. An ageless child of the century, he has become one of its venerable ancients.

To mark the start of Fiedler's ninth decade, Irving Malin and I have assembled this volume. The contributions, most of which were written expressly for this project, are organized into three

sections. The first consists of statements by Fiedler himself, including a recent self-assessment—on the occasion of receiving the
Hubbell Award—as well as a reprint of his most influential essay.
The second section collects essays that analyze Fiedler's writings,
examining him as more than just the author of *Love and Death in
the American Novel* and *The Return of the Vanishing American;* among
the subjects studied are Fiedler's literature textbook, his memoir,
his fiction, and his studies of science fiction, of archetype, and of
Shakespeare. The final section of this volume consists of tributes,
by some who have known him personally and by others who testify
to extended acquaintance with an extraordinary author's formidable work.

Chronology

1917	March 8, Leslie Aaron Fiedler born in Newark, New Jersey
1938	B.A., New York University
1939	M.A., University of Wisconsin, Madison
	Marries Margaret Shipley
1941	Ph.D., University of Wisconsin, Madison
1941–42	Assistant professor of English, University of Montana
1942	Enlists United States Naval Reserve
1946	Discharged from U.S. Naval Reserve with a rank of lieutenant junior grade
1946–47	Rockefeller Fellow, Harvard University
1947–48	Assistant professor of English, University of Montana
1948	"Come Back to the Raft Ag'in, Huck Honey!" published in *Partisan Review*
1948–52	Associate professor of English, University of Montana
1951–53	Fulbright lecturer, Universities of Rome and Bologna
1953–64	Professor of English, University of Montana
1954–56	Chairman, Department of English, University of Montana
1955	*An End to Innocence*
1956	As Heavy Runner, named a chief of the Blackfoot Indian tribe
1958	*The Art of the Essay*
1956–57	Christian Gauss Lecturer, Princeton University
1960	*Love and Death in the American Novel*
	No! In Thunder
1961–62	Fulbright lecturer, University of Athens
1963	*The Second Stone*
	Pull Down Vanity and Other Stories
1964	*Waiting for the End*
	The Continuing Debate (with Jacob Vinocur)
1965	Professor of English, State University of New York at Buffalo
	Back to China

11

1966   *The Last Jew in America*
          Love and Death in the American Novel, revised edition
1967   Arrested on charge of maintaining premises where
          marijuana used
1967–68   Visiting professor, University of Sussex
1968   *The Return of the Vanishing American*
1969   Associate Fellow, Calhoun College, Yale University
          Being Busted
          Nude Croquet and Other Stories
1970–71   Guggenheim Fellowship
1971   Visiting professor, University of Vincennes
          The Collected Essays
1972   Drug conviction reversed
          Named Samuel L. Clemens Professor, SUNY Buffalo
          The Stranger in Shakespeare
          Cross the Border—Close the Gap
          Divorces Margaret Shipley
1973   Marries Sally Smith Andersen
1974   *The Messengers Will Come No More*
1975   *In Dreams Awake*
1977   *The Leslie Fiedler Reader*
1978   *Freaks: Myths and Images of the Secret Self*
1979   *The Inadvertent Epic*
1981   *English Literature: Opening Up the Canon* (with Houston
          Baker, Jr.)
1982   *What Was Literature?*
1983   *Olaf Stapledon: A Man Divided*
1991   *Fiedler on the Roof: Essays on Literature and Jewish Identity*
1996   *Tyranny of the Normal: Essays on Bioethics, Theology and
          Myth*
1998   National Book Critics Circle Ivan Sandrof Lifetime
          Achievement Award

Anthropophagi

R. H. W. DILLARD

With their heads tucked into their vests
    Our friends, the everyday scholars,
Frost, Snow, or Williwaw, note the literary "best"
    In perfect harmony with their peers, but must
Nonetheless stand in awe of Leslie Fiedler
    Who has actually read it all, all
Of it, the good, the bad, the wheedlers,
    The whiners, the bold and visionary,
With something worth saying to say
    About them all, and not something
We've already read somewhere else. Okay,
    I know that he's often out of step,
Inaccurate on occasion, or even downright
    Duplicitous (eh, Huck honey?),
That he can with no effort stir up a fight
    And be exiled to the children's table
At the Banquet of the Great, but, hey,
    The man's a writer, read his poems,
Or read a novel, *The Second Stone* say,
    So funny and smart and just plain good
That I gave it a vote for the Faulkner Prize
    (I was a judge) in 1963, although
I knew that Pynchon's *V.*, no surprise,
    Would win the award (Fiedler was Fiedler
Already; Pynchon was Promise), but I needed
    That vote on my conscience (not off it),
A tip of my hat in private, though defeated,
    To the prodigious feats (that's Hitchcock,
The 39 Steps, if you don't get it), fictive
    And creative of this literary Mr. Memory
Who remembers with a skill apparently instinctive
    Everything he's ever read (or maybe he just

13

Takes good notes, who knows?) and knows how
      And when to use it to bowl the reader over
Or, as in the novel I mentioned just now,
      The Second Stone (the epigraphs),
To break the reader up. The only other
      Person I've ever known to read and remember
So very much (and he's certainly no brother
      To Fiedler, but can I help it, who I know?)
Is Colin Wilson, and that's another story.
      But here's my point, those anthropophagi
I mentioned, those devotees of a priori
      Criticism, those ideologues and theory
Touters with their heads buried in their chests,
      Should take note of Fiedler and just look up,
Should (as Vivian de Sola Pinto, unimpressed
      By a visiting lecturer at Nottingham,
Once shouted out, "Read the book, sir, read
      The book!") read the book! Read the books,
Not just the books "about" the books, screeds
      Of continental garble, read Poe,
Actually read him, read Twain, read Robinson,
      Read the women and the men, like Fiedler
Read everything from Shakespeare to Stapledon,
      And read them well, not just to fit a template
Or make a point dozens have already made.
      Talk about preaching to the converted:
Post-structuralism [or insert here your own fad
      Of choice] makes the grimmest cult,
New Nikes on every foot, look positively free.
      And I guess I've made my own point as well,
That I honor Leslie Fiedler and will be
      Always indebted to him, his insight, his wit,
His wisdom, but this seems like a good place for a tale,
      A true one, one that goes back to 1966
When I was emceeing a reading for *The Girl
      In the Black Raincoat*, George Garrett's
Amazing anthology (see if you can find it
      In a used book store, the Fiedler story
"Four Academic Parables," to my mind, is
      Worth the price alone), while high above,
Locked in low clouds and drifting fog,
      Leslie Fiedler circled (we could hear the plane

As it groped by, time and again), the audience agog,
    A group reading and going well, a rock band
And go-go girls, quite an event, but everyone aware
    Of Fiedler curving overhead. Then suddenly
At the door the lost traveller appeared, every hair
    In place, with the rosiest cheeks I've ever seen
On a man, the brightest eyes, clearly having a ball.
    The room arose as one and burst
Into standing applause. So should we all.

Leslie Fiedler
and
American Culture

Part I

Hubbell Acceptance Speech

LESLIE FIEDLER

Churlish as it may seem, I propose today—before thanking you properly—to reflect a little on the ironies implicit in your giving me this award. Let me begin by making it clear that unlike most of you and those you have thus honored before, I am not a professional scholar specializing in American literature, but an unreconstructed amateur, a dilettante who stumbled accidentally into your area of expertise. I have, as you are surely aware, never been a member of the American Literature Section of the MLA. Indeed, if my failing flesh had permitted me to attend this luncheon, it would have been the first time I have ever attended one.

This is not, let me assure you, out of mere snobbishness, but because I would have felt an interloper, an uninvited guest. After all, in graduate school I took no courses and wrote no papers on American literature, concentrating instead on the poetry of the Middle Ages and the English Seventeenth Century under mentors who believed and sought to persuade me that only second-rate minds wasted their time in studying American books. I did not even then, however, share their elitist beliefs, convinced indeed that the canon should be opened even wider than the pioneers of American Studies were then proposing.

In fact, in a review of *The Literary History of the United States,* which I wrote shortly after getting my final degree, I scolded its editors for having sought to canonize only those classic American authors already dead and sanctified by the passage of time, while ignoring still living and problematical modernists like T. S. Eliot and Ezra Pound. Nonetheless, I was not sure (and indeed, I have doubts to this very day) that any writers, living or dead, who embody in our own tongue our own deepest nightmares and dreams ought to be taught in American classrooms. Would it not be better, I wondered, to keep them sources of private delight rather than turning them into required reading for students in quest of good grades and teachers seeking promotion and tenure.

21

In any case, for nearly a decade after I had myself become an instructor, I taught no courses in American writers nor did I publish anything about them; though, of course, I did continue to read them secretly in silence, not breaking that silence until one day in 1947 when quite inadvertently I found myself writing my infamous little essay, "Come Back to the Raft, Ag'in, Huck Honey!"

I had been reading to my two sons (then seven and nine), as I was accustomed to do at bedtime, a passage from *The Adventures of Huckleberry Finn* about Huck and Jim on the raft; and afterwards between sleeping and waking, I found myself redreaming Twain's idyllic dream of inter-ethnic male bonding and the flight from civilization. Then, I awoke fully to realize how central that erotic myth was not just to our literature but to our whole culture and rushed to my desk to get the insight down before it vanished forever. The little prose lyric which it insisted on becoming I sent off immediately to the *Partisan Review*—the kind of little magazine publication in which, in those benighted times, was still more of a hindrance than a help to academic advancement.

To my surprise, however, it was widely read (or more often misread) and responded to in the academy as well as out. Not that it was generally admired. On the contrary, it was either dismissed as a *boutade*, a joke in bad taste, or condemned as a calumny of the tradition it purported to explore and a travesty of scholarship. Needless to say, among those condemning it on the latter grounds were the sort of scholars who had at that point been awarded the honor you bestow on me today.

A half century later, however, that much maligned essay has refused to die. I myself reprinted it in my first book, *An End to Innocence*, where it was flanked by a dozen or so other pieces, some literary, some autobiographical or political—but all more like what academics of the old school would have called "mere journalism" rather than "true scholarship." Yet it has appeared since in many languages; and, in another ironic turn of the screw, it has become assigned reading in university classes in literature. In addition, it was this volume that persuaded those with no sense of where I was really coming from or heading to, that I was—however misguided and perverse I might be—a would-be scholar of American letters.

Certainly, it was that misapprehension which led to my being granted a Fulbright Fellowship to Italy, where I discovered I was expected to lecture (as I had never yet done at home) on the literature of my native land. Though I thought of myself as a comparatist, a mythographer, a literary anthropologist, anything but an "Americanist," I felt disconcertingly at ease in that new role. This was (I have come since to realize) because as a stranger in a strange land, I was able to teach our books as a literature in a foreign tongue. Indeed, at the University of Bologna my own language was so unfamiliar to the students I addressed that I had to lecture in theirs. In any case, what I ended up trying to do was to translate the parochial insights I had sketched out in "Come Back to the Raft" into more universal terms; which is to say, treating our literature not in isolation but in relation to Western culture as a whole—or more specifically, to deal with it as the first postcolonial literature of the modern world.

To do so properly, it soon became clear to me, would require more than a handful of irregularly scheduled lectures; and so, on my return home, I began to plan what turned out to be a rather formidable series of books, four in all, which together constituted a critical history of our literature from the end of the eighteenth century to the last decades of the twentieth. It took me nearly three decades to complete that project, and, indeed, I did not start *Love and Death in the American Novel,* the first of those books, until seven or eight years after I had conceived it. Though that volume has turned out to be finally the best known and most highly respected of all my works, initially it baffled and dismayed many of its readers—mostly, perhaps, because of its generic ambiguity.

Librarians have classified it either as literary history or criticism, but I have always considered it a work of art rather than scholarship, since it seeks not to prove its most outrageous theses but to charm the skeptical into a willing suspension of disbelief. More specifically, I think of it as a gothic novel in scholarly disguise: haunted like the dark novels so central to our tradition, by ghosts out of the European past which our white founding fathers fled, along with vengeful spectres of the Native Americans they displaced and menacing shadows cast by the Africans they enslaved to work the soil. But as its title indicates, its themes are erotic as well as thanatic, though, to be sure, its eros is as dark as thanatos, eventuating not in happy heterosexual unions, but in foredoomed male bonding, brother-sister incest, and necrophilia.

Moreover, to make clear that the tale it seems to tell is mythic rather than factual, poetic rather than prosaic, I eschewed such conventional academic trappings as footnotes and bibliographies. So, too, I spoke not just in the solemn and magisterial third person, but also in the informal first; thus permitting myself to indulge in high rhetoric and low humor. For this reason, the reaction of more conventional scholars was overwhelmingly negative, as it was to the three succeeding volumes, *Waiting for the End, The Return of the Vanishing American* and *What Was Literature,* so that for while it seemed as if I were to be doomed forever to be labelled a disturber of the peace, an *enfant terrible,* "the wild man of American Letters."

But nothing is forever, of course. As I approach my eightieth year, I am made aware by occasions like this that I have come to be thought of as a perfectly respectable scholar, an Americanist *par excellence.* I must confess to being pleased a little, but even more I am dismayed—wanting to cry out against such misapprehensions, to protest that I have remained a jack of all fields and master of none, continuing to write and speak as I have from the first, about whatever moves me at the moment. And this has turned out to be not just the literature of many nations and eras beside my own: ancient Greek tragedy, the classic Chinese novel, Old Provençal poetry, the English Victorian novel, Kafka and James Joyce, Jaroslav Hasek and Chrétien de Troyes, and especially Shakespeare and Dante. I have also dealt with subjects as remote from my presumable field of expertise as theology and psychology, voting studies and the war in Vietnam, Japanese woodblock engravings, pornography and comic books, sideshows and circuses, bio-ethics and organ transplants. I have talked about them, moreover, not just in the classroom and at gatherings of my fellow-academics, but to trade unionists, nurses and dermatologists, as well as on talk shows presided over by Dick Cavett and William Buckley, Merv Griffin and Phil Donahue—earning myself a listing in *Who's Who in Entertainment.*

Similarly, I have less and less often published in academic journals (never in the PMLA), preferring to appear in magazines aimed at a nonprofessional audience, like *The Nation, The New Republic, Psychology Today, Esquire* and (most scandalous of all) *Playboy.* Despite all this, I am presently praised by the sort of scholars who first ignored me, then vilified me (sometimes while stealing my ideas without acknowledgment)—though, to be sure, it is only for what I have written about American literature.

Even more disturbingly, I am now routinely quoted in jargon-ridden, reader-unfriendly works I cannot bring myself to read, and am listed honorifically in the kind of footnotes and bibliographies I have always eschewed. But most disturbingly of all, as a result (in a culture where nothing fails like success) some younger, future-oriented critics have begun to speak of me as old-fashioned, a member of a moribund establishment. I was, however, heartened when Camille Paglia, the most future-oriented of them all, the *enfant terrible,* in fact, of her generation, as I was of mine, was moved by a new edition of *Love and Death in the American Novel,* to write, "Fiedler created an American intellectual style that was truncated by the invasion of faddish French theory in the '70s and '80s. Let's turn back to Fiedler and begin again."

Her words not merely reassure me that I am, still, not P.C. They also make me aware that whatever I have written about it has always been from an essentially American point of view and in an essentially American voice; and that therefore I am in the deepest sense an "Americanist"—a true colleague (despite their original doubts and my own continuing ones) of all those who have earlier received this award and you who so graciously bestow it on me now. As such a colleague, I feel free to say in conclusion—straight out and without irony—what I hope you realize I have been—in my customary perverse and ambivalent way—trying to say throughout these remarks, *thank you, thank you very much.*

Come Back to the Raft Ag'in, Huck Honey!

LESLIE FIEDLER

It is perhaps to be expected that the Negro and the homosexual should become stock literary themes in a period when the exploration of responsibility and failure has become again a primary concern of our literature. It is the discrepancy they represent that haunts us, that moral discrepancy before which we are helpless, having no resources (no tradition of courtesy, no honored mode of cynicism) for dealing with a conflict of principle and practice. It used once to be fashionable to think of puritanism as a force in our lives encouraging hypocrisy; quite the contrary, its emphasis upon the singleness of belief and action, its turning of the most prosaic areas of life into arenas where one's state of grace is tested, confuse the outer and the inner and make hypocrisy among us, perhaps more strikingly than ever elsewhere, *visible*, visibly detestable, the cardinal sin. It is not without significance that the shrug of the shoulders (the acceptance of circumstance as a sufficient excuse, the sign of self-pardon before the inevitable lapse) seems in America an unfamiliar, an alien gesture.

And yet before the continued existence of physical homosexual love (our crudest epithets notoriously evoke the mechanics of such affairs), before the blatant ghettos in which the Negro conspicuously creates the gaudiness and stench that offend him, the white American must make a choice between coming to terms with institutionalized discrepancy or formulating radically new ideologies. There are, to be sure, stopgap devices, evasions of that final choice; not the least interesting is the special night club: the "queer" café, the black-and-tan joint, in which fairy or Negro exhibit their fairy-ness, their Negro-ness as if they were mere divertissements, gags thought up for the laughs and having no reality once the lights go out and the chairs are piled on the tables by the cleaning women. In the earlier minstrel show, a Negro performer was required to put on with grease paint and burnt cork the formalized mask of blackness; while the queer must exaggerate flounce and flutter into the convention of his condition.

26

The situations of the Negro and the homosexual in our society pose quite opposite problems, or at least problems suggesting quite opposite solutions. Our laws on homosexuality and the context of prejudice they objectify must apparently be changed to accord with a stubborn social fact; whereas it is the social fact, our overt behavior toward the Negro, that must be modified to accord with our laws, and the, at least official, morality they objectify. It is not, of course, quite so simple. There is another sense in which the fact of homosexual passion contradicts a national myth of masculine love, just as our real relationship with the Negro contradicts a myth of that relationship; and those two myths with their betrayals are, as we shall see, one.

The existence of overt homosexuality threatens to compromise an essential aspect of American sentimental life: the camaraderie of the locker room and ball park, the good fellowship of the poker game and fishing trip, a kind of passionless passion, at once gross and delicate, homoerotic in the boy's sense, possessing an innocence above suspicion. To doubt for a moment this innocence, which can survive only as *assumed,* would destroy our stubborn belief in a relationship simple, utterly satisfying, yet immune to lust; physical as the handshake is physical, this side of copulation. The nineteenth-century myth of the Immaculate Young Girl has failed to survive in any *felt* way into our time. Rather, in the dirty jokes shared among men in the smoking car, the barracks, or the dormitory, there is a common male revenge against women for having flagrantly betrayed that myth; and under the revenge, the rather smug assumption of the chastity of the revenging group, in so far as it is a purely male society. From what other source could arise that unexpected air of good clean fun which overhangs such sessions? It is this self-congratulatory buddy-buddiness, its astonishing naïveté that breed at once endless opportunities for inversion and the terrible reluctance to admit its existence, to surrender the last believed-in stronghold of love without passion.

It is, after all, what we know from a hundred other sources that is here verified: the regressiveness, in a technical sense, of American life, its implacable nostalgia for the infantile, at once wrong-headed and somehow admirable. The mythic America is boyhood—and who would dare be startled to realize that the two most popular, most *absorbed,* I am sure, of the handful of great books in our native heritage are customarily to be found, illustrated, on the shelves of the children's library. I am referring, of course, to *Moby Dick* and *Huckleberry Finn,* so different in technique and language, but alike children's books or, more precisely, *boys'* books.

There are the Leatherstocking Tales of Cooper, too, as well as Dana's *Two Years Before the Mast* and a good deal of Stephen Crane, books whose continuing favor depends more and more on the taste of boys; and one begins to foresee a similar improbable fate for Ernest Hemingway. Among the most distinguished novelists of the American past, only Henry James completely escapes classification as a writer of juvenile classics; even Hawthorne, who did write sometimes for children, must in his most adult novels endure, though not as Mark Twain and Melville submit to, the child's perusal. A child's version of *The Scarlet Letter* would seem a rather farfetched joke if it were not a part of our common experience. Finding in the children's department of the local library what Hawthorne liked to call his "hell-fired book," and remembering that *Moby Dick* itself has as its secret motto "*Ego te baptizo in nomine diaboli,*" one can only bow in awed silence before the mysteries of public morality, the American idea of "innocence." Everything goes except the frank description of adult heterosexual love. After all, boys will be boys!

What, then, do all these books have in common? As boys' books we should expect them shyly, guiltlessly as it were, to proffer a chaste male love as the ultimate emotional experience—and this is spectacularly the case. In Dana, it is the narrator's melancholy love for the *kanaka*, Hope; in Cooper, the lifelong affection of Natty Bumppo and Chingachgook; in Melville, Ishmael's love for Queequeg; in Twain, Huck's feeling for Nigger Jim. At the focus of emotion, where we are accustomed to find in the world's great novels some heterosexual passion, be it "platonic" love or adultery, seduction, rape, or long-drawn-out flirtation, we come instead on the fugitive slave and the no-account boy lying side by side on a raft borne by the endless river toward an impossible escape, or the pariah sailor waking in the tattooed arms of the brown harpooner on the verge of their impossible quest. "*Aloha, aikane, aloha nui,*" Hope cries to the lover who prefers him to all his fellow-whites; and Ishmael in utter frankness tells us: "I found Queequeg's arm thrown over me in the most loving and affectionate manner. You had almost thought I had been his wife . . . he still hugged me tightly, as though naught but death should part us twain . . . Thus, then, in our heart's honeymoon, lay I and Queequeg—a cosy, loving pair . . . he pressed his forehead against mine, clasped me around the waist, and said that henceforth we were married."

In Melville, the ambiguous relationship is most explicitly rendered; almost, indeed, openly explained. Not by a chance phrase or camouflaged symbol (the dressing of Jim in a woman's gown in *Huck Finn*, for instance, which can mean anything or nothing at all), but in a step-by-step exposition, the Pure Marriage of Ishmael and Queequeg is set before us: the initial going to bed together and the first shyness overcome, that great hot tomahawk-pipe accepted in a familiarity that dispels fear; next, the wedding ceremony itself (for in this marriage like so many others the ceremonial follows the deflowering), with the ritual touching of foreheads; then, the queasiness and guilt the morning after the *official* First Night, the suspicion that one has joined himself irrevocably to his own worst nightmare; finally, a symbolic portrayal of the continuing state of marriage through the image of the "monkey rope" which binds the lovers fast waist to waist (for the sake of this symbolism, Melville changes a *fact* of whaling practice—the only time in the book), a permanent alliance that provides mutual protection but also threatens mutual death.

Physical it all is, certainly, yet somehow ultimately innocent. There lies between the lovers no naked sword but a childlike ignorance, as if the possibility of a fall to the carnal had not yet been discovered. Even in the *Vita Nuova* of Dante, there is no vision of love less offensively, more unremittingly chaste; that it is not adult seems beside the point. Ishmael's sensations as he wakes under the pressure of Queequeg's arm, the tenderness of Huck's repeated loss and refinding of Jim, the role of almost Edenic helpmate played for Bumppo by the Indian—these shape us from childhood: we have no sense of first discovering them or of having been once without them.

Of the infantile, the homoerotic aspects of these stories we are, though vaguely, aware; but it is only with an effort that we can wake to a consciousness of how, among us who at the level of adulthood find a difference in color sufficient provocation for distrust and hatred, they celebrate, all of them, the mutual love of *a white man and a colored*. So buried at a level of acceptance which does not touch reason, so desperately repressed from overt recognition, so contrary to what is usually thought of as our ultimate level of taboo—the sense of that love can survive only in the obliquity of a symbol, persistent, obsessive, in short, an archetype: the boy's homoerotic crush, the love of the black fused at this level into a single thing.

I hope I have been using here a hopelessly abused word with some precision; by "archetype" I mean a coherent pattern of beliefs and feelings so widely shared at a level beneath consciousness that there exists no abstract vocabulary for representing it, and so "sacred" that unexamined, irrational restraints inhibit any explicit analysis. Such a complex finds a formula or pattern story, which serves both to embody it, and, at first at least, to conceal its full implications. Later, the secret may be revealed, the archetype "analyzed" or "allegorically" interpreted according to the language of the day.

I find the complex we have been examining genuinely mythic; certainly it has the invisible character of the true archetype, eluding the wary pounce of Howells or Mrs. Twain, who excised from *Huckleberry Finn* the cussing as unfit for children, but who left, unperceived, a conventionally abhorrent doctrine of ideal love. Even the writers in whom we find it attained it, in a sense, dreaming. The felt difference between *Huckleberry Finn* and Twain's other books must lie in part in the release from conscious restraint inherent in the author's assumption of the character of Huck; the passage in and out of darkness and river mist, the constant confusion of identities (Huck's ten or twelve names; the question of who is the real uncle, who the true Tom), the sudden intrusions into alien violences without past or future, give the whole work, for all its carefully observed detail, the texture of a dream. For *Moby Dick* such a point need scarcely be made. Even Cooper, despite his insufferable gentlemanliness, his tedium, cannot conceal from the kids who continue to read him the secret behind his overconscious prose: the childish, impossible dream. D. H. Lawrence saw in him clearly the boy's Utopia: the absolute wilderness in which the stuffiness of home yields to the wigwam, and "My Wife" to Chingachgook.

I do not recall ever having seen in the commentaries of the social anthropologist or psychologist an awareness of the role of this profound child's dream of love in our relation to the Negro. (I say Negro, though the beloved in the books I have mentioned is variously Indian and Polynesian, because the Negro has become more and more exclusively for us *the* colored man, the colored man *par excellence*.) Trapped in what have by now become shackling clichés—the concept of the white man's sexual envy of the Negro male, the ambivalent horror of miscegenation—they do not sufficiently note the complementary factor of physical attraction, the archetypal love of white male and black. But either the horror or the attraction is meaningless alone; only together do they make sense. Just as the pure love of man and man is in general set off against the ignoble passion of man for woman, so more specifically (and more vividly) the dark desire which leads to miscegenation is contrasted with the ennobling love of a white man and a colored one. James Fenimore Cooper is our first poet of this ambivalence; indeed, miscegenation is the secret theme of the Leatherstocking novels, especially of *The Last of the Mohicans.* Natty Bumppo, the man who boasts always of having "no cross" in *his* blood, flees by nature from the defilement of all women, but never with so absolute a revulsion as he displays toward the *squaw* with whom at one point he seems at the point of being forced to cohabit; and the threat of the dark-skinned rapist sends pale woman after pale woman skittering through Cooper's imagined wilderness. Even poor Cora, who already has a fatal drop of alien blood that cuts her off from any marriage with a white man, in so far as she is white cannot be mated with Uncas, the noblest of redmen. Only in death can they be joined in an embrace as chaste as that of males. There's no good woman but a dead woman! Yet Chingachgook and the Deerslayer are permitted to sit night after night over their campfire in the purest domestic bliss. So long as there is no mingling of blood, soul may couple with soul in God's undefiled forest.

Nature undefiled—this is the inevitable setting of the Sacred Marriage of males. Ishmael and Queequeg, arm in arm, about to ship out, Huck and Jim swimming beside the raft in the peaceful flux of the Mississippi—here it is the motion of water which completes the syndrome, the American dream of isolation afloat. The notion of the Negro as the unblemished bride blends with the myth of running away to sea, of running the great river down to the sea. The immensity of water defines a loneliness that demands love; its strangeness symbolizes the disavowal of the conventional that makes possible all versions of love. In *Two Years Before the Mast,* in *Moby Dick,* in *Huckleberry Finn* the water is there, is the very texture of the novel; the Leatherstocking Tales propose another symbol for the same meaning: the virgin forest. Notice the adjectives—the virgin forest and the forever inviolable sea. It is well to remember, too, what surely must be more than a coincidence, that Cooper, who could dream this myth, also invented for us the novel of the sea, wrote for the first time in history the sea story proper.

The rude pederasty of the forecastle and the captain's cabin, celebrated in a thousand jokes, is the profanation of a dream; yet Melville, who must have known such blasphemies, refers to them only once and indirectly, for it was *his* dream that they threatened. And still the dream survives; in a recent book by Gore Vidal, an incipient homosexual, not yet aware of the implications of his feelings, indulges in the reverie of running off to sea with his dearest friend. The buggery of sailors is taken for granted everywhere, yet is thought of usually as an inversion forced on men by their isolation from women; though the opposite case may well be true: the isolation sought more or less consciously as an occasion for male encounters. At any rate, there is a context in which the legend of the sea as escape and solace, the fixated sexuality of boys, the myth of the dark beloved, are one. In Melville and Twain at the center of our tradition, in the lesser writers at the periphery, the archetype is at once formalized and perpetuated. Nigger Jim and Queequeg make concrete for us what was without them a vague pressure on the threshold of our consciousness; the proper existence of the archetype is in the realized character, who waits, as it were, only to be asked his secret. Think of Oedipus biding in silence from Sophocles to Freud!

Unwittingly, we are possessed in childhood by these characters and their undiscriminated meaning, and it is difficult for us to dissociate them without a sense of disbelief. What—these household figures clues to our subtlest passions! The foreigner finds it easier to perceive the significances too deep within us to be brought into focus. D. H. Lawrence discovered in our classics a linked mythos of escape and immaculate male love; Lorca in *The Poet in New York* grasped instinctively (he could not even read English) the kinship of Harlem and Walt Whitman, the fairy as bard. But of course we do not have to be conscious of what possesses us; in every generation of our own writers the archtype reappears, refracted, half-understood, but *there*. In the gothic reverie of Capote's *Other Voices, Other Rooms,* both elements of the syndrome are presented, though disjunctively: the boy moving between the love of a Negro maidservant and his inverted cousin. In Carson McCullers' *Member of the Wedding,* another variant is invented: a *female* homosexual romance between the boy-girl Frankie and a Negro cook. This time the Father-Slave-Beloved is converted into the figure of a Mother-Sweetheart-Servant, but remains still, of course, satisfactorily black. It is not strange, after all, to find this archetypal complex in latter-day writers of a frankly homosexual sensibility; but it recurs, too, in such resolutely masculine writers as Faulkner, who evokes the myth in the persons of the Negro and the boy of *Intruder in the Dust.*

In the myth, one notes finally, it is typically in the role of outcast, ragged woodsman, or despised sailor ("Call me Ishmael!"), or unregenerate boy (Huck before the prospect of being "sivilized" cries out, "I been there before!") that we turn to the love of a colored man. But how, we cannot help asking, does the vision of the white American as a pariah correspond with our long-held public status: the world's beloved, the success? It is perhaps only the artist's portrayal of *himself,* the notoriously alienated writer in America, at home with such images, child of the town drunk, the hapless survivor. But no, Ishmael is in all of us, our unconfessed universal fear objectified in the writer's status, as in the outcast sailor's: that compelling anxiety, which every foreigner notes, that we may not be loved, that we are loved for our possessions and not our selves, that we are really—*alone.* It is that underlying terror which explains our incredulity in the face of adulation or favor, what is called (once more the happy adjective) our "boyish modesty."

Our dark-skinned beloved will take us in, we assure ourselves, when we have been cut off, or have cut ourselves off, from all others, without rancor or the insult of forgiveness. He will fold us in his arms saying, "Honey" or "Aikane"; he will comfort us, as if our offense against him were long ago remitted, were never truly *real.* And yet we cannot ever really forget our guilt; the stories that embody the myth dramatize as if compulsively the role of the colored man as the victim. Dana's Hope is shown dying of the white man's syphilis; Queequeg is portrayed as racked by fever, a pointless episode except in the light of this necessity; Crane's Negro is disfigured to the point of monstrosity; Cooper's Indian smolders to a hopeless old age conscious of the imminent disappearance of his race; Jim is shown loaded down with chains, weakened by the hundred torments dreamed up by Tom in the name of bulliness. The immense guilt of guilt must not be mitigated any more than the disparity of color (Queequeg is not merely brown but monstrously tattooed; Chingachgook is horrid with paint; Jim is portrayed as the sick A-rab died blue), so that the final reconciliation may seem more unbelievable and tender. The archetype makes no attempt to deny our outrage as fact; it portrays it as meaningless in the face of love.

There would be something insufferable, I think, in that final vision of remission if it were not for the presence of a motivating anxiety, the sense always of a last chance. Behind the white American's nightmare that someday, no longer tourist, inheritor, or liberator, he will be rejected, refused, he dreams of his acceptance at the breast he has most utterly offended. It is a dream so sentimental, so outrageous, so desperate, that it redeems our concept of boyhood from nostalgia to tragedy.

In each generation we *play out* the impossible mythos, and we live to see our children play it: the white boy and the black we can discover wrestling affectionately on any American sidewalk, along which they will walk in adulthood, eyes averted from each other, unwilling to touch even by accident. The dream recedes; the immaculate passion and the astonishing reconciliation become a memory, and less, a regret, at last the unrecognized motifs of a child's book. "It's too good to be true, Honey," Jim says to Huck. "It's too good to be true."

Part II

The Prophetic Textbook

Irving Malin

I want to be perverse. I propose to read closely a textbook, *The Art of the Essay,* that Fiedler published in 1958. This textbook, which appeared a few years before *Love and Death in the American Novel,* clarifies Fiedler's abiding interests and obsessions. It is, thus, an intriguing document, one that, like his dissertation on Donne, offers a "secret" passage into his written world.

The book is divided into three large sections: "The Discovery of the Self"; "America" (containing a selection of "Americans on Native Places," "As Europeans See Us," and a "Coda"); and "Ourselves and Our Culture" (containing essays on "Mass Culture" and "High Culture"). Fiedler offers introductions to each section, selections of essays, and even a series of questions about the essays. I assume that such an anthology is an "occult" autobiography; it is for students and Fiedler himself.

In the introduction Fiedler writes: "Precisely because the essay is the most familiar of literary forms, it is the one of which we are least likely to be conscious." The sentence is fascinating; he in effect takes the "familiar" form and "transforms" it into an "unconscious" revelation. He refers to the essay as a "kind of printed confession," an exchange, if you will, between "our best 'I' and an ideal 'you.'" He ends the introduction with this sentence: "Plagued by the problems of sentence structure and subordination, bored by his own writing, and his teachers' dull admonitions, the student will perhaps find it refreshing to be reminded of what it is all for—of what the essay can be as an art form and a grace of life." Fiedler attacks the academic world—it consists of "boredom" and "dullness"—and he hopes to save it by offering the student a fresh way of perception, a mode of looking at school and world as fields of energy, formal beauty, and "grace of life." The entire introduction, written in an informal manner, is unusual for a textbook. Who else would use such phrases as a "grace of life" or "printed confession" in a textbook? Obviously, this textbook is highly personal. Of course, all textbooks are personal in

some sense, but we usually don't relate them to the anthologist's
other writings, except in a routine way. We don't usually view the
textbook as part of the author's canon. The fact that I am doing
so demonstrates that I have been subtly influenced by Fiedler.

In the introduction to "The Discovery of the Self" Fiedler begins with this sentence: "The essay begins . . . with the discovery
of the self." Although he doesn't define the "self"—he doesn't
make it an ambivalent construction—he does regard the "self" as
skewed, complex, and peculiar. He writes about the beginnings of
the essay: "inwardness and personality (what is called in fiction
'character') become the chief concerns of literature; the interest
of thinking and reading men shifts from what is representative
in a given person, what he stands for in terms of a class, to what
is peculiar in him: to his individuality rather than his humanity."
Fiedler is already implying that the "peculiar" is what interests
him. He is crossing genres or, at least, questioning rigid lines of
demarcation. Is it any wonder that he will later refer to *Love and
Death* as a kind of gothic novel, to other books as the "inadvertent epic"?

Perhaps every sentence of the introduction is coded—consciously or unconsciously—or reflective (Am I peculiar in these
statements?) Fiedler credits Montaigne as the "urbane, ironical,
skeptical" father of the essay: "the feel of his work is something
midway between that of an overheard conversation of a man with
himself and of the confidence of one friend to another in a world
where a code of courtesy protects us from embarrassing revelation
and tedious insistence upon a point." Fiedler is using Montaigne
as his "secret sharer"; his own essays are full of tension, they are
ambivalent gestures of intimacy and secretiveness. (There is a
sense of opposition, of battling forces.) They are "midway" texts:
bold explorations, not final solutions.

After he makes a few comments about his selections—I will
comment on these later—he links all of his selections to a sense
of inwardness: "It is a belief that the essential clue to the self lies
not so much in the society outside the man as to the child within
him." Notice the oppositions of "the child *within* him and the
society *outside* of him. Fiedler tends to look for *clues;* he is a literary
detective of sorts. And he will stress the child—the id underlying
the ego, to use simplistic, outdated words. But I am not sure that
he ever informs us of the methods by which the child becomes
the adult. And perhaps, he doesn't explore language itself, words
rather than tones. He seems to believe in a close reading of motives; he refuses to read words closely. His introduction ends with

the hope that by reading the essays he has chosen, the student will "search" for the self: "the search for the self becomes the search for the child one was, and in some disconcertingly essential way still is." But I am somewhat troubled by such words as "essential"; it dismisses "existential" or "fashioned" or "performing" selves.

I want now to look at the essays Fiedler has chosen. The first essay is Montaigne's "Of Presumption." It is a moving text because it seems to presume that there is no validity in stable ways of self-exploration. It is filled with ironic reversals, with turns and counterturns. Montaigne claims, for example, that he has never created anything that has offered complete satisfaction (including this essay). But at the same time we feel that he is proud of his "incapacities," of his "failures." The essay is complex, surprising, contradictory. Montaigne, in effect, elevates his "weakness" into "strengths" (or vice versa). The entire essay is fueled by subtle ironies. It mirrors in an odd manner Fiedler's introduction.

I am fascinated by Lamb: "Two Letters to Coleridge" and "Two Attempts at an Autobiography" (to use Fiedler's titles). The "letters" adopt a different tone from the "attempts at an autobiography." Lamb tries to give an honest account of his problems with his sister, his need to act as her guardian. He is confessional. But he omits references to her—and to the tragic consequences of her madness—in his attempts at autobiography. Again we are offered conflict and ambivalence. It is, of course, striking that Lamb creates another self in Elia, one who seems to be untroubled. There is a rupture in the self, a kind of delusional division. This rupture, like Montaigne's reversals, stresses that the self is tenuous—it can crack at any moment.

Fiedler is then ready to offer us Fitzgerald's classic "The Crack-Up." These notes are completely ruptured. Fitzgerald's main point seems to be that the self is always on edge, that it can never be secure. It fears (and loves?) divisions. Every moment is dangerous, haunted by the "imagination of disaster" (James's phrase).

Fiedler's choice of essays is remarkable—he next proceeds to give us one by S. J. Perelman. Perelman is a master—like West—of surrealist comedy. (He writes about his feelings when he buys a suit. He cannot see himself in the mirror; the mirror "distorts" his figure.) Perelman questions the image we have of ourselves; he suggests that it is warped by self-love. His language is decidedly perverse; it alternates between slang and arcane words. The language, in a sense, reflects the dislocation of self. It is wonderfully strange.

The other essays in this section are familiar. They include Greene's "The Revolver in the Corner Cupboard," Baldwin's "Stranger in the Village," and an excerpt from Stein's *Autobiography of Alice B. Toklas*.

Greene's essay describes his childhood attempts to play Russian roulette as a way of giving excitement to his somewhat dreary, boring life. He wants—like Fitzgerald—to escape from his daily normal existence into one of adventurous primitivism. Obviously, he is divided. The gun is a kind of drug, opening a possible new world of death. The fact that Greene underplays the craziness of his adolescence, that he is matter-of-fact, unnerves us. Style, we can say, fights content in a studied, ironic way. He writes at the end: "One campaign was over, but the war against boredom had got to go on."

Baldwin's well-known essay concerns the stranger in the village. He is a kind of dark presence in the European world; he seems to be attractive *and* repulsive to the citizens who cannot certify his status. He is, to use his words, a "living wonder." Baldwin does not know how to respond to his European citizens. At times he rages against the fact that he is not taken as a *person;* that he is transformed into a kind of dark ghost (now that is ambivalence!)

The interracial drama in the essay looks forward to Fiedler's concern with race in most of his writings, to Caliban in the volume on Shakespeare, to the duplicities of Mark Twain. And, of course, it is marked by the deeper psychology of Jung. The last line of Baldwin's essay is: "This world is white no longer, and it will never be white again." Isn't the line an oddly prophetic one for the reader of Fiedler's future works?

Stein writes about Hemingway. But her comments are transmitted through Toklas. There is a complex play of subversions and maskings. Stein appears as Toklas; Hemingway appears as a creation of Stein. The identities are so fluid that this last selection in the first section seems to be the perfect end. Identity is oppositional, dynamic, performative; the "self" is now open to complex questioning.

In his introduction to "America" Fiedler suggests that "the search for identity leads outward as well as inward, and the sensitive observer turns his eye on the place he knows least: the place from which he begins or the one in which he chooses to end, the place from which he has fled or the one to which he comes after his flight." These words have mythological resonance. Although each person has his own identity, his signature, he seems to be acting in a recurring, universal drama.

Fiedler suggests that literature, unlike social science, holds the mysteries of identity. It tells us more than statistics; it offers "sights remembered and feelings relived." It is true in a personal way. It is, indeed, a product of a "quarrel with experience." Therefore the essays are revelations of the true Princeton (by Bishop) or the true "High School" (by Cowley). But truth for Fiedler is a fiction, a necessary lie for the author. There is a play of appearances, of hallucinatory presences. Places and selves are never what they seem to be.

One of the most interesting selections is Henry Miller's description of a "soiree in Hollywood." (The very fact that Fiedler includes Miller in a 1958 anthology for students is outrageous.) Hollywood is, of course, the dream world of America or, better yet, the creator of "America," an "America" that has never really existed. The entire piece is satirical, demonstrating the falsity, the fictional quality of the place. Miller delights in listing the oddities: "elocution lessons, psychic readings, institutes of religion, astronomical demonstrations. . . ." These oddities stun or "wobble" him. Part of the humor of the piece is that Miller portrays himself as a rational observer. He is, indeed, as "nutty" as the place. The essay becomes a highly dramatic transfiguration. Stability of place and visitor is destroyed in a joyous "nightmare." (Oxymoron rules.)

Fiedler includes his own well-known "Montana: or The End of Jean Jacques Rousseau." Montana is, for him, not the Romantic paradise. It is a dangerous place because it doesn't conform to the usual descriptions. It, like Hollywood, is full of nervous contradictions. (Consider that "Montana" and "Hollywood" are partially *mythical* places.) It offers contradiction between "actuality and the dream." I am rash indeed; I don't even believe that actuality exists; it is a word, not a world. I assume that I am more self-contained than Fiedler; the world is created by me.

The text is filled with favorite words of Fiedler: "trick" "inner feelings," "complicity," "stereotypes," "consciously," "reinvented." I suggest that these are repeated in the later, systematic works. They create the full shock we feel in reading Fiedler. I wonder whether or not he is forcing me to be unbalanced. His language is a weapon and a gift. Sometimes I reach the point of wondering whether Fiedler is Fiedler. (I should state here that Fiedler plays with his own name. Why does he include his middle initial "A" at times? Why does he play with his ambiguous first name? What's going on?) To quote him: "There is, of course, no easy solution. . . ." Solutions may, in fact, be a dream.

In the selections included in "As Europeans See Us," we find three essays which are especially significant. Matthew Arnold writes one entitled "America Is Not Interesting"; D. H. Lawrence writes "The Spirit of the Place" (a chapter from *Studies in Classic American Literature*); Sartre writes on "American Cities." These essays are valuable for several reasons.

Arnold's essay, excerpted from *Civilization in the United States*, deplores the fact that our country lacks fine paintings, that it depends on imitations of European art. American architecture is "pretty and coquettish," not beautiful. Of course, he doesn't define these important words; he simply employs them (assuming that men of culture will immediately understand them). Arnold is, in many ways, the precursor of Trilling who, unlike Fiedler, always takes the safe path, invoking "sincerity" and "culture." (It is, of course, amusing that Trilling had to be inauthentic to survive in the academic world; he could never trace his spiritual roots. He was an academic actor.)

Arnold, in his civilized manner, claims that America lacks distinction; it is full of "tall talk," "inflated sentiment." The very fact that Arnold sees only the "surface" of art forces him to avoid the perversity of Poe or Ryder, the strangeness of "civilization." Are not the highest products of civilization those that fight the gentility of civilization? And what, in heaven's name, is civilization? Isn't it another word for good manners?

Arnold assumes that America lacks "elevation," lofty idealism. He refuses to see that we have the beauty of jittery tension, that our art refuses to be smooth, high, full of light. We have the "power of darkness"—to quote Harry Levin's wonderful phrase—and we seek, in our art, an eternal battle against interesting ideas. We seek "deities of unholiness," paradoxes which fight the notion of calm wisdom praised by Arnold. We yearn to say "No! in Thunder."

Lawrence, in opposition to Arnold, understands that America is a special, spectral place—the home of new myths, new masks. We fight the "masters" (Arnold); we rebel against the "old parenthood" Lawrence is, without doubt, an influence on Fiedler because he refuses to see or to write calmly. He rants; he prays for magic, for "IT," some force that has been tyrannized by civilization: "We are not the marvelous choosers and deciders we think we are. IT chooses for us and decides for us." America, for Lawrence, has an original spirit, a spirit embodied by the terrifying New Mexico sun.

Sartre begins his description of America by admitting that "my eyes were not accustomed to the skyscrapers and they did not surprise me; they did not seem like man-made, man-inhabited constructions but like rocks and hills." He mentions "turbulent soil." He describes American communities: "communities are born as they die—in a day." I assume that, like Lawrence and Fiedler, he delights in the (con)fusion of light and dark, of death and life. He is open to "brick houses" that are "the color of dried blood." America, for these visitors, is almost a body full of blood and unsteady vibration. Sartre notes shrewdly that in America nothing is "definitive," nothing is arrested.

I assume that Fiedler deliberately chooses Sartre and Lawrence to oppose Arnold. Both writers are haunted; both believe in momentary flashes of insight. Their styles have a kind of "disordered beauty," an "unfixed form." They unconsciously remind us that Europe and America are, in odd ways, states of mind, archetypal dreams.

In the third section, "Ourselves and Our Culture" (divided into "Mass Culture" and "High Culture"), Fiedler again plays with opposition. He writes in his introduction: "The essayist cannot consider for very long the relationship between the self and the society which forms it without coming to terms with the ways in which most men become aware of that relationship. "Ordinary people" act out; their scripts (life-scripts) come from what they see daily: television. Television, athletic "rituals," films "celebrate the beauty of violence." Fiedler is perhaps easy here because he doesn't indicate the "ugliness" of violence, of "acting out," but he recognizes that we are spectators, not readers. When he speculates at length about "sub-art," he relates it to dream. He implies that our existence is at times so filled with dream that we can barely recognize *fact*. (Don't our papers seem to be fictional? Don't they glorify or magnify the amusing scandal, the violent event, the weird hoax?) Popular culture, whether we like it or not, is always before us, and it forces essayists to find the secrets for its verve and appeal.

Liebling's essay, "Ahab and Nemesis," is on the match between Rocky Marciano and Archie Moore. (The title subtly conflates high art and violent entertainment.) He refuses to write in newspaper language, to use such simple words as "crushed" and "bloody." Perhaps he actually believes that a "fight" is our equivalent to ancient ritual. Thus he writes this typical sentence: "What he [the trainer] has taught Rocky in the four years since I last saw him fight is to *shorten the arc* of most of his blows without losing

power *thereby,* and always to follow one hard blow with another—
'for instance'—delivered with the other hand, instead of *recoiling*
to watch the *victim* fall" (my italics). The sentence contains unusual
words that are not often employed by pulp writers. These words
somehow elevate the event, making it resemble ancient ritual: "victim" and "shorten the arc" could easily be used in a Greek tragedy
or *Moby-Dick.* "Form" and "content" are "at odds" (excuse the
pun). The result is "high journalism," perhaps even "art," so that
Liebling emerges as more than a hack. Would any ordinary sports
writer end an essay with this personal sentence: "I felt the satisfaction because it proved that the world isn't going backward, if you
can just stay young enough to remember what it was really like
when you were really young." The fighters—the spectacle itself—
are as golden as the old, classic boxers: they remind Liebling of
his youthful explorations in the ring.

Norman Podhoretz's essay, "Our Changing Ideals, As Seen on
TV," is a complex investigation of the American family in sitcoms.
He writes about the mother: "A good woman is not so much *by*
as *on* the side of her husband. If she asserts her personality too
forcefully, we may be sure that calamity will result." He does not
approve of the "role" played by the mother, but the very fact that
he recognizes her role indicates that television limits (or creates?)
"reality." Evil is out-of-place in domestic drama because it will
upset the viewer. Television, for Podhoretz, is good in that "the
retreat to the home, then, means a retreat from 'environment'—
from the competitive world of business and politics which men-
aces amiable human relations and does not yield easily to compromise and good will." I am startled by the possible lack of irony.
Does Podhoretz believe that domestic "drama" offers *peace?* Does
he really think he is "honest" in his depiction; that television itself
is worth such close consideration? Perhaps he has been influenced
by his mentor, Trilling. And perhaps this early essay reveals his
present concern for "family values."

The last section on "High Culture" begins with an interesting
sentence: "The essayist must finally learn to comment not only
on raw experience and on popular attempts to 'ritual' and 'myth'
to come to terms with it." The sentence implies a belief in cogni-
tive progress, in epistemological voyage. The essayist must come
to terms with "high art," "which is, to say, on man's subtlest and
loveliest means of ordering and understanding his life." (I have
italicized "loveliest" because it demonstrates Fiedler's aesthetic
sense.) For Fiedler "the crown and climax of the essay is literary
criticism." And by "literary criticism" he means neither theory

nor journalism. How interesting that he hates "theory"! Isn't his own criticism subtly theoretical? Doesn't he simply *hide* theory?

There are three well-known essays—well-known now—by Baudelaire on Poe, Poe on Hawthorne, and Melville on Hawthorne. When these essays were written they were bold assessments of "new writers." (I have always believed that the mark of a significant critic is that he dares to recognize genius before others. Think of Fiedler on Barth and Hawkes.)

Baudelaire discovers Poe in 1852; he views him not as the hack or lunatic most Americans believed but as a true visionary. He writes: "I prefer Edgar Poe, drunk, poor, persecuted, to a calm and virtuous Goethe or Walter Scott." He, of course, sees Poe as his double and, in many ways, he uses the essay to justify his own art. (But don't the best critics choose to write about their "doubles"? Don't we feel the strong attraction? Am I surely not one of the "best" critics, writing on Fiedler because he *led* me to the Gothic, to American Jewish writers?)

Poe's essay on Hawthorne again seems to be personal; by praising certain qualities in Hawthorne—his fondness for the intensity of the short story, his use of dark psychology, his fastidious style—he is surely using his appreciation as a way of exploring his own fictional world. Poe continually refers to "concealed" meaning, to masquerade. How ironic that his essay itself is a secret message!

I turn at last to "Hawthorne and His Mosses" by Melville. Surely the essay is literally criticism of the highest order. Remember the famous sentence: "For spite of all the Indian-summer sunlight on the hither side of Hawthorne's soul, *the other side*—like the dark half of the physical sphere—is shrouded in a blackness, ten times black" (my italics). Melville is aware of "the other side." Isn't he also aware that he is secretly writing a kind of love letter to Hawthorne?

If we were to see these three essays as "reflections"—on the anthologist's part, on the author's part—then we would be capable of recognizing the reasons for Fiedler's choices. He is using them, in fact he is using the entire textbook, as an "occult" guide to the literary work he is writing: *Love and Death in the American Novel.*

The textbook—which is usually not listed in the Fiedler canon—is as close to autobiography as *Being Busted.* It is a thrilling achievement filled with the ironic joy of an academic fighting the academic world by employing a textbook—yes, a textbook!—to declare his profound other side, his peculiarity. How perverse! How original! How prophetic!

Andromeda on the Rocks: The Irony of Belonging in *The Last Jew in America*

Joseph Dewey

> *I reckon I got to light out for the Territory ahead of the rest, because Aunt Sally she's going to adopt me and sivilize me and I can't stand it. I been there before.*
>
> —*Huck Finn*

> *What, for instance, has happened in the middle of the twentieth century to Huckleberry Finn: loneliest of Americans; eternally and by definition uncommitted; too marginal in his existence to afford either conventional virtue or ordinary villainy; excluded . . . from marriage and family; his ending ambiguously suspended between joy and misery; condemned to the loneliness which he desperately desires."*
>
> —*Waiting for the End*

Never bothered much by contradiction, America conceived of itself as home for the homeless, a resting place for the restless, the discontented, the dispossessed—for those, in short, with little regard for settling in or for the settled in. The literary testimony produced by such a culture, not surprisingly, has never valued fitting in—indeed, the defining characters in our literature, from Rip van Winkle to Tyrone Slothrop, move (un)easily to the margins, risk awkward positions of deep vulnerability, postures of alienation and isolation, and there touch the darker, deeper stirrings untested (and far more to the point unsuspected) by those who stay securely within social structures. Leslie Fiedler has long argued that the identity of the American character is necessarily found along its margins, among outsiders, freaks, misfits, and strangers.[1] In his 1966 trilogy of interrelated stories, *The Last Jew in America*, his central characters wind up in places where they do not belong, in vaguely threatening or starkly inhospitable spaces. For instance, in the first offering, "The Last Jew in America," a handful of Jews, mostly first-generation Eastern European immigrants who have long succumbed to the attractive comforts of America and have consequently forfeited much of their religious

46

identity, gather (reluctantly) in a Catholic hospital amid the decid-edly a-Semitic landscape of the American Far West to conduct a Yom Kippur service for a dying friend. In the second, "The Last WASP in the World," a WASP poet, a sagging and wrinkling Lo-thario who attends a Jewish wedding out of affection for an ex-mistress, is caught quite drunkenly kissing a different ex-mistress by his wife, a woman all too accustomed to such infidelities. In the third, "The First Spade in the West," a black restaurateur helps home a drunken customer, a gay gigolo newly (and secretly) married to one of the town's richer dowagers, and, in the odd heat of moral indifference, he beds down the ancient bride herself while the groom is passed out, only to find her quite dead the following morning.

In each story, Fiedler's characters end up exactly where the prototype American literary—and historic—icons have always found themselves: bereft of the comfortable reassurance of place, the confident sense of belonging. It is surely no coincidence that the explorers Lewis and Clark figure so prominently in each of these stories—they are the quintessential expression of the Ameri-can restlessness, of our disdain for the comforts of civilized and settled space, of our fascination (and our terror) over the irresist-ible need to step out and there to touch in ourselves the satisfying sense of authenticity that is the sweet reward of such defiant explo-ration. As such, Lewis and Clark represent what has always been for Fiedler the defining energy of the American literary experi-ence: the embrace of vulnerability, the wonder of alienation, the benediction of homelessness. Indeed, Fiedler's characters here are offered what Lewis and Clark were offered: the opportunity to define their spiritual and emotional identities against the hard reality of a profound isolation.

Yet each character rejects isolation; each feels the compelling urgency to network, to settle in, or to disappear into the larger social crowd. As such, these are harsh and unforgiving narratives of failure. Unforgiving, perhaps, because Fiedler understands that these characters should, by rights, touch the enlarging power of alienation: one, an immigrant Jew who fancies himself a latter-day prophet in the desert wastes of Montana; another, a love poet in an age that routinely sentences its poets to obscurity in the academic gulag; the other, a black in midcentury racist America. But none maintains the strategy sufficient to find in such isolation its benediction. Amid a complex of secondary characters who do survive despite being denied place—Jews, gays, African Ameri-cans, Native Americans, academics—and amid a complex of cultural referents that each suggest the splendid agony of isolation and the necessity of life as a pilgrimage—in addition to Lewis and Clark, Fiedler invokes the mythic Andromeda, the Marranos of Inquisition Spain, the tormented blues singer Leadbelly, the damned Don Giovanni, the roaming Miles Standish, the doomed Pagliacci, George Eliot's hungry Daniel Deronda, Tchaikovsky's tragic Evgeny Onegin—Fiedler's three central characters understand only the conservative logic of belonging. But to belong here leads to the sacrifice of authenticity, the parody of self-importance, the surfeit of material comfort, a distracting busyness about the horizontal plane, the denial of authentic love, inevitable role-playing and pretense, and, ultimately, a vicious devolution into the simply animal. We must learn Fiedler's notion of what constitutes heroics by observing those who fail miserably. It is as if we must infer the argument of Huck Finn without Huck himself but rather by watching the sorry hypocrisy of the Duke and the Dauphin.

I

We begin with Jacob Moskowitz. Surely, much about Jacob's life should have created the contemporary prophet he fancies himself to be. After seventy years of Job-scale suffering—a family exterminated in Hitler's camps; a failed affiliation with leftist political causes; a wife who never found a way to accommodate life in the spare wastes of the Far West and who died slowly of loneliness amid chatty faculty wives; a daughter who died too young and too distant (the sole memory that he permits of the long-dead girl is a painful moment when she, as a teenager, awkwardly avoided an encounter with him downtown, no doubt, he reasoned, fearing his heavy accent and his social gracelessness would embarrass her in front of her friends); an uninspiring academic position for thirty-odd years in the zoology department that, because he lacks any academic qualifications, makes him little more than a glorified cage cleaner; and friends who consider him a pest— Jacob's life has given him ample reason to affirm the efficacy of a God. Like testamental prophets, Jacob is homeless (he lives in a rented half of a house—on Mountainview Avenue, yet), alienated, stubborn, crabby, suspended between the necessary misery of the moment and the tonic anticipation of the approaching joy of the after-life.

Apparently so compelled, he recruits among the lapsed Jews in Lewis and Clark City ten men, sufficient to conduct on behalf of a dying friend the somber ritual of atonement and repentance that marks Yom Kippur. Those he tabs resist—they cite their heavy schedules, their antipathy toward the ancient practices of their religion, their disquieting pride in children who have married out of the faith. With apparent courage, Jacob persists—he undertakes to assert the vibrant argument of religiosity in the wasteland about him, the world of assimilators, of friends who have *elected* to become the last Jew, of those who mistake money sent to the United Jewish Appeal for a religious exercise. Staging the Yom Kippur service is, on the surface, a most heroic exercise. And to Jacob's credit, the service is completed—and as Jacob returns to his rented half-a-house and heats his dinner of Campbell's chicken noodle soup, he resolves to dedicate what is left of his days to becoming the town's Jew, the lingering conscience of his race, bringing the practices of Judaism to whomever he encounters, even (he declaims) going door to door. It would appear a most striking revitalization of the spiritual dimension and Fiedler's unqualified offering of the possibility of a prophet who resolves to live out his days where American characters have always thrived: along the margins.

Why, then, does this story not feel affirmative? Why do we close the tale with the uncomfortable notion that Jacob Moskowitz is not the heroic character he imagines himself to be, the keeper of the faith in a faithless era—but is (as his canned soup suggests) a poor imitation, a mock-prophet, a dangerous and self-deluded counterfeit, who resists the authentic role of the prophet and indeed who mocks the fundamental argument of Judaism and who cannot ultimately embrace the difficult move toward the margins. What bothers the reader is what apparently does not bother Jacob—he is nearly devoid of the spiritual dimension. Fiedler cautions us that this self-styled prophet from Montana is entirely anchored to the immediate. After all, each year during student orientation Jacob tells incoming freshmen that college should be about the "good life" (14) and how to lead it. He is the only community resident who refuses to bow his head during an elaborate memorial service for one of the town's leading lights. He is unsettlingly proud over how he has kept his body strong despite his seventy years. His sole childhood memory is his radical violation of a Yom Kippur fast. Jacob, punished rather than illuminated by a life of suffering, acknowledges early on that not for a moment does he embrace the notion of God. The decision to

pursue the Yom Kippur service is done only against the fast approach of mortality—not his friend's but Jacob's own death; he
admits that he himself had not many Yom Kippurs left. It is the
sorriest sort of faith, one pressured by the chilling approach of
death and, hence, urged by the crudest egoism.

The service itself is a mockery of the ritual. The participants
are uneasy over the service—their own lapsed Judaism telling.
The antiseptic hospital surroundings and the general atmosphere
of imminent death (and heavy Catholicism) oppress. The men's
teenage sons, with their black leather jackets and unkempt hair,
slouch in the corners and snicker throughout the service; the
aging lady librarian who attends appears to keep her hearing aid
off; the men shuffle and stare uneasily, self-consciously, during
the ritual. Miles Standdish, who attends the service despite a long
history of being most uncomfortable with his Judaism, becomes
violently nauseous in reaction to the ritual wine. When the dying
man dramatically refuses to continue the service until the room's
wall crucifix has been removed, such insistence is laughed at by
the others, dismissed as the narrowest superstition. When the dying man chants the haunting Kol Nidre, he seems not to be praying at all but rather "acting praying" like "Al Jolson in *The Jazz
Singer*" (40). As the service ends, the dying man, despite a near
collapse in exhaustion and despite being part of a religious service
that hinges on notions of forgiveness, immediately demands (with
breath that is appropriately "thin and sour" [41]) that Miles
Standdish leave. Jewish tradition, of course, argues that atonement
for offenses done to others can come not from God but only from
sincere reconciliation with the offending party—the dying man's
simmering (and unexplained) dislike of Miles and his peremptory
ejection of him from the hospital room sadly undermine and
ultimately mock the validity of the Yom Kippur service.

But the sorry mock-ritual played out in the Catholic hospital
does not prepare the reader for the disturbing close of the story
when Jacob reveals a most disconcerting mockery of his pretense
to religiosity. Indeed, in a pattern that Fiedler will follow in each
of the tales, Jacob at narrative close mutates into his own worst
stereotype.[2] After the hospital ritual, one of Jacob's longtime
friends, a jeweler named Max, heatedly denies the validity of the
afterlife, accuses Jacob of interfering with their friend's recovery
and perhaps even hastening his death. In a snit, Max even sells
his share of the world-to-come to Jacob for a nickel—a monetary
transaction that Jacob negotiates as soullessly as Shylock, even de-
manding Max bring down the price from the original offer of a

dime. Later that evening, Max telephones Jacob, presumably to
"buy" his share of eternity back (Jacob is sure the man's Catholic
wife would not have found the purchase amusing).

But Jacob will not even listen. Too proud of his two shares in
the afterlife, he puts the receiver on a nearby hassock, shuts out
what he dismisses as "squawking on the other end" (50). Jacob,
impressed by the apparent power he has secured by his "purchase," calmly shuts out his longtime friend, a man whose influence years earlier had saved Jacob's university appointment when
his longstanding association with socialist causes had nearly cost
him his job. Forsaking the nearby space heater and the living
room lamp, Jacob closes in a chilly, forbidding darkness. Emotional debts now mean nothing. Negotiating shares in the afterlife
(as if such negotiations were even under his sway), dispassionately
tuning out a friend, Jacob closes the story distressingly at odds
with the spiritual dimension he had so profusely endorsed. Suddenly, his spiritual reclamation smacks of dark irony. Yes, he de-
termines he will become the town's practicing Jew—but first thing
next week. It is a stalled and, hence, suspect reclamation. We need
only remind ourselves of Jacob's university job—a zoologist—to
suggest that Jacob becomes the most distressing cartoon of the
American literary canon—the animal man, the creature of the
immediate who lacks the viability of soul necessary for authentic
life on the margins.

II

Much like Jacob Moskowitz, the prophet without a soul, Vin
Hazelbaker is a love poet without a heart. In poems that have
slowly ossified in anthologies, poems that Hazelbaker himself dis-
owns during onerous celebrity readings, Hazelbaker hymned the
wonder of love, the bonds of fidelity, and the strength of a love
that does not alter even when circumstances alter—all the while
indulging a life of raw sensual satisfactions, bedding women, married or single, without much interest in commitment or in constancy. Like Jacob Moskowitz's Yom Kippur service, Hazelbaker's
poems mock the authentic experience and leave their practitioner
ill-equipped for life on the margins, the spare and unsettling ge-
ography most fitting for poets—and for prophets. Vin Hazelbaker
begins and ends a creature of the immediate, an aging sensualist
who moves about any roomful still fancying himself a Perseus
casting about for an Andromeda, a damsel in distress who re-

quires his saving touch. Despite poetry that celebrates love, he is unimaginatively priapic, the slenderest encounter in the busiest room turns him rock hard (*"Help,* they would be calling, *please, someone help,* as all women called always" [62, italics Fiedler's]). Vin moves through the story a love poet whose erection is so persistent that it becomes starkly ironic. In the opening pages at the wedding reception, Vin drunkenly kisses his own goddaughter, the bride, and finds himself aroused as she leans her strong young body against his—a reaction all the more disturbing because of the persistent rumors that she may be his daughter.

As he does with Jacob, caught between his Eastern European roots and his adopted America, between tradition and assimilation, Fiedler suspends his love poet between two worlds (hoping perhaps that both characters, like Huck on the river, will come to relish how thoroughly they belong to neither). Vin moves between the traditional world of love and commitment and the more contemporary arena of sexual athleticism and casual involvements. Indeed, Vin moves literally—through two rooms during the wedding reception. In one, he finds a wide circle of dancing, sweating guests celebrating with drunken abandon the Jewish wedding of his goddaughter. Vin is fascinated by the frenetic choreography of the traditional steps. He considers the elements of the vanishing tradition such dancing recalls—the thin weeping virgin-bride, the solemn sanctity of the vows, and the trembling anticipation of the wedding night itself, traditions that he understands (given his own sexual résumé) are threatened by contemporary licentiousness. The dancing circle attempts to pull Vin into its embrace—but he resists. He cannot find a place within such tradition.

But before Vin leaves the room, an ancient woman, believing Vin to be the rabbi, insists that Vin dance with her. As they dance, she tells of her family, her sense of its rootedness and of her place within it. With determination, against swollen and heavy legs, she moves about in the traditional steps. Her conversation slips easily into Yiddish, which Vin, of course, cannot follow. But Vin is moved by the woman's resiliency and by her faith in institutions, and he responds in the only way he can express emotions—he kisses her full on the mouth and assures her that had he danced with her on her wedding night, her husband would have been without a bride, a crude remark that speaks of his own lifestyle of easy fornications, a remark so wildly out of place that (like Jacob Moskowitz's Yom Kippur service) it mocks the truer emotions that Vin is no doubt struggling to register. He is then moved to tell her the truth, that he is no rabbi—such a revelation prompts the expected results. Shocked, she pulls away in disgust, leaving him alone. He is left suddenly—and promisingly—apart.

But he is quickly escorted down a narrow and twisting staircase to a windowless room where, to pounding rock and roll and amid the sweet fog of marijuana and the blinking lights of a juke box, young sweaty couples gyrate in grotesque contortions that mimic the sexual activity they are most assuredly anticipating. Again, Vin stands apart, watching. Which is the world of Vin Hazelbaker? He is moved by the nostalgia represented by the aging woman with whom he dances—but authentic connection is clearly impossible, she and her world belong to a moment long vanished, indeed to a culture that is not even his to claim. But Vin is no more comfortable in the world of the young, despite the lifestyle suggested by his considerable inventory of random sexual involvements. His has been a life of love entirely devoid of love, a life whose sole childhood memory is of his paramedic deflowering by a Native American whore back in Lewis and Clark City—a blasphemy of the experience of love akin to Jacob's sole childhood memory, the blasphemous breaking of the Yom Kippur fast. Not surprisingly, when Vin finds himself alone with Miriam, an ex-mistress to whom he confesses (despite his marriage) that he has always loved her best, he can express such emotional need only through a hard, pressing kiss delivered clumsily across turned-over garbage cans in a littered alley outside the wedding reception, a sorry performance (one that recalls the Yom Kippur service) whose potentially critical importance is undercut first by a group of taunting black kids and then, more alarmingly, by the intervention of Vin's wife, who reveals the sad effects of a lifetime spent discovering such infidelities: she refuses any confrontation but rather makes an awkward, if telling, observation about how marriage had become "a joke, a gag, a gasser" (86).

Like Jacob Moskowitz, who morphs into Shylock, Vin will close his narrative by becoming his own worst stereotype—in this case, nothing less than a Nazi. We close the narrative at the apartment of the bride's mother, an ex-mistress of Vin's. Vin has been driven to the apartment by his wife and his two ex-mistresses. With drunken carelessness, the women begin to strip Vin, which he takes (naturally) as the most promising sort of foreplay. He prepares for the ultimate excess of sensualism, a *ménage à quatre*. But rather than pursue such decadence, the women complete the stripping and move to leave Vin to sleep off his bourbon. He is incensed, his sensual appeal (despite his erect prong) so curtly denied, and he hurls disquieting epithets at the retreating women.

Such a tantrum climaxes with his taking a wild swing at his wife and hitting instead the beautiful Miriam—smacking her between her "two wide tearful eyes" (102). It is a shocking moment, one that reveals Vin's core problem, his inability to connect with women (indeed with anyone) save on the animal level. Hurt, he hurts back, his emotional register never crawling above the animal. He stands shockingly revealed—as when Jacob connives over shares in the afterlife. Vin's wife denounces Vin, calls him a "vicious, self-important, aging shit" and a "loathsome brute." Then, in a moment of brutal honesty, she levels Vin—she calls him a "Nazi" (102). Vin's sensualist agenda, so apparently harmless as he swings amid women he is so certain want him to bed them, is laid bare in a single brutal moment as the fundamental assumption behind the most horrific philosophy of the twentieth century, the casual denial of the human dimension to others.

Vin is left alone, in the dark, naked, bleeding (from a zipper cut as the women had stripped him). It is a position—as when Jacob listens to the Kol Nidre under the shadowy crucifix—that promises the epiphanic revelation of the powerful suasion of alienation. But Vin cannot accept such a position. Vin struggles to locate a telephone, intent to project himself through the night's void, to tap out any number that might promise connection. It is then we are finally told of the letter that Vin has kept in his pocket all day. We learn that on a visit some months before to Lewis and Clark College, Vin had encountered a shy graduate student, Ardith Eugenia Sparrow. Even as his reading bored the gathered university elite who fidgeted and even left early, even as he is surrounded after his reading by the insufferably smug, Vin is momentarily impressed by the Sparrow woman, who comes up to him and reassures him enigmatically that, yes, someone in the audience did understand. Vin assumes the mysterious woman has responded to his love poetry, that here this frail woman had somehow resisted the cynical contemporary collapse of love into casual carnality. And that night, even as Vin moves toward the obligatory rendezvous with yet another married (and insufferably shallow) coed and takes her in his hotel room, the image of the other woman stays with him. He imagines her alone in bed reciting his poetry into the lonely darkness.

Her letter, however, has revealed that, far from the ethereal, she does indeed understand Vin exactly—her letter is a bold request for Vin to fuck her, its bald carnality underscored by her use of the jarring expletive, by an italicized "please," and by several exclamation points. Still reeling from the letter's revelation, Vin is in perfect position to end the sorry pretense that has become his life and to step out into the unsettling element of alienation. But he rejects it, terrified by its implications. We close with Vin, alone and naked in the dark silence, his erection inexplicably taut, screaming helplessly into a dead phone, that phone and the stiff erection both suggesting that Vin will not embrace: the uselessness of connection. Like Jacob, Vin fears the sole element that engenders the authentic spiritual sensibility—for prophets and poets—in this horrific century: the crippling beauty of isolation. A superannuated sensualist, interred in the immediate; a poet without production, too content with celebrity; a lover who defines love by the twitch of a skirt, the heft of a buttocks, the cut of a blouse, the texture of the flesh, the availability of a bed, Vin only momentarily touches his isolation. Panicked at one point, he sees that he is not Perseus but more like Andromeda herself in the icy black sea or, more disturbing, like the rock itself. But he cannot find his way to the complex resilience that might embrace, as Huck Finn does, such a spiritual condition. Rather, he clings to the dead telephone, screaming for help until his voice fails, as hopeless as Jacob smugly clinging to his illusory promissory notes for the afterlife.

III

We save the most distressing case for Fiedler's close. "The First Spade in the West" is deceptively comic—a sort of anecdote, or extended joke, about an aging white woman, Elmira Gallagher, apparently killed by the act of making love to a well-endowed black man, a sort of racist variation on the "oldest joke in the world" (179), the one about the old man who dies trying to please a young bride. Its close is deceptively affirmative—black businessman Ned York appears to have found his way to acceptance by the white community of Lewis and Clark City, voted as the Kiwanis Man of the Year despite the harrowing night when he beds the dowager Elmira, newly remarried, who then dies on him the following morning. That distressing imbroglio neatly finessed, Ned York prepares to take his place. He is Andromeda rescued—but we cannot embrace such hokey celebration because Fiedler's admiration, after all, is for Andromeda on the rocks.

In Ned York, Fiedler examines the deep hypocrisy of those who work to belong. Like Jacob and like Vin, Ned should by rights be apart. He is a halfbreed—part black, part Native American, his

father a drifter, his mother a barmaid in a speakeasy. He begins
as a boxer—venting his deep rage in the ring—but he had long
since given up the fight. Ned tries now to pass for white—he
married a white woman; he refuses to pursue strident civil rights
activism; he shamelessly promotes his "high-class Cocktail
Lounge" (128) among the town's toney white upper class with
their "juicy expense accounts" (128); he measures success by material trappings; he panders to white social authority—the Chamber
of Commerce and the Kiwanis Club—seeking the benediction of
the Kiwanis Club by baldly politicking for its Man of the Year
designation, although acknowledging that the tokenism of the
gesture renders its bestowal virtually meaningless. He reveals distressing bigotries that suggest his embrace of the white middle
class has gone quite deep—particularly his nasty biases against
Native Americans and against gays; he nurses glasses of cold milk
as antidote for a burgeoning ulcer. When the narrative opens,
Ned agrees to entertain the late night hip white crowd at his
lounge by singing a traditional blues song recorded by Leadbelly,
a much-tormented black artist whose authentic experience of dis-
placement and alienation is parodied by Ned, who clearly feigns
the pain in such blues work. It is like the Kol Nidre sung by
matinee idol Al Jolson, Ned acknowledges that he barely knows
the chords and strums the guitar mechanically with his neatly
manicured fingers—indeed, he forgets the song halfway through.
Cheerfully, he abandons the stage: "Anybody can sing, but somebody's got to make the drinks" (127). Indeed.

Like Jacob and Vin, Ned is given to us without the complication
of sympathy. Like them, he is unattractively shallow—he makes
no effort to understand the murals ("red and white splotches"
[130]) he had commissioned for his lounge wall, secure only that
they reek of class. He is proud of his son, an ex-professional foot-
ball player, largely because of his inflated income apparently unaware how such a profession merely reinforces the traditional
notion that blacks in American society find reputation most readily in the sports arena; and Ned is proud of his daughter's array
of high school honors, although he is told bluntly by one of the
musicians in his bar's band that her selection had more to do with
her classmate's uneasiness at her being the only black in the
school. The man calls the daughter a "freak" (132), an epithet
that would naturally attract Fiedler as richly promising but one
that Ned greets angrily by swinging wildly at the man. Ned wants
only to be accepted as white. The darkly comic relationship between the gay gigolo and the aging dowager—he yells obscenities

at the bewildered old woman, certain that drinking impairs her hearing, and later pitches quarters into her abundant open cleavage as she slumps drunkenly over the bar and even takes bets on the accuracy of his tosses—surely suggests Fiedler's cold assessment, à la Twain, of the affluent white society Ned so hungers to be a part of: its icy hypocrisy, its moral shallowness, and its thorough pretense, a gay (who made a reputation in local repertory theater by playing the exaggerated machismo of Stanley Kowalski) now playing gigolo to a drunken dowager-*qua*-blushing bride.

Like Jacob and Vin, Ned will be maneuvered to a promising position apart but there will only expose his own triviality and, ultimately, will devolve into his own worst stereotype. For most of the narrative, Ned plays with bland indifference the Stepin' Fetchit role (indeed, he describes himself with pride as descendant of the black slave who served under Lewis and Clark). He attempts to ingratiate himself with the rich white customers, singing the Leadbelly riff for their drunken amusement. When Elmira's party stumbles into the club quite late, Ned suffers the indignities of their racial slurs and even offers them drinks on the house. And when the gay man, who is celebrating (or perhaps forgetting) his secret marriage to the aging wealthy woman, passes out at his table, Ned even agrees to help deliver all 220 pounds of him to the couple's secluded lake estate. Once there, he will be reduced to playing the ultimate Stepin' Fetchit variation: the Mandingo stereotype, the black stud, at once powerful and powerless, called upon to service a blushing and aging daughter of the Old South who is darkly fascinated by legends of black endowments (Elmira admits to such a pedigree even as she zips herself into a scanty "black lace thing" [158] and suddenly forces a hokey accent).

Although Ned's easy willingness to "haul the ashes" of a married woman on such cold impulse (the logic he offers is really only that she is available and hence fuckable) speaks to his insensitivity and to his slippery moral makeup, it is his behavior the following morning, after he finds her dead, that recalls Jacob Moskowitz and Vin Hazelbaker, who in their narratives move to positions when they freely discount the humanity of those about them. He evidences no regard for the dead woman after finding her in the grotesque post–cardiac arrest position; he thinks, oddly amused, that he must have been just too much for her. He calmly dresses, straightening his tie "just right" (164). Yes, he fumes, but only over the precarious position of his secret past as a petty crook given the inevitable involvement of the local police. When a friend,

a gay musician from the club, shows up for a fishing date with
the husband, Ned agrees (after coolly negotiating with the man
for his help) to restage the woman's death by placing her gay
husband, still very much passed out, in bed with the corpse so
that when he finally revived he would assume, undoubtedly to his
amazement, that not only had he had sex with his new wife but
that he had sufficient potency apparently to kill her. It is profoundly theatrical—a performance of suggestion and of the suasion of appearances.

Indeed, the police fall for the ruse, and the entire episode
becomes something of a local joke. But, as in Fiedler's other narratives, we close on a most disturbing moment. We end appropriately on stage. Elmira is given a public memorial service—her
casket, a gaudy silver and white, is put on the stage of a downtown
theater, the renovation of which she had spearheaded. The theater fills with the local (decidedly white) power structure. There
on stage, in a posture that brings the narrative directly to the
theme of performance and inauthenticity, is Ned; he is accorded
what might seem a position of some import—he is a pallbearer.
But such work is, after all, merely a glorified Stepin' Fetchit—he
carries the coffin on stage and, two hours later, will carry it off.

Meanwhile, he stands on stage dressed absurdly (in accordance
with the dead woman's will) in full cowboy regalia, one of four
pallbearers—the others, the gay widower himself, the gay beatnik
who helped Ned cover the death, and one of the town's few Jews.
It is a quartet of the alienated, the misfits, each a contemporary
variation of the Huck Finn prototype, each in the costuming of
our culture's abiding figure of strength and isolation. With merci-
less satire, Fiedler closes the narrative with this quartet of community pariahs joining in the singing of the state song, an ardent
affirmation of the existing social structure that talks of tolerance
but, in fact, baldly rejects acceptance. Even the song participates
in Fiedler's larger theme of inauthenticity—for all its evocation of
the sweeping majesty of Montana, the anthem was written by a
hack showtune writer from back East, a hoofer stranded in the
state when his road show went bust. But Ned, on stage and proud
in his supremely superficial way of how well his costuming fits,
considers himself located, presumes that he now belongs—even
though, despite being the Kiwanis Man of the Year, he still cannot
get a haircut in town; miscegenation is still a crime in his state; a
nearby town actually sponsors a Pancake and Watermelon Jambo-
ree to honor a black retiring as the local high school's "general
handyman" (yet another glorified Stepin' Fetchit); and, looming

above the memorial service, the theater's new massive mural of Lewis and Clark simply excludes the hardy slave, Ned's ancestor, who strove mightily to ensure the success of that enterprise.

We leave this sham-Negro, this sham-cowboy, shamming emotions on stage as part of a sham-funeral service that is in its very theatricality a mockery of the traditional ritual. Ned has played out his life on stage, a life by fakery, chameleon inauthenticity, and imitation (he decides in the aftermath of the woman's death that his own bar can be easily made over into a Gay Nineties decor—sure, why not), pandering shamelessly for acceptance by manipulating appearances and by discounting as simply irrelevant his legitimate racial identity. Fiedler damns such superficiality the only way he can—he bestows on New York the empty gift of place. He is Man of the Year, an honor that, like Jacob's Yom Kippur service and Vin Hazelbaker's love poetry, is so emptied of authentic emotion it becomes parody.

The position of spiritual alienation and dislocation that is so much at the dark heart of the American experience is suggested then by the Jew, the poet, and the African American; Fiedler affirms the possibility of that position by reviling his own characters—a Jew, a poet, and an African American—who work so diligently to empty their status of its authentic, if disturbing, spiritual dimension. Fiedler cannot brook their easy charades. Whether Jacob, so supremely confident and trafficking in shares of the afterlife, or Vin, so paralyzed by the sharp intuition of his alienated status, or Ned, so validated by his triumphant social positioning, Fiedler cautions against the compelling urge to belong. He offers three stark portraits of those who busy themselves about the horizontal plane of experience, who become unsettling parodies of self-importance accepting lives that never touch the authentic (God, beauty, integrity) because they refuse to acknowledge the most provocative assessment of the human condition proffered by American literature: the deep terror and concomitant joy of isolation. We are left with the disturbing figure of Ned York, the first of what we fear will become a long line of "spades," Fiedler invoking the loaded epithet as a way of underscoring his own displeasure at the moral cowardice of those who opt for strategies of placement and who, in the process, void their character and become little more than caricatures.

NOTES

1. Mark Royden Winchell makes this point at some length as a focal theme of Fiedler's criticism, although he does not apply the notion to *The Last Jew.*

Of all of Fiedler's fascinating examinations of outcasts, freaks, and outlaws, a particularly relevant argument can be drawn from *Waiting for the End,* published shortly before *The Last Jew,* in which Fiedler argues that the Jewish-American and African American fictions of midcentury could find their way into the national argument only by tapping the larger spirit of the American experience. He cites Huck Finn as the embodiment of this compelling urge to distrust the social structure as inherently soul-deadening.

2. Fiedler's free use of stereotypes in this collection proved something of a problem for reviewers. See Bellman's particularly nasty review that cites the stereotypes as inept characterizations, apparently unaware of the possibility that Fiedler, ever the astute critic of contemporary culture, might be invoking so many stereotypes deliberately.

WORKS CITED

Bellman, Samuel I. "In Groups within Groups." Rev. of *The Last Jew in America. Saturday Review,* 30 July 1966, 31–32.

Fiedler, Leslie. *The Last Jew in America.* New York: Stein and Day, 1966.

Winchell, Mark Royden. *Leslie Fiedler.* Boston: Twayne, 1985.

Freakshow: Normality, Self, and Other in Leslie Fiedler's Short Stories

BROOKE HORVATH

"You, whoever you are . . ."

—Walt Whitman

From "Come Back to the Raft Ag'in, Huck Honey!," *The Jew in the American Novel,* and "The New Mutants" to *The Stranger in Shakespeare, Freaks,* and *Tyranny of the Normal,* Leslie Fiedler's criticism and social commentary have been obsessed with norms, their oppressive elusiveness, their complicity in the construction of otherness. As he told *Newsweek* in 1984, "I began . . . by writing about ethnic outsiders—blacks, Indians—then about excluded generations and genders—adolescents, women—and finally about physiological abnormalities—freaks. I'm more interested in defining what's human by the marginal than by the central."[1]

Fiedler's short fiction likewise reveals a fascination with marginalized and sometimes self-loathing outsiders: the economically, culturally, or emotionally impoverished; failed or otherwise alienated artists and intellectuals; compromised radicals; dubiously assimilated Jews; the physically or mentally infirm; self-abusive misfits; homosexuals in the days before Stonewall. Often the stories include obvious examples of socially designated "others": Mrs. Jovanich in "Let Nothing You Dismay," a Jew who cannot forget the horrors of Nazi Germany and whose Christmas Eve presence explodes a family's illusions of assimilation; Warren, the self-anointed but inconsequential intellectual of "The Teeth," who delights in enhancing his already considerable repulsiveness; Milton Amsterdam of "Pull Down Vanity!," a New York Jew fresh from Texas who at a Missouri writers' conference feels himself "an intruder and a spy" (*Nude Croquet,* 189); Ham, the dream-haunted black protagonist of "The Stain," rejected by both the white world and the Communist Party with its promises to remake

61

that world; the reservation "Indians" of "Bad Scene at Buffalo Jump," told by a local professor that, despite the squalor and anonymity of their lives, they enjoy a fulfillment of the American Dream superior to that attained by their white "exploiters" (*Nude Croquet*, 253–54).

If Fiedler's work has, as John McGowan asserts, constantly concerned itself with "people on the margin of culture who embody its deepest fears and deepest urges,"[2] the stories collected in *Nude Croquet* show necessarily an equal interest in those ("the central") who scapegoat these marginal others as a means of sustaining the myth of their own normality. But to say this is to argue that what the short stories reveal—the deep fear the marginalized other exposes—is that everyone inhabits the margins: to define the "human by the marginal," these stories suggest, is to expose the arbitrariness of any definition of "the central"—or to erase the normal as a meaningful category. In story after story, those not scapegoated are tyrannized by their need to belong among the ostensibly normal, a need that can drive them to insist upon a superior normality through rigorous displays of those attributes thought to be essential to a life at the center. In the end, to borrow a phrase from *Love and Death in the American Novel*, they become "monsters of virtue" (75) or, better, monsters of (superior) normality.

As Fiedler writes in the introduction to *Tyranny of the Normal*, "for all of us able to think of ourselves as 'normal,' there is a more ultimate Other' (xiii)—someone in contrast to whom the normal comes into being—and in that volume's title essay, explaining our culture's widespread fascination with physiological malformation, Fiedler observes that "those wretched caricatures of our idealized body image . . . are really a revelation of what in our deepest psyches we recognize as the Secret Self. After all, not only do we know that each of us is a freak to someone else; but in the depths of our unconscious (where the insecurities of childhood and adolescence never die) we seem forever freaks to ourselves" (*Tyranny*, 152). Everyone, in short, is someone else's other; everyone is his or her own other.

"Dirty Ralphy," for instance, presents two outsiders viciously scapegoating each other with normality the prize. The narrator, a Jew, recalls his childhood nemesis Ralphy, the day he punched out two of Ralphy's teeth, and the sudden revelation that rather than be damned to the childhood hell reserved for those labelled cowards, he "could harm what [he] hated" (*Nude Croquet*, 77) and so enter the paradise of normal adolescent machismo. Ralphy, unlike the narrator, lives dysfunctionally down "a mean alley" (77), and like that alley he is "filthy as we [the narrator's friends and family] were convinced it was a sin to be, crawling about in some lonely game amid the garbage and old boxes . . ." (78). The narrator asserts that Ralphy "did not live like other children," marked as he was by "the stigma of poverty" and hence very much at odds with the narrator's family, their clean rooms and shining glasses of milk.

Praising his cleanliness-is-next-to-godliness upbringing, the narrator confesses,

I was glad really . . . that my father worked hard and did not drink, that my mother mended and scrubbed for us, that we ate and went to bed at regular times—and above all, that we were Jews who could never be dirty or wanton or drunk, and who even washed our hands each time after going to the toilet. (79)

In his world, as the narrator acknowledges, "Dirty Ralphy became for me . . . the extreme revelation of what awaited those who, outside our law and election, began by not washing their hands, and plunged through extravagance, poor diet, and dirtiness toward final depravity" (79).

The need for Ralphy to fill the role of pariah is likewise made explicit:

We [the narrator's family] were almost alone in that small town, one of the three families of Jews, and it must be forgiven me if I imposed on a grimy addled boy the burden of symbolizing, at the level of contempt, the community that excluded us. When I walked past the cropped lawns, the white Gentile houses from which I had been taught to expect hostility, I had to believe . . . that behind their ostensible peace and security lay the real horror betrayed by Dirty Ralphy. (79–80)

Ralphy, then, functions for the narrator as an outsider's scapegoat, the means by which the narrator clings to his place among the chosen, a synecdoche of the hypocrisy that is Gentile propriety. The narrator knows that, from the standpoint of his neighborhood—and arguably America at large (the story was first published in 1947)—as a Jew he resides always among the marginal others. If Ralphy's cries of "dirty Jew" (80) spark shame in the narrator, causing him to run, "tear-stained, frightened" (78), home to his father, his father's response—to drag the boy back to Ralphy's alley for a fight—permits the use of Ralphy to escape a shameful cowardice ("'God damn it, no son of mine will grow up a coward!'" his father growls [78]) by asserting over this blustering but vulnerable goy a physical superiority that signals a superior normality.

But if besting Ralphy with a lucky punch and hiding behind supercilious hygiene placate the narrator, he never forgets the deeper ostracism of being a Jew, one of those who, Ralphy jeers, "killed our Christ!" (80): "outcast and fetid though [Ralphy] was, before my exile and blame *he* was the oppressor" (81). This awareness leaves the narrator alienated even from the rest of his boyhood crowd in their disdain for Ralphy: "Though in detesting him, I seemed one with the pack, I felt no kinship. Mine was a deeper difference than poverty or filth . . ." (81). It is in fact this more radical otherness that Ralphy seeks to exploit through his hurled epithets, which reverse the grounds for alienation and election, and it is the narrator's acceptance of his outsider status that leads to his unwanted identification with Ralphy.

When older (and when, like so many of Fiedler's narrators, he has perhaps begun to read Marx and Engels), the narrator says he even began to feel "remorse for my contempt of Ralphy, and could only believe him a victim, our hostility a disguise for social guilt, an uneasy hatred of what nurtured and defined our comfort" (80). Entertaining fantasies in which he rescues Ralphy "from packs of well-fed, over-dressed kids" and wins the boy's gratitude (80), the narrator confesses the allure of this other, of "what lurked in me too, under my rehearsed values and responses: a voluptuousness of abandonment, a hunger for filth and debasement; and I could not help knowing that there was complicity, a choice, a moral flaw beyond the plea of social fate in his plight" (80). The narrator understands, in short, both that his comfort's meaning requires the palpable presence of the uncomfortable and that "normality" is not inherent or God-given but "rehearsed," chosen, and therefore arbitrary, conditional, revocable.

The "real horror betrayed by Dirty Ralphy" (80) is not, however, only the narrator's recognition that neither Jewishness nor tidy respectability is any safeguard against ghettoization and the "uneasy hatred" of others. The horror lurks equally in the narrator's ecce-homo confrontation with his secret self and inability to sustain his fleeting commiseration, his imperfect awareness that to save Ralphy would be to save himself. But even in reverie, the narrator finds himself repulsed by Ralphy's "sour breath" and "half-mad insolence" (80)—by what should not matter but cannot be gotten past.

Or say that the horror resides in the story's closing pages wherein the narrator, now grown, is startled to learn from his mother that Ralphy was not the boy with whom he once fought, nor was Ralphy the vocal anti-Semite of the narrator's memories. Ralphy Goldenberg, the narrator's mother explains, was himself Jewish, and it was the tax commissioner's son, Arthur Wilcox, whose unavenged slurs stopped only when his family moved out of the neighborhood:

> "Momma—" I began, "Momma—" but I let it go, as that smell, sour and sunless and unforgotten, the smell of the injured, assailed me in that quiet room. Once more my blow fell, once more and forever to the mocking applause of a faceless Arthur, and bleeding over his teeth, as if bowed before me, crouched the Jew Ralphy. (82)

The final horror unintentionally revealed by Ralphy is that the scapegoated will unwittingly betray themselves in the effort to attain a dubious normality. Either Ralphy has bullied the narrator with ethnic invective to conceal his own Jewishness and distract attention from his poverty while laying claim to a more fundamental connection to the normal world—Gentile if not genteel—or the narrator has displaced his anger and shame at being a Jew among goyim onto a safe target, the doubly assailable because twice-othered Dirty Ralphy, elevating income and stable respectability over ethnicity as the grounds for normality—a self-deception so complete it denies the bond the narrator has felt between himself and the outcast down the alleyway.

In his introduction to *Freaks: Myths and Images of the Secret Self,* Fiedler notes that of the "primordial fears" set free through confrontations with the physically abnormal, insecurities about "our tenuous individuality" are embodied in Siamese twins: "In joined twins the confusion of self and other, substance and shadow, ego and other, is . . . terrifyingly confounded," shattering the illusion that a distinction exists between "we and them, normal and Freak" (35, 36). "Dirty" Ralphy and the "dirty Jew" he torments are, in terms of self and other, normal and abnormal, psychologically joined twins, as the adjective they share suggests. Each senses himself in the other, rebels against the othering that bond imposes, and pays the price of hatred, denial, self-delusion, and self-victimization.

If "Dirty Ralphy" is the story of outsiders pitted against one another, each abusing the other to gain entrance to normality, "Nobody Ever Died from It" is Hyman Brandler's story of a gay shoe salesman, Abie Peckelis, who knows that he is and always will be an outsider who exists for others as a means of defining the limits and attributes of their normality, that he is a tool in the construction of life-enhancing illusions spun by the likes of Hyman at the expense of himself and others like him. What is revealed by Hyman's description of Abie and his behavior during a store Christmas party are the tactics of a man who has decided to seize every opportunity to give the lie to the belief that normality belongs to anyone, by turning the shoe store where he works into his private freakshow.

Abie—who likes sometimes to refer to himself as "Florence" and who has been arrested for "impersonating a female" (160)—has a number of things working to marginalize him: a nellie queen (an exaggeratedly feminine gay) given to vamping, shrilly voiced crude sexual humor, and lewdly theatrical gestures, he is also a poorly educated drug user with a criminal record. Hyman, who has told the Peckelis story at parties "a hundred times" (*Nude Croquet,* 156) during the twenty-one years that have passed since the two worked together, likes to paint Abie as an exotic degenerate:

> I begin always by describing Peckelis: the identical oily ridges of his marcelled hair, and sullen droop of his fat lips, the eyelids as heavy as if hewn in stone. . . . the face of a wicked queen in an Assyrian bas-relief; a face ravaged by passions it does not understand. . . . an ugly body, uglier because borne with such outrageous assurance of its allure: the swollen female breasts visible beneath the sag of the coat from the padded shoulders, the movement of the hips a parody, savage and tender, of womanly charm. (156–57)

Although Hyman scoffs at Abie's assurance of his allure, the hundred retellings testify to a fascination that is, as the Fiedler of *Freaks* knows, at least partly a result of Abie's epicenism and transvestism—the fascination of the radically other.

What Hyman has been slow to realize is that for Abie, as Robert Gorham Davis has remarked is the case for almost all of Fiedler's fictional characters, "the lie as myth is life-giving" (76).[3] Abie is definitely homosexual, but—as he has confided to Hyman (159, 161)—he is also to a large degree feigning the role expected of him by the normals he condemns, donning the behavioral accouterments of the "funny man" (163) with the smirking superiority

of one who finds that to *épater les bourgeois* is life-enhancing, thera-
peutic. His assault on others—which his fellow salesman, the
lapsed social Max, can manage only when stinking drunk—is relentless: "Excuse me," he addresses a woman giggling at his antics
on the bus, "Lean over a little further—maybe you'll fall over on
that face. It could only be an improvement" (161); and wheeling
on a gaggle of eavesdroppers in the store, he cries, "Dogs! What
are you listening to? Come closer, you might miss something. Garbage!" (160). But provocation is unnecessary: a customer chosen
at random can become the victim of Abie's joking attempt to sell
her an "assblaster" brush ("Good for the hair around the hole," he
croons [163]), and at other times he will suddenly "[grab] himself
between the legs" to "scream in an anguished falsetto," "Oh! oh!
oh! I thought I had it, but I lost it!" (162).

Abie's self-defensive, bizarrely self-glorifying strategy is to con-
front those who find him an amusing or shocking curiosity with
the fragility of the wall behind which they gawk and titter. Indeed,
Hyman recalls that Abie "preferred for stooges large Negresses,
who would roll their eyes shyly; middle-aged matrons with foreign
accents; or the very old, the half-deaf, the obviously genteel"
(162). In the context of 1956, when "Nobody Ever Died from It"
first appeared, this list is largely a catalog of explicitly (blacks) or
implicitly (the old) marginalized others. However, that it concludes
with the "genteel"—those of decorous propriety, refined conven-
tionality—explodes the notion that any "us" exists finally as distinct from "them."

Abie's scorn extends to those with whom he works. He may be
an outsider, but as his choices of customer-victims indicate, his
ostracism does not imply tolerance for those differently othered:
the bitter, failed socialist Max, still secretly loathing the "boozh-
wahzee" and demonstrating his scorn by drunkenly trampling the
doll he has bought his daughter (165, 172); the black porter
George, who metamorphoses during the store's Christmas party
(thrown by the store's Jewish manager for his mostly Jewish employees) into a "jig" left lying unattended with a broken leg in the
basement (171); Greenie, the store's oldest employee, who will
because of his age "be fired inside of a month or two" (165);
Mr. Z., the manager, toasting this "big happy family" and singing
parodies of Yiddish songs (accompanied by the cashier, long sus-
pected of being an anti-Semite) but behind his back held up by
Max and Hyman as a capitalist exploiter (170, 167).

Recipient of Abie's severest scorn, however, is Murphy the cop,
symbolic representative of the enforcers of normality. Appearing

toward the end of the party, Murphy jokingly dances with Abie, then gooses him obscenely with his nightstick to the fascinated delight of the others. If Murphy cannot see the embarrassing part he plays in making the pitiful Abie what he is, neither can Murphy appreciate the hatred that bubbles up through Abie's humiliation. As the shoe-dog fakes sexual gratification at the end of Murphy's billy, he silently mouths Yiddish curses directed at the cop: "'May he swell up—may he be hanged; may he burn like a candle . . .'" (171). As Abie had confided earlier to Hyman, attempting to diminish the distance he knows Hyman perceives separating the two, "I only make fun for the boys" (161)—and to get along by pretending to be what others wish him to be.

If age, race, ethnicity, gender, and politics render everyone in the shoe store an outsider of one sort or another, Hyman, fourteen years old when the events recounted occurred, is the most marginal of them all. He is told repeatedly by everyone to go home as the party begins, and a few weeks earlier, he reveals, he had been along with Abie the butt of one of the hose girls' jokes when enlisted by them to deliver to Abie a sexual gag gift (158). Hyman may protest that they "did not deliberately mock me," but he also confesses that he would "have given alot to be able to kid with the hose girls as some of the salesmen did" (158). In fact, although he self-importantly drops the names of authors he is reading and claims Freud has taught him too much to find the girls' joke funny, he cannot join the laughter surrounding Abie's gift because he doesn't really get it: only a few weeks earlier his mother had given him "a little book about sex and procreation" (158), the older Hyman recalls as a way of indicating the naïveté of his younger self beneath the smug mask he typically sported. Indeed, if his age guarantees his otherness, Hyman's self-image exacerbates it. At fourteen, he has made it generally known that he is a political radical who is writing a novel about his fellow employees, and he basks childishly in Mr. Z.'s references to him as a genius, doubtless an offhand and possibly insincere compliment but one Hyman seemed at the time to believe was true. He is, however, so peripheral to the others that no one can remember his name, calling him throughout the story "Herman" despite his efforts to correct them.

During the Christmas party, observing Hyman's reactions to the goings-on, Max calls the boy's bluff: "Feeling pretty *superior*, ain't you, snotnose. Su-per-i-or, that's a fancy word for a shoe-dog," attacking a moment later with "Oh, you know the score all right! We're just wage slaves, white-collared, yellow-bellied boozhwahzees. Ain't that right, Comrade Genius?" (168, Fiedler's emphasis). Similarly, outside the store as the party breaks up, Abie also turns on Hyman, who has attempted to avoid being noticed and so spoken to by Peckelis lest the bus-stop crowd become aware of the acquaintance and presume more. "Dog!," Abie shouts, "Don't try to hide. I know you already. False! You're like all the rest—*false!*" (174). It is a fair response to Hyman's denial of a man who has only wished to be his friend, who has offered the boy advice about the importance of getting an education and being good to one's mother, who has dropped his guard to reveal "his loneliness, his faith in my [Hyman's] understanding" (161) only to find himself betrayed by Hyman's "revulsion" (170), his bus-stop denial, and twenty-one years of homophobic anecdotes.

The reasons behind Hyman's response to Abie are clear: Hyman cannot afford, then or later, the guilt by association he believes a friendship with Abie would entail. He flushes with embarrassment when Max refers to Abie as "your pal" (164), and his constant retelling of this story seems the assertion of his own normality within a self-selected community of normals: "Woe betide [anyone hearing the story for the first time] if he sits there straight-faced or only snickers politely. He is written off forever as a *shmuck*" (156). As a young, sexually inexperienced Jew whose education and aspirations set him apart from the others, whose name no one can be bothered correctly to remember, Hyman simply cannot risk further alienation from his sense of superior normality that a hint of homoeroticism would impute, if only in his own mind. His normality, at any rate, can be asserted time and again through such distancing ploys as referring to Abie as "that god-damn fairy" (170).

As an adult (who appears again in "An Expense of Spirit" as a lonely misanthrope), Hyman continues to feel his status uncertain: he becomes, as the years pass, merely a writer manqué who has spent his life enduring rejection slips and selling shoes. The sense of specialness, of superiority, that permitted the buttressing of his ego at the expense of the inferior, abnormal other, has faltered. He begins his story by mocking his own failure to become a writer and the absurd compromise that has left him instead the owner of his own soon-to-open shoe store, "The New Bon-Ton Bootery":

Store or no store, I am what I am. Each day when I shave, I look at the middle-aged shoe salesman under the lather, and suddenly I want to weep or giggle—I hardly know which. Here is the face of a man

who at thirty-five has published nothing, who owns his own store, who
has even sent himself a floral horseshoe inscribed: Success! (155)

The pathetic irony of the floral horseshoe cannot be missed; nor
can Hyman overlook the fact that neither novel nor store will
change what he essentially is, nor will either be enough to buy
him an unflappable normality in a world filled with Abie Peckel-
ises. Hyman Brandler has finally learned the limits and debilitat-
ing demands of normality. If his failures have taught him "that
the only answer is to laugh" (156), his melancholic chuckle is now
directed at himself—and at the folly of everyone who attempts to
compensate for a sense of failed normality through role-playing,
scapegoating, or drink, illusions of their own superior specialness
as defined by religion or politics or social class, or a retreat into
misanthropic solitude.

Hyman closes his story with the recollection of joining the bus-
stop crowd in their laughter at Abie: "I smile smugly to myself at
the nuttiness of Abie Peckelis—I who at fourteen believe I have
never betrayed anything, and know that I never will" (174). But
Hyman at thirty-five knows otherwise: just as his opening self-
deprecation concedes but forgives his self-betrayals, these closing
lines acknowledge that twenty-one years ago by denying Abie he
betrayed both Peckelis and himself by purchasing a place in the
crowd at his potential friend's expense.[4]

"Nobody ever died from it" (166), the hose girls tell Hyman
when, the Christmas party in full swing, they attempt to get the
boy liquored up. But the women's words, a glib exercise in bonho-
mie, are patently inaccurate as far as both alcohol and the corro-
sive, potentially lethal effects of a coercive normality are
concerned. Like "Dirty Ralphy," "Nobody Ever Died from It" exposes the tenuousness of all norms and the cruel grotesquerie
that can reside within efforts to inhabit the ostensibly normal.
Those who see the world through normal-colored glasses may say
otherwise. They may praise sentimentally if condescendingly the
lives of othered individuals, as does Professor Baro Finkelstone,
speaking foolishly at a "Conference on Indian Affairs" about the
lives of those he hardly understands ("Bad Scene at Buffalo
Jump," *Nude Croquet*, 253). Or they may exploit their otherness to
their own selfish advantage, as the poet Milton Amsterdam does
to secure the affection of a writing conference's "full coven" of
aging midwestern "poetesses" ("Pull Down Vanity!," *Nude Croquet*,
176, 209) and, less platonically, the passionate attention of a pretty
but sexually frustrated young secretary ("'Oh my darling,' she

sobbed, 'you do like me, you *do!* My poor Milton, my poor, *poor* Jew" [227]).

But however the othering implicit in constructions of normality may be used, those constructions are always, these stories suggest, founded upon the lie of essential difference. Thus, in "The Stain," Ham, startled by some boys' use of the word "nigger," reflects:

> His being, as they said, "colored" was not for *him* a fact, only for the others, the whites—and their definition he felt imposed on him from without: a distinction of fear, a discrimination of contempt: a stain. *Their* stain, he cried in his head bitterly, *their* shame!
>
> He could see his face now . . . the broad nose, gross lips, the tight nap of hair that even he could dream on no hero. From childhood on, his picture books, the movies had proposed to him a mythical American face, thin-nosed, smooth-haired, grayish-pink, before which he must confess his own face a failure, a blemish. (*Nude Croquet*, 248; Fiedler's emphases)

But Ham knows as well that, as regards blacks and whites, "there is no real difference between us, nothing which corresponds to the outer difference, only what they have invented—*their* lie":

> But he knew that if it were really a lie, if they were truly alike . . . their guilt must be his guilt, too, their stain somehow also his stain. Either the internal blackness was a human blackness, the dark failure of everybody, or else there was *no* stain. . . . (249)

Employing allegory and parable, folk tale, black humor, and slice-of-life realism, the stories collected in *Nude Croquet* variously pursue the causes and consequences of coercive normalizing— from the ultimate othering of death and estrangement from one's own wife and child in "The Fear of Innocence" to the otherness endured historically by entire groups of people ("The Dancing of Reb Hershl with the Withered Hand"), from the otherness that can surprise one with a change of geographical and cultural locale ("Let Nothing You Dismay," "Bad Scene at Buffalo Jump") to the reciprocity of otherness lying in wait whenever the sexes meet ("The Girl in the Black Raincoat") or private insecurities over- whelm ("Nude Croquet," "The Teeth").

Regardless, Fiedler's point, as he himself has elsewhere put it, is that finally *"there are no normals"* (*Tyranny of the Normal*, 153; Fiedler's emphasis)—which agrees with what is increasingly understood to be the case today. Thus, in his recent book on stuttering Marty Jezer dismisses the vogue in his youth of providing psychological explanations for all personal problems with a dismissive "as if perfection were the norm"[5], and Michael Bérubé, writing on Down Syndrome, argues that "the 'normal' is not a category that exists on its own: it requires the creation of various 'abnormals,'" these only seemingly natural categories turning on "a distinction between kinds of variety we will agree to overlook—differences that don't make a difference—and kinds of variety for which we will create social institutions that 'administer' to those with 'special needs.'"[6]

In *Nude Croquet*'s twelve stories, which upon their appearance were often as not perceived to fall somewhere outside the margins of acceptable short fiction,[7] Fiedler, notorious for styling himself a "presumptuous outsider" (*Tyranny of the Normal*, ix), would seem to be making a point he has made at least since *Love and Death in the American Novel:* that if "maturity involves the ability to believe the self normal" (*Freaks*, 31), we are outsiders to the world of maturity. It is for Fiedler ironically a world in which forces conspire toward mandatory normality—as in medical decisions today regarding the "removal of life supports" from "malformed neonates" (*Tyranny*, 148)—leaving "those of us allowed to survive by the official enforcers of the Norm . . . free to become even more homogeneously, monotonously . . . supernormal, however that ideal may be defined" (*Tyranny*, 155).

If "they" are abnormal because not we, Fiedler's short fiction usefully suggests that, upon closer scrutiny, there is no "we" anywhere. In story after story, what passes for the normal collapses to reveal in what pathetically grotesque prisonhouses of cards many of us have attempted to make uncharitable homes for ourselves.

NOTES

1. Quoted in David Gates, "Fiedler's Utopian Vision," 11.
2. John McGowan, "Leslie A. Fiedler," 94.
3. Davis' comments on Fiedler's fiction are particularly interesting in light of the argument being forwarded here. Davis finds Fiedler—and his characters—preoccupied with "lies, ambiguities, confusions of identity" (74), his characters' "social and ethnic status" as well as whatever ideas they may voice "primarily interesting as chosen or enforced role-playing" in stories in which the quest for identity pits "inwardly desperate people against other desperate people" (76).
4. Mark Royden Winchell disagrees, judging Hyman "a successful storyteller but a failed novelist" because lacking "human understanding." In support of this reading, Winchell points to the story's closing lines ("I smile smugly to myself

. . ."), which, because rendered in the present tense, imply Hyman's "continuing lack" of that indispensible understanding (Winchell, *Leslie Fiedler*, 118).

Ronald Bryden's reading is closer to the one forwarded here, although focussed on Fiedler more than on Hyman Brandler: "Abie Peckelis is gross, epicene, humiliating and two-parts mad; the satisfaction he gets from being goosed with a policeman's night-stick is human animality at its most abject. This, Mr. Fiedler seems to say, is what you build sentimental theories of tolerance about, this is the thing itself. He can afford to, for in the end he manages to accept Abie, with all his horror, as equal, human, pitiable as all men are" (241).

5. Marty Jezer, *Stuttering*, 31.

6. Michael Bérubé, *Life as We Know It*, 207–8.

7. Guy Davenport, for instance, with his customary aplomb, observes that Fiedler "abuses the art of telling a story. . . . he makes certain that what he tells is as far from a story as one can get. There is no plot; there are no characters that one can see in one's imagination; and, triumph of triumphs over what one would think was utterly impossible, there is no style" (123). Similarly, Ronald Bryden, although more sympathetic, judges those stories first gathered in the collection *Pull Down Vanity and Other Stories* (later expanded as *Nude Croquet*) as distorted beyond "the possibility of thinking of them . . . as art" (239).

WORKS CITED

Bérubé, Michael. *Life as We Know It: A Father, a Family, and an Exceptional Child.* New York: Pantheon, 1996.

Bryden, Ronald. "My Son the Frontiersman." Rev. of *Pull Down Vanity*. In *The Unfinished Hero and Other Essays*. London: Faber, 1969. 239–42.

Davenport, Guy. "Over-Told, Half-Told, Well-Told." Rev. of *Nude Croquet*. *National Review*, 4 November 1969, 1123.

Davis, Robert Gorham. "Leslie Fiedler's Fictions." *Commentary*, January 1967, 73–77.

Fiedler, Leslie A. *Freaks: Myths and Images of the Secret Self.* New York: Simon and Schuster, 1978.

———. *Love and Death in the American Novel*. 1960. Rev. ed. New York: Stein, 1966.

———. *Nude Croquet: The Stories of Leslie A. Fiedler*. New York: Stein, 1969.

———. *Tyranny of the Normal: Essays on Bioethics, Theology & Myth*. Boston: Godine, 1996.

Gates, David. "Fiedler's Utopian Vision." *Newsweek*, 9 January 1984, 11.

Jezer, Marty. *Stuttering: A Life Bound Up in Words*. New York: Basic Books, 1997.

McGown, John. "Leslie A. Fiedler." In *Modern American Critics since 1955*, vol. 67 of *Dictionary of Literary Biography*, edited by Gregory S. Jay, 90–96. Detroit: Gale, 1988.

Winchell, Mark Royden. *Leslie Fiedler*. Twayne's United States Author Series 492. Boston: Twayne, 1985.

The Importance of *Being Busted*

STEVEN G. KELLMAN

I first read *Love and Death in the American Novel* in college in 1965, when no reputable literary critic either began or ended a sentence with the pronoun *I*. One still observed an academic quarantine against evidence of the author. "Poetry is not a turning loose of emotion, but an escape from emotion," decreed T. S. Eliot; "it is not the expression of personality, but an escape from personality" (764). Yet, though John Berryman, Allen Ginsberg, Robert Lowell, and Sylvia Plath were already projecting their own distinctive identities into their poetry, for the *poètes manqués* who became professors, analyzing literary texts still meant concealing spoors of the slovenly self. Against the New Critical ideal of impersonality that still dominated intellectual life in 1960 (when it was published), Fiedler announced, heretically, that *Love and Death* "is finally a very personal book, in which I attempt to say with my own voice out of my own face (all masks abandoned) what I have found to be some major meanings of our literature and our culture" (13). By the end of a tumultuous decade, the conventions of academic discourse were changed utterly, and Fiedler was an overt agent of that change.

Fiedler would later call his most famous book "a vast horrific-comic overview of American fiction" (*Being Busted*, 53). Raw with youthful pluck but ripe with seasoned insight, *Love and Death*, written when Fiedler was already on the verge of forty, was dazzling in its affectionate command of the American—and Western—canon and brilliantly mischievous in its pioneer project of outing Huck Finn, Ishmael, Natty Bummpo, and other quintessentially American white males who, we began to notice, preferred the company of dark-skinned men. However, before its provocative thesis came the volume's Preface. Because so often perfunctory or platitudinous, prefaces are justly neglected. But this one is a classic of the genre, a powerful piece of personal writing that, especially in its final paragraph, might be Fiedler at his most compelling, and intimate.

74

The author pays extraordinary tribute to William Ellery Leonard: "It was he who first not merely told but showed me—showed in the rich, tragic quality of his own being as well as by the excitement that he engendered in the classroom—that literature is more than what one learns to read in schools and libraries, more even than a grace of life; that it is the record of those elusive moments at which life is alone fully itself, fulfilled in consciousness and form" (15–16). Leonard was Fiedler's teacher at the University of Wisconsin, but though the former student refers to his mentor as "a great and, I hope, unforgotten teacher, as well as a rebel, poet, translator, and essayist" (15), it is likely that for most readers Leonard is unforgotten only because he was never known in the first place. However, Fiedler himself—also a teacher, rebel, poet, translator (of Dante), and essayist—makes continuing claims on our memory because his luscious prose embodies just those qualities of empathy and incandescence for which he honors the older man. Fiedler's eulogy for his ancient professor amounts to an eloquent assertion of his own professional credo:

> No one who has been his student can regard literary criticism as anything less than an act of total moral engagement, in which tact, patience, insolence, and piety consort strangely but satisfactorily together; nor can anyone who once listened to him believe that the truth one tries to tell about literature is finally different from the truth one tries to tell about the indignities and rewards of being the kind of man one is—an American, let's say, in the second half of the twentieth century, learning to read his country's books. (16)

This grandiose but glorious defense of literary criticism as something more than mere interpretive proficiency, "an act of total moral engagement," is a fitting prologue not merely to Fiedler's impassioned attempt to examine the tradition of the American novel, and the currents of American culture. It is a gloss on all the author's twenty-something books, not least on his most personal, *Being Busted,* an enduring blend of tact, patience, insolence, and piety.

The ordeal of tenure at American colleges and universities institutionalizes the opportunistic vice of self-seeking. But self-searching is a quality discouraged by the disinterested dedication to precision demanded by New Criticism. Published in 1969, *Being Busted* was certainly not the first instance of personal writing published by an American professor; Margaret Mead and Joseph Wood Krutch, among other scholars, had earlier abandoned the formalist fiction of *impassibilité.* However, the book anticipates

many of the qualities celebrated three decades later in the autobiographical narratives of Cathy Davidson, Henry Louis Gates,
Jr., Sandra Gilbert, Alice Kaplan, Frank Lentricchia, Susan Rubin
Suleiman, and other faculty authors. "I find it endlessly fascinating to tell the young how it is with me, just as I did to inform
the old about my own state when young," confesses the antic
Fiedler. "And I have always found my auditors, old and young,
equally interested" (55). Readers of various ages are likely to be
equally interested, if not endlessly fascinated, even three decades
after the book's publication.

Being Busted owes its genesis to Fiedler's arrest, on April 28,
1967, on charges of maintaining premises—his comfortable home
in Buffalo's posh Central Park neighborhood—where narcotics
were used. It devotes many but not all of its pages to an account
of the police raid and its consequences for the author. However,
in Whitmanesque fashion, Fiedler begins *Being Busted* by insisting
on the representativeness of both its narrator and narrative. Not
only does he suggest that every atom that belongs to him as much
belongs to you, but he also sets about to demonstrate the continu-
ity of 1967 with the rest of his own life and of his own life with
American cultural history in the mid-twentieth century:

> Essentially then, this is, despite its autobiographical form, a book not
> about me, or indeed individuals at all, so much as one about cultural
> and social change between 1933, when I just missed being arrested,
> and 1967, when I made it at last. (7)

Hence Fiedler begins his story on Bergen Street in Newark in
1933, when, at the age of sixteen, three years after first reading
Karl Marx, he barely avoids being jailed along with a buddy for
inciting a crowd with leftist oratory. The next chapter then jumps
to Missoula in 1958, where the maverick professor leads a successful struggle to oust the president of the University of Montana,
who was hostile not only to Fiedler but also to the unorthodox
colleagues that he, as department chairman, recruited. However,
the victor, a lightning rod for local resentment of the university
as a haven for alien ideas and behavior, himself falls victim to a
campaign of vilification. After twenty-three years in Missoula,
weary of suffering smears from bigots and philistines, Fiedler
moves on to the State University of New York at Buffalo, where—
despite and because of the fact that he has never smoked marijuana—he agrees to be faculty sponsor of a student organization
that advocates its legalization. As a Jewish intellectual sympathetic

to youthful rebels, the fifty-year-old professor becomes the special target of yahoo police. They induce a confused young woman to betray the hospitality she has received from Fiedler and his wife. After planting marijuana in their house, she informs on them.

Being Busted offers much beyond the circumstances of its author's misadventures of being busted in Buffalo in 1967. It is a vivid evocation of several times and places—not only Newark, Missoula, and Buffalo but also Colorado and China, where Fiedler spent World War II in Navy intelligence; Harvard, where he studied on the GI bill; Italy and Greece, where he lectured, and hectored; and Amsterdam, southern France, and Brighton, where he traveled while his marijuana case was making its way through American courts. *Being Busted* is not a full-fledged autobiography; it skips large swathes of the author's life. It is a polemical memoir organized around the theme of dissidence. "I like disturbing the peace, whenever that peace seems to me the product not of mediation but of torpor and fear" (55), explains Fiedler, who recounts numerous instances in the United States and Europe of his success at disturbing the peace and who, in recounting those instances, sets out to disturb the reader's torpid, fearful peace.

For most of his career, Fiedler has been tagged with the epithet "controversial," a label that he rightly resents as a means of stigmatizing the thinker while slighting his ideas. Nevertheless, a bit of pride seems to dilute the irritation with which he quotes a colleague's judgment that Fiedler is "the most controversial professor of literature in America since Irving Babbitt" (84). In *Being Busted,* Fiedler assumes the role of combat reporter, reporting on the contemporary *Kulturkampf* between young and old and combatting the complacencies of either side. Fiedler counsels himself: "Be faithful to your ambivalence" (100), a dictum certain to rankle zealots of every stripe. But Fiedler is even ambivalent about his ambivalence. Early on, he says of the book: "Its true subject is the endless war, sometimes cold, sometimes hot, between the dissenter and the imperfect society" (7). That would appear to situate Fiedler firmly in the camp of the dissenter, except that he also finds himself at odds with organized dissent. He depicts himself as a pharmacologically abstemious *pater familias* manifestly uncomfortable when hailed as champion of pot-smoking polymorphous perversity. He was, along with Buckminster Fuller, Ché Guevera, Timothy Leary, and Benjamin Spock, one of the very few figures over thirty trusted by the young. And he was trusted

by them merely because he was so mistrusted by his own generation, a fact that undercut any trust he had for either.

At the time, another outspoken American Jewish author, Norman Mailer, was demonstrating his own estrangement from conventional political polarities by ascribing to himself the oxymoron
"Left Conservative." *Armies of the Night* (1968) is Mailer's account
of being busted, at an antiwar demonstration outside the Penta-
gon, and it shares many qualities with the book that Fiedler published a year later, not least the author's discomfort with being
cast in the role of guru to Jacobin youth. Both works are self-
conscious performances by eristic literary celebrities who place
themselves at the center of the drama, and at the margins of
respectability. Mailer's epic description of himself, as "a warrior,
presumptive general, ex-political candidate, embattled aging enfant terrible of the literary world, wise father of six children, radical intellectual, existential philosopher, hard-working author,
champion of obscenity, husband of four battling sweet wives, amiable bar drinker, and much exaggerated street fighter, party giver,
hostess insulter" (153), anticipates the drollery if not the connubial
constancy of Fiedler's auto-portrait:

> not just, not even primarily, the professor who was busted for pot and
> maligned, much less the pot-happy corrupter of the young, but a
> refugee from the urban East, as well, who lived in Montana for nearly
> a quarter of a century, a thirty-years married father of six kids; a
> critic, teacher, and committee-member; a writer of fiction and verse;
> a maker of jokes, good and bad; a translator of Dante. (230)

Like Mailer, who begins his book by berating a version of events
at Washington's Ambassador Theater that was published in *Time*,
Fiedler offers his words as an antidote to numbing lexicons of
journalism and legalese. Mailer flaunts his verbal extravagances
as an overt weapon against "totalitarianese, which is to say, techno-
logese, which is to say any language which succeeds in stripping
itself of any moral content" (315). Fiedler, who shares Mailer's
enthusiasm for boxing, as solitary combat and as metaphor for
the literary enterprise, jabs back at headlines and captions that
reduce him to such stereotypes as "POT PROFESSOR" (230) and
"hip literary critic" (231). The courtroom transcripts and forensic
pronouncements that Fiedler reproduces diminish him by translating him into the simplified jargon of jurisprudence. He chafes
at the way that even his own lawyer renders him as a case. "But
my lawyer has had to content himself with writing a brief, that is,

my story" (254), notes Fiedler, on the penultimate page of *Being Busted*. In effect, the book that Fiedler writes in response to the way that others have appropriated his experiences into their own prose is a way of restoring the author to his own full life.

But *Being Busted* is a selective memoir, not a full life, except to the extent that for Fiedler *being busted* is not the discrete event that occurred in Buffalo on April 28, 1967. It is an ontological condition, the state of embattlement, which suffuses the author's entire life and, by endowing it with design, renders it full. Being busted, insists Fiedler, is a universal and routine phenomenon: "All up and down our land, bust follows bust ever more rapidly, although without visible effect—by now, they are an end in themselves" (235). Offering himself as defendant in a class action suit in which every individual—because the very notion of individuality—has a stake, he embraces his own oppression, as an agent that enables him "to come to terms with a larger piece of my life than had been touched by the Buffalo Narcotics Squad, but whose real shape and meaning I perceived for the first time only after those cops had entered it, so tangentially and so late" (247). Fiedler shares with Hamlet, for whom all Denmark is a dungeon, a sense of being psychically busted. He paints Buffalo, like his native Newark, in penal drab—"just as unspectacularly ugly, and just about the same middling size as the city in which I was born" (91). Yet he exults in the antic spirit that defies incarceration and asserts its own irreducible singularity.

Fiedler concludes *Being Busted* with a disquisition on Fourth Amendment rights and the erosion of privacy that is sometimes as sententious as the homily on dehumanization with which Mailer concludes *The Armies of the Night*. Though he claimed in *Love and Death* to be abandoning all masks, Fiedler is aware that candor is the most cunning veil. *Being Busted* reveals by concealing. It elides vast stretches of the author's life that elude the focus of the memoir's theme, and, even when recounting the marijuana bust that is the proximate basis for the book, Fiedler withholds essential information about his codefendants, his own wife and children, including even their names. In fact, no one in *Being Busted* but the author himself is nonymous, "and even he," notes Fiedler, "is most often referred to by the anonymous designation of 'I.'" However, he proclaims his Whitmanesque ambitions by adding: "But 'I' is, of course, the true name of us all, of the reader as well as the other actors in the book, or at least would be in the similar books each of us might write" (7). Call him Ishmael, or call him simply "I," he is the articulate proxy for the troubled reader.

Fiedler reports that while living in Montana, he was renamed Heavy Runner by the Blackfoot tribe that ceremonially adopted him. Brave Heavy Runner has left deep tracks.

WORKS CITED

Eliot, T. S. "Tradition and the Individual Talent." In Hazard Adams, ed., *Critical Theory Since Plato* (Fort Worth, TX: Harcourt Brace Jovanovich, 1992): 761–4.

Fiedler, Leslie. *Being Busted.* New York: Stein and Day, 1969.

———. *Love and Death in the American Novel.* Revised ed. New York: Stein and Day, 1966.

Mailer, Norman. *The Armies of the Night: History as a Novel, The Novel as History.* New York: New American Library, 1968.

The Akedah (the Binding of Isaac) in Shakespeare's *Merchant of Venice*

Jay L. Halio

Leslie Fiedler's *The Stranger in Shakespeare*[1] shows, above all, that Fiedler is no stranger to Shakespeare. His analyses of several major plays as well as poems and sonnets reveal, like so much of his other work, an uncommon perception—uncommon not only in its depth of seeing but in its ways of seeing. Sadly, his book has been unjustly ignored by professional Shakespeareans, many of whom approach Shakespeare's work these days with various agendas, often taking a polemical, not to say antiliterary, approach. But *The Stranger in Shakespeare* demonstrates what real sensitivity and close reading, coupled with vast knowledge, can do to illuminate further what generations of scholars and critics have poured over and still pour over in an attempt to pluck the heart out of Shakespeare's mystery.

As one might expect, Fiedler, an observant Jew, devotes a whole chapter in his book to *The Merchant of Venice*. Shylock is, after all, one of Shakespeare's archetypal "strangers" who emerges as the leading figure in the play, notwithstanding that its title actually refers to Antonio. In Fiedler's chronology, Shylock follows Joan la Pucelle in *1 Henry VI* and anticipates Othello and, finally Caliban in *The Tempest* as the principal embodiments of the stranger in Shakespeare. About their commonality as strangers I shall have nothing to say, for on that subject Fiedler's book is quite sufficient. But one aspect of *The Merchant of Venice*, which Fiedler has only touched on, deserves more attention. It is a subject that most commentators have neglected, if they have perceived it at all, although it lies at the heart of the play's most dramatic episode, the so-called Trial Scene in act 4.

Like the Moor, the Jew as stranger has been well documented, and Fiedler shows the ways in which Shylock's alien qualities are important in Shakespeare's play. He also shows how, in the view of many in Shakespeare's time, Jews represented a menace to all

Christian males. In his recent study, James Shapiro goes into still greater detail to illustrate the particular kind of threat Shylock with his knife symbolized. Circumcision, practiced by Jews but not Christians, was regarded by the latter as emasculating. The Jew pursuing a Christian, knife in hand upraised (as in the jacket design for Shapiro's book, taken from Thomas Coryate's *Crudities*, 1611), constituted a serious threat to Christians in the English Renaissance.[2] No matter that the threat was purely imaginary; it found its basis in myth and legend, perhaps best remembered in Chaucer's *Prioress's Tale* and the story of Hugh of Lincoln. Nor did the myth die with the Renaissance. As Fiedler reminds us, it persisted to our own century in the infamous Beiliss case in Czarist Russia, in the Nazi exterminations and the calumnies of Streicher, and so on (124).

But the threat to Christian manhood that Jewish circumcision represented was not all. Fielder and after him Shapiro also refer to the cannibalistic implications of several of Shylock's speeches with regard to Antonio and the revenge the Jew seeks against his Christian oppressor.[3] Cannibalism was yet another charge against Jews dating from medieval times; Jews ate their victims and consumed Christian blood for ritual purposes, or so the myth went. The irony, as Shapiro points out, is that to support the myth Christians had to invert what they knew from Scripture, i.e., that Jews were (and are) strictly forbidden to drink or eat blood.[4] But what Shakespeare wrote as metaphor could easily, like many metaphors, be taken literally. Shylock will "feed fat the ancient grudge" he bears Antonio; he will "go in hate to feed upon / The prodigal Christians"; he will exact his pound of flesh to "feed" his revenge against Antonio.[5] But of course, Fiedler says, "Shylock does not actually eat Antonio, does not even really want to eat him, except maybe in dreams, even though he does want him dead, feeling him—along with all his friends and doubles—as rebellious Christian sons, who, in seeking to destroy Judaism, have turned against the father of Jews and Christians alike, the patriarch, Abraham" (111). Interestingly enough, the metaphors of eating disappear from the text in act 4, Fiedler notes, "replaced by the image of the threatening father with a knife, a special variant of the ogre archetype derived not from fairy tales, but precisely from the story of Abraham and Isaac in the Scriptures of the Jews" (111).

Just at this point of high fascination, Fiedler turns aside to something else: the cognate myth of "the ogre's daughter." True, he picks up the story of Abraham and Isaac briefly later on, identifying Shylock with the patriarchal Abraham, both in act 4 and earlier in one of Shylock's oaths: "O father Abram, what these Christians are" (1.3.157). But it is precisely in act 4 that the analogy between Abraham and Shylock is most pertinent and requires explication. As Antonio bares his breast so that Shylock, knife in hand, can extract his pound of flesh, Shakespeare presents us with a nearly exact image of the Akedah, or the Binding of Isaac, with which Shakespeare and his audience were well acquainted— not only through the story in Genesis but through the mystery plays that had been enacted and were still known by the end of the sixteenth century, when Shakespeare wrote his play. Fiedler rightly reminds us that in Jewish lore, Isaac was at this time thirty years old or more (118). The identification with Antonio is thus even closer.

Why has this analogy not been perceived earlier and by others? Perhaps it is because, as Fiedler says, in Christian imagination Isaac in this episode was viewed not a grown man but as a child, and Antonio is no child. Earlier in the scene, moreover, Antonio calls himself a "tainted wether of the flock" (4.1.113), associating himself not with the son Abraham intends to sacrifice but with the ram eventually used instead. Shakespeare thus appears to move from one analogy to another, seemingly at cross purposes, while all the while focusing nonetheless on the Genesis story, which he undoubtedly had in mind as he wrote his play.[6] Like Abraham, Shylock is saved from an inhuman pagan act by the intervention of another being, in this case Portia, whose angelic qualities we might otherwise dispute but who here, at any rate, functions very much like the angel in the Akedah. She saves both Antonio and—following the Akedah, more to the point—Shylock. She saves him from committing a horrendous act, one that would violate not only his religion but his humanity as well. It is not for nothing that at the beginning of this scene, when Shylock is adamant in his revenge, the Duke calls him "an inhuman wretch" (4.1.3), and Graziano damns him as an "inexecrable dog" (127) whose desires are "wolvish, bloody, starved, and ravenous" (137).

The extreme horror of the act Shylock intends must be understood in its full biblical context. Throughout the Pentateuch Jahweh issues commandments, dutifully recorded by Moses, many of which are clearly designed to distinguish and keep separate the children of Israel from the heathen tribes surrounding them, especially as they enter the land of Canaan promised them from of old. For example, the commandment not to seethe a kid in its mother's milk (Exodus 23.19)[7] derives from a chant that initiates in a pagan mystery cult intoned as they proceeded through their rites of passage.[8] Similarly, prohibitions against intermarriages were designed to maintain the integrity of the Israelites as a people.[9] One of the worst practices among heathen religions was the institution of child sacrifice, and the Akedah represents (among other things) one of the most important commandments enjoined upon the ancient Hebrews—not to engage in such ungodly practices.[10]

Portia thus saves Shylock from a terrible form of apostasy, from becoming an anti-Jew. As the scene progresses, he is forced to become an apostate of another sort—a Christian. But for the moment he is saved from a worse fate. What he intends as the scene opens will separate him from all his tribe. The oath he has taken in the synagogue[11] is blasphemous, to say the least. He has told Tubal, his co-religionist, exactly what he means to do (3.1.119–23). Significantly, Tubal does not respond. Nor does Tubal—or any other Jew from among all those in Venice—accompany Shylock into the Duke's court. By his intended action, Shylock has separated himself from everyone—Jew and Christian alike. He has become a stranger indeed, a stranger to his family— to Jessica, his daughter, who has absconded from his house of "hell"; to his friends among the money-lenders in Venice—Tubal and Chus; and to everyone else, most of all, perhaps, to himself and his religion.[12] Despite his hatred towards Antonio for bringing down the price of usance in Venice (1.3.40–42), his feelings modulate as the dialogue in that scene progresses; in fact, he indicates quite clearly to the merchant and Bassanio that he wants to become friends with them, to forgive and forget the insults that in the past they have heaped upon him (134–35). For this reason, apparently, he reverses himself later on when he decides to accept Bassanio's invitation and go to dinner at his house, although earlier he had expressed complete disdain for dining with him and his Christian friends.[13] By the middle of the play, however, after Jessica's elopement with Lorenzo and their theft of his wealth, about which Solanio and Salarino mercilessly taunt him (3.1.21–38), he has become utterly embittered. This bitterness then alienates him altogether from his better self, from whatever noble impulses he may have earlier entertained, such as loving his enemies and lending money to them at no interest (1.3.134–38), unheard of for a moneylender and a Jew in those times.

What happens to Shylock later in the play we all know and recognize as his forced conversion. If the conversion is successful—and Shakespeare wisely does not dramatize it—Shylock will be a stranger no more. He will have succeeded, but now against his will, in becoming one of "them." However repugnant we find this conclusion, or however we try to justify it in historical terms, it remains problematical for modern audiences. Some recent productions have tried to evade the issue. In Jonathan Miller's National Theater production, Shylock uttered an offstage cry of anguish such that we might think he has died—of heartbreak? of suicide?—and the voiceover Kaddish at the end of 5.1 suggested as much. In a more recent modern-times production (the Royal Shakespeare Company in 1993, with David Calder as Shylock), the conversion at the end of 4.1 did not signify very much. In this secular age, it would not. Earlier, in another RSC production, Patrick Stewart's Shylock flipped off his yarmulka and accepted conversion readily enough: a "bad" Jew from first to last, he was only interested in saving his life and reclaiming as much of his estate as the Christians allowed him, so that he could go on making money.[14] But all these are interpretations. Shakespeare's point is to redeem Shylock from his "strangeness." How well he succeeds, we do not know. Shylock, claiming illness (as well he might), leaves at the end of 4.1, asking merely that the deed of gift for Jessica and Lorenzo, which Antonio has demanded, be sent after him to sign (391–93). And that is the last we see of Shakespeare's Jew.

NOTES

1. Fiedler, *The Stranger in Shakespeare* (New York: Stein and Day, 1972). References hereafter are given in the text.

2. See James Shapiro, *Shakespeare and the Jews* (New York: Columbia University Press, 1996), 113–30.

3. See, e.g., Fiedler, *Strangers*, 109–11; Shapiro, *Shakespeare*, 102–5, 109–11.

4. Shapiro, *Shakespeare*, 109.

5. *The Merchant of Venice*, 1.3.44; 2.5.14–15; 3.1.50–51. All quotations from this play are from the edition I have edited (Oxford: Oxford University Press, 1993).

6. Note, for example, the many references in the play to names and events taken from Genesis; for example, the story of Jacob and Laban that Shylock recounts to Antonio, 1.3.74–87. See also the Introduction to my edition, 22 and 49, note 1.

7. The commandment is repeated at Exodus 34.26 and Deuteronomy 14.21. In the third citation it follows "for thou art a holy people unto the Lord thy God."

8. As a former colleague of mine, David Ward, discovered while doing research for a book on T. S. Eliot. (Private communication.)

9. See, for example, Exodus 34.16 and Deuteronomy 7.1–3.

10. For this reason, the production of *The Merchant of Venice* by the Royal Shakespeare Company in 1987, with Antony Sher (a South African Jew) as Shylock, was particularly offensive. At the opening of 4.1, Sher intoned various

Hebrew prayers, purportedly taken from the Passover Haggadah, in which the ten plagues against Pharaoh and the Egyptians are recounted, among them (last and finally most effective) the slaughter of their first-born male children. But human sacrifice as such is, as the Akedah shows, most assuredly *not* a Jewish practice. For the prohibition against child sacrifice, see Leviticus 18.21 and the comment on the Akedah by Dr. J. H. Hertz in his translation of the *Pentateuch and Haftorahs,* 2d ed. (London: Soncino Press, 1970), 201.

11. See 3.1.119–23, 4.1.225.

12. This is why Laurence Olivier's portrayal in the National Theatre production, directed by Jonathan Miller in 1970, showing Shylock wrapped in a traditional *tallis,* distorts what is happening to Shylock. Unless it was meant to emphasize Shylock's hypocrisy, which did not seem to be either Olivier's or Miller's intention, the religious trappings in 3.1 were inappropriate, as was the Kaddish recited as voiceover at the end. But Miller's interpretation stemmed from a particular agenda. See James Bulman's analysis in *Shakespeare in Performance: The Merchant of Venice* (Manchester: Manchester University Press, 1991), 75–100.

13. True, he says he will "go in hate" (2.5.14), but his motives here, as in 1.3, remain mixed. Indeed, the play is filled with inconsistencies and contradictions, as Norman Rabkin has shown in "Meaning and *The Merchant of Venice,*" *Shakespeare and Meaning* (Chicago: University of Chicago Press, 1981), 169–88.

14. For a discussion of this interpretation, directed by John Barton, and a comparison with David Suchet's Shylock, also at the RSC and directed by Barton, see "Exploring a Character: Playing Shylock," in John Barton, *Playing Shakespeare* (London: Methuen, 1984), 169–80.

Fiedler and the New Criticism

MARK ROYDEN WINCHELL

Over the past three decades, Leslie Fiedler's attacks on the New Criticism have become increasingly pronounced, at times even strident. In "Cross the Border—Close the Gap" (1970), he identifies "the unconfessed scandal of contemporary literary criticism" as the vain attempt "to explain, defend, and evaluate one kind of book" with standards invented for a very different kind of book (*CBCG*, 270).[1] "The second or third generation New Critics in America," he writes, ". . . end by proving themselves imbeciles and naifs when confronted by, say, a poem by Allen Ginsberg, a new novel by John Barth" (271). In *What Was Literature?* (1982), he contends that by the 1960s, it had become apparent that the New Critics had "exhausted their small usefulness." Although "their analyses had made possible some reforms in pedagogy, and had even illuminated a handful of neglected lyric poems, chiefly by John Donne, . . . they had done nothing to explain the great novels of their own tradition, or to encourage any new achievement in that genre." Fiedler even believes that the influence of the new critics on poetry "served to inhibit rather than spur new experiments after 1955" (*WWL*, 71).

Despite these denunciations and the image that Fiedler has long projected of being a barbarian at the gates of literary respectability, his relations with the New Critics have not always been hostile. Although his earliest essays appeared most often in *Partisan Review* and the *New Leader*, Fiedler submitted work to John Crowe Ransom's *Kenyon Review* from the very beginning of his career. When none of these early submissions was accepted, Fiedler expressed his pique to Ransom in a letter dated October 19, 1947. "It requires a stubborn act of faith to send you more of my stuff," he writes. "Yours is the only publication from which in my year + a half of submitting material I have received nothing but the dumb rebuke of a form rejection slip. In most cases I get at least some acceptance—in all, decent + interested notes of rejection. I should be less than frank, if I did not say that these anonymous pale slips of yours irk, annoy (and even, tho I am a resilient fellow, discourage) me. I like, in general, your taste, but am equally fond of my own pieces. What is it?"[2] This letter produced a detailed reaction to the story submitted with it, along with Ransom's invitation to review for his magazine. Over the next decade, Fiedler would be a frequent contributor to the *Kenyon Review* and was even named a Kenyon Fellow in Criticism for 1956.[3]

One should be careful not to read too much into Fiedler's relationship with Ransom and the *Kenyon Review*. Although Ransom is often regarded as the godfather of the American version of New Criticism and the *Kenyon Review* as its unofficial house organ, the truth is actually more complicated. The *Kenyon Review,* and the original series of the *Southern Review* before it, were remarkably eclectic journals, which were equally hospitable to contributions from Southern Agrarians and New York intellectuals.[4] Moreover, the New Criticism itself was never as monolithic as conspiracy buffs would have us believe. The term "New Criticism" (with its built-in obsolescence) was inadvertently coined by Ransom when he used it as the title of a book he published in 1941. He might just as well have called the book "Some Recent Trends in Criticism," because the figures he discusses were espousing different critical methods. I. A. Richards and William Empson are treated as psychological critics, T. S. Eliot as an historical critic, and Yvor Winters as a logical critic. (The fact that Ransom did not find any of these approaches to be entirely satisfactory is indicated by the title of his final chapter—"Wanted: An Ontological Critic.") What all these men had in common was an interest in criticism as opposed to the old philological scholarship.

The new interest in criticism began at the University of Cambridge with the pedagogical experiments of I. A. Richards in the late 1920s. In America, its greatest currency has also been as a method of teaching literature. (Beginning in the mid-thirties, a series of spectacularly successful textbooks edited by Cleanth Brooks and Robert Penn Warren sparked a classroom revolution that is still very much with us.)[5] At the same time, literary journalists and a few iconoclastic college professors were discovering that the old critical methods were not adequate to interpret and evaluate the radical innovations of modernism. While encouraging the search for new exegetical techniques, the first generation of modernist critics were remarkably undogmatic about the ways in which one might read a literary text. Unfortunately, a later generation of "New Critics" threatened to turn what had once been an innovative approach to literature into a stale orthodoxy. As

Christopher Clausen has noted recently: "A bright student who knew little history, no philosophy, and no foreign languages could learn to analyze literary structures in terms of a small number of technical concepts. After that, nothing more was needed than a good anthology . . . , a supply of paperbacks, and perhaps, for the adventurous, a subscription to the *Kenyon Review*."[6]

In her history of the *Kenyon Review*, Marian Janssen argues persuasively that Ransom himself had begun moving away from the New Criticism by the early 1940s and that, contrary to conventional opinion, the *Kenyon Review* had effectively ceased to be a New Critical journal by the time Fiedler was contributing to its pages. (In addition to Fiedler, Kenyon fellowships in criticism were awarded in the 1950s to such varied and heterodox individuals as Irving Howe, R. W. B. Lewis, Richard Ellmann, and Howard Nemerov, while the thoroughly conventional New Critic Robert Wooster Stallman found his application repeatedly turned down.) In reading Fiedler's essays from the early fifties, it is clear that he found the New Criticism to be a useful, perhaps even necessary, touchstone against which to measure his own evolving view of literature. We see this process at work in his essay "Toward an Amateur Criticism," published as part of a critical symposium in the Autumn 1950 issue of the *Kenyon Review*.

By endorsing an "amateur" criticism, Fiedler is rejecting not only the New Criticism but all systematic approaches to reading literature. Although he is reluctant to call himself a romantic, he believes that doctrinaire anti-romanticism can lead to a fatal contempt for the imagination. Making a point with which Ransom certainly would have agreed, Fiedler argues that the chief enemy of literature in our day is the "'liberal' or scientific mind, with its opposition to the frivolous and the tragic, its distrust of such concepts as the Devil, Genius and Taste, and its conviction that it is impertinent to ask just how many children Lady Macbeth *did* have" (*TAC*, 562).[7] By definition, the amateur critic would be one who loved literature and conveyed a sense of pleasure in writing about it. In two important respects, his vocation is similar to that of the poet: "First, he must join in irony and love what others are willing to leave disjoined, and second, he must be willing to extend awareness beyond the point where the lay reader instinctively finds that quality profitable or even possible" (562). The critic also possesses a third responsibility that is only an option for the poet—the obligation to be comprehensible.

If Fiedler's warning against critical jargon was useful in 1950, it sounds downright prophetic nearly half a century later. In an

age when readers of professional criticism are all too often mes-
merized by the glossolalia of post-structuralist theory, it is easy to
forget that the purpose of criticism is to clarify, not to obscure.
"In *intent*," Fiedler reminds us, "the good critic addresses the
common reader, not the initiate, and that intent is declared in his
language. That in fact there are in our own time few general
readers in the Johnsonian sense, is completely irrelevant. The primary act of faith that makes criticism possible compels the critic
under any circumstances to speak as if to men and not to specialists. The compulsory comprehensibility of the critic is not a matter
of pandering to indolence, prejudice or ignorance, but of resisting
the impulse to talk to himself or a congeries of reasonable facsimi-
les of himself" (563).

Fiedler next attacks one of the cardinal tenets of the New Criticism—the notion that literary evaluation must always be intrinsic
to the work itself. Not only does this belief contribute to the further atomization of modern life, but it is also a canard that is
honored more in the breach than in the observance. As he correctly notes "even the terms of 'aesthetic' criticism, complexity,
irony, simplicity, concreteness, betray themselves as metaphors one
element of which rests on ethical preconceptions" (566). Although
Fiedler does not develop this point, it is interesting to note how
the technical judgments of the New Critics often presuppose a
particular view of reality. When Cleanth Brooks is analyzing particular poems in *The Well Wrought Urn*, he uses such intrinsic aesthetic terms as wit, irony, and paradox; however, his more general
theoretical comments later in that same book hold that a poem is
to be judged by its "coherence, sensitivity, depth, richness, and
tough-mindedness."[8] As sound as this position may be, it represents a moral rather than a merely literary point of view. Different
aesthetic judgments would certainly be rendered by someone who
preferred an incoherent, insensitive, shallow, superficial, and sentimental interpretation of reality. Fiedler thinks it proper that the
critic's view of literature be influenced by his moral and religious
beliefs and regards talk about intrinsic criticism as disingenuous
nonsense.

Fiedler is not rejecting the value, only the sufficiency, of close
reading. He believes that "the point is not to choose between the
complementary blindness of the 'formalists' and the 'historians,'
but to be more aware than either: to know, if possible, when one
is making aesthetic judgments and when philosophical or ethical
ones, or, at least, to realize when one is confused" (*TAC*, 564). In
other words, because there are pitfalls in every known system of

criticism, it is best to avoid all systems and rely on one's own intuition and tact to make correct literary judgments. The most obvious objection to this position is that we are left with no standards by which to criticize the critic. The one advantage shared by critical systems, whether aesthetic or ideological, is that we have some notion of whether or not the critic is a competent practitioner of his own craft. Unfortunately, Fiedler's "amateur" criticism can easily lead to relativism and subjectivism. To escape this dilemma, it is necessary to validate one's judgments by appeal to some external source of authority, whether it be popular opinion or elitist taste.

Because Fiedler's position since the 1960s has become increasingly populist, it is surprising to discover that his earliest critical writings were distrustful of the *vox populi*. In the Kenyon symposium, he argues that even the amateur critic must oppose those who hold that Carl Sandburg is superior to Wallace Stevens simply because Sandburg "is much admired by high school students and the teachers of high school students" (569). He goes on to say that "the critic must stand against the attempt to replace the consensus of expert judgment with popular suffrage. He must resist that deep-rooted hatred of excellence that seeks to pass itself off through sentimental analogies as essential to democracy" (569). Throughout his essay, Fiedler constantly invokes the concept of "taste" and argues for an aristocracy of taste. What he envisions is a battlefield of critical judgment, in which conflict among the most sensitive readers establishes the kind of protean hierarchy that T. S. Eliot had in mind in "Tradition and the Individual Talent." Fiedler believes that criticism should not be "a rival to the attempt to achieve final hierarchies, but rather a handmaiden. The only way to find out if a poet is immortal is to kill him; Milton and Wordsworth slain have risen; Cowley and Shelley are rotting in their tombs" (570).

Fiedler contends that voice is more important for a critic than method. The polemical article (more often a book review than a full-length critical thesis) is the perfect vehicle for criticism. "The occasional piece discourages the framing of elaborate vocabularies, and encourages a tone committed to communication and sociability" (571). Such an article avoids the opposite extremes of technical jargon (here typified by Kenneth Burke) and the "grey, standard, glutinous prose" of reference books such as *The Literary History of the United States* or middlebrow journals such as the *Saturday Review of Literature* (571–72). "The true language of criticism," Fiedler writes, "is the language of conversation—the voice of the dilettante at home. Its proper materials are what the civilized, outrageous mind remembers and chooses to connect, not what the three by five cards scrupulously preserve or the printed glossary defines" (572). One hears this conversational voice in critics as diverse as "Longinus," Nietzsche, Coleridge, and D. H. Lawrence. "One feels in their tone and texture an assurance that the works of art being discussed have really *happened* to the men that discuss them, and have been ingested into the totality of their experiences" (572).

After spending more than a dozen pages condemning critical systems and methodologies, Fiedler confesses that he finds himself "more and more drawn" to myth criticism. Unlike more scientific and rationalist approaches, myth criticism expresses a proper reverence for the mysteries of artistic creation and offers an intriguing standard for evaluation in the concept of "mythoplastic power, that goes beyond the merely formal without falling into the doctrinal and the dogmatic." An additional advantage is that "writers like Dickens and R. L. Stevenson, who have fared ill at the hands of the historical and formalist critics alike, reveal the source of their persistent power over our imaginations in the light of myth doctrine" (574).[9] Whereas a criticism based on aesthetics or ideology tends to be divisive and reductive, myth criticism offers the possibility of cultural synthesis. It enables the critic "to speak of the profound interconnections of the art work and other areas of human experience, without translating the work of art into unsatisfactory equivalents of 'ideas' or 'tendencies'" (574).

Fiedler's next major attempt to differentiate his position from that of the New Criticism came in another journal widely identified with the movement he was attacking. "Archetype and Signature," which would become one of Fiedler's best known and most frequently anthologized works, originally appeared in the Spring 1952 issue of the *Sewanee Review*. Although this essay is most important as an affirmative rationale for myth criticism, it is also a spirited attack on what Fiedler regards as the inevitable excesses of a purely intrinsic approach to literature. Referring to his enemies as the "anti-biographists," Fiedler argues that formalist critics, of whatever stripe, have made a fatal error in reducing the poem to mere words on a page. When I. A. Richards defines a poem as an "experience," he is rejecting the notion that it might also be an "imitation," an "expression," or a "communication." If, as Richards strongly implies, literary language is non-referential, then it is divorced from the rest of human experience. Although no one could have foreseen it at the time, it was precisely this notion that lay the philosophical groundwork for the deconstructionist contention that all language is simply an arbitrary system of linguistic signs with no objective meaning.[10]

Fiedler believes that extreme literary formalism is based on the nominalist assumption that we can speak of individual poetic texts but not of something so general as poetry itself. Although he does not mention them by name, and may not even have had them in mind, Fiedler has identified the major weakness in the position of the Chicago neo-Aristotelians. In the Spring 1948 issue of *Modern Philology,* the neo-Aristotelian godfather R. S. Crane had proclaimed his nominalist credentials in an essay entitled "Cleanth Brooks; or the Bankruptcy of Critical Monism." Crane castigates Brooks (and, by implication, the entire fraternity of New Critics) for trying to define the nature of poetry rather than content themselves with discussing the specific characteristics of individual genres of poems. If Brooks's *The Well Wrought Urn* focuses almost entirely on analyzing particular poems, his grand design is to remake the canon of English *poetry* or at least to establish aesthetic criteria on which to judge the existing canon.

Although he prefers to deal in broad generalities, Fiedler does mention a few other critics by name in "Archetype and Signature." In discussing the importance of knowing a writer's intentions, he dismisses what he calls "Wimsatt and Beardsley's ponderous tract on the Intentional Fallacy" (*AS,* 28). Even though a poem may contain more or less than what its author intended, Fiedler argues, we must speak of what it obviously aims at to judge what it actually achieves. (By such a standard, intentional farce would be good art, whereas unintentional camp would not be.) Certainly, if W. K. Wimsatt and Monroe C. Beardsley were not willing to concede that much, their position would be absurd. If one reads their "ponderous tract," however, it becomes clear that they are making the more limited and sensible point that a writer is not always the best *judge* of his or her own work and that sincerity is no excuse for ineptitude.

Fiedler is also guilty of caricature when he suggests that Wimsatt and Beardsley believe "that there is no poem except the poem of 'words'" (*AS,* 28). However much William K. Wimsatt may have distrusted archetypal criticism,[11] he was just as skeptical of the sort of extreme formalism that would treat a work of literature as something palpable and mute. When the Chicago critics tried to make a fetish of the poem as artifact, Wimsatt rebuked them in terms with which Fiedler would undoubtedly agree. "[I]f anything about poetry is clear at all," Wimsatt writes, "it is that a poem is not really a thing, like a horse or a house, but only *analogically* so. . . . [A] poem is, if it is anything at all, a verbal discourse; . . . hence it is a human act, physical and mental. The only 'thing' is the poet speaking."[12]

In attempting to defend the uses of biography in literary criticism, Fiedler also challenges T. S. Eliot's belief that "a poem succeeds, as a poem, insofar as it is detached from the subjectivity of its maker" (*AS*, 27). Such a belief denies the poet's right to speak with any decisive authority about his own work. If such a poet were to protest "against some critical analysis or interpretation which sees to him wrong on the basis of his special biographical knowledge, he reveals that the poem is not truly 'successful,' or even worse, that he has never read 'Tradition and the Individual Talent'" (*AS*, 28). One does not need to worship at the shrine of St. Thomas Eliot to think that Fiedler may be dismissing "Tradition and the Individual Talent" too glibly. In discussing the dialectical relationship between the individual writer and his cultural inheritance, Eliot is dealing with concepts closely related to archetype and signature. If he exaggerates the importance of impersonality in art, he may simply be compensating for the equal but opposite exaggeration of the romantics. Nearly two decades later, Fiedler himself would ponder the tension between self-assertion and self-effacement in art ("*Chutzpah* and *Pudeur*" [1969]) without ever mentioning Eliot's classic essay.

If his attacks on Wimsatt, Beardsley, and Eliot are not entirely convincing, Fiedler is certainly on solid ground when he ridicules Thomas and Brown's *Reading Poems*, an anthology that prints poems "out of chronological order and without the names of the authors attached, lest the young reader be led astray by what (necessarily irrelevant) information he may have concerning the biography or social background of any of the poets" (29). One suspects that this text is a variation on the far more famous experiment that I. A. Richards conducted in the 1920s. Richards gave a total of thirteen unidentified poems to his students at Cambridge and asked for critical responses. Confronting the text without the benefit of history or biography, the students not only varied widely in their judgments, but also fell prey to every conceivable form of misreading. This project led to the publication of Richards's groundbreaking work *Practical Criticism* in 1929.[13] However valuable such an experiment may have been as a diagnostic exercise, it was not meant to exclude context from the *teaching* of literature. The first generation of New Critics understood the value of context. It was only their second-rate imitators who reduced the movement to the level of self-parody.

Even though he may have been somewhat reticent in naming names, the New Critics were never in doubt that Fiedler had them in mind when he attacked the "anti-biographists" in "Archetype and Signature." In *Literary Criticism: A Short History* (1957), which he wrote in collaboration with W. K. Wimsatt, Cleanth Brooks devotes more than a page to critiquing Fiedler's essay.[14] He charges that the notion of the archetype is really a disguised attempt to define "a privileged poetic subject matter. . . . [because] any great poem must be an acceptable rendition of this special poetic content."[15] The problem with this objection is that Fiedler has not catalogued a limited number of archetypes from which a great poem must be written. It is clear from his essay that his notion of the archetype is expansive enough to admit virtually any subject matter that can be rendered in song and story. A more plausible charge is that Fiedler's understanding of myth is too broad rather than too narrow.[16]

If Brooks has difficulty with Fiedler's notion of the archetype, the signature gives him problems as well. He argues that "in Fiedler's conception, a poem is not an object to be known; it is rather a clue to an event in the poet's psyche" (713). This characterization would cast Fiedler in the unlikely role of psychobiographer. Although he most assuredly does regard the poem as "an object to be known," Fiedler believes that a familiarity with the poet's life can aid in the act of knowing. If he sees the poem as a clue to anything beyond itself, it is to the collective dreams of a people. He uses literature not so much for psychoanalysis as for spiritual anthropology. In his discussion of the Southern community in *William Faulkner: The Yoknapatawpha Country*, Cleanth Brooks does much the same thing superbly well.

Although *Literary Criticism: A Short History* did not appear until five years after the publication of Fiedler's essay, Brooks's initial response to "Archetype and Signature" was almost immediate, coming in the Winter 1953 issue of the *Sewanee Review*. Entitled "A Note on the Limits of 'History' and the Limits of 'Criticism,'" this defense of the New Criticism is actually the last installment in a running debate between Brooks and Douglas Bush over the meaning of Marvell's "Horatian Ode." While defending himself against the attacks of Bush's traditional historical scholarship, Brooks felt compelled to add a few words about Fiedler's more general assault on aesthetic formalism. In essence, he sees Fiedler's myth criticism and Bush's old historicism as opposite sides of the same coin.

Although he admits that Bush and Fiedler would find each other to be strange bedfellows, Brooks notes that both are attempting to restore biographical and historical considerations to the analysis of literature. Summarizing Fiedler's "neat, almost jaunty survey of recent literary history," Brooks writes: "If I may fill in some names, Mr. Fiedler might presumably see Mr. Bush as the thesis (the old fashioned historical scholarship), me as the antithesis (the doctrinaire antibiographer), and himself as the triumphant synthesis."[17] There are, however, other ways of looking at the situation. Eschewing dialectics for dichotomy, Brooks sees formalism as the only pure criticism and all other approaches as hybrids of nonliterary disciplines.

"In their concern for the break-up of the modern world," Brooks writes, "Mr. Bush, Mr. Fiedler, and a host of other scholars and critics are anxious to see literature put to work to save the situation." Although Brooks professes to share his adversaries' desire to redeem our disintegrating, deracinated culture, he thinks it dangerous to confuse religion and poetry. Such confusion, he argues, serves neither God nor art: "though poetry has a very important role in any culture, to ask that poetry save us is to impose a burden on poetry that it cannot sustain. The danger is that we shall merely get an ersatz religion and an ersatz poetry."[18]

The judicious distinctions that Brooks makes clearly delineate the fundamental differences between the New Criticism and Fiedler's approach to literature. Brooks and other New Critics of an orthodox Christian persuasion accept the conventional Judeo-Christian separation of the sacred from the profane. Fiedler, however, subscribes to the mystical tradition that sees religion not as a specific category of experience, but as the underlying reality of all experience. Although Fiedler speaks of mythos and archetypes (terms that do not carry the sectarian baggage of "religion"), he is clearly dealing with what he regards as spiritual and metaphysical realities. Brooks endorses a religion of incarnation. Fiedler believes just as passionately in a literature of incarnation. For him, the words of a poem are never merely words, but some primordial Word made flesh.

NOTES

1. Leslie Fiedler's works are quoted in text using the following abbreviations: *AS*, for "Archetype and Signature," in *A Fiedler Reader*, 24–43 (Briarcliff Manor, NY: Stein & Day, 1977); *CBCG*, for "Cross the Border—Close the Gap," in *A Fiedler Reader*, 270–94; *TAC*, for "Toward an Amateur Criticism," *Kenyon Review*

12 (Autumn 1950): 561–74; *WWL*, for *What Was Literature?: Class Culture and Mass Society* (New York: Simon & Schuster, 1982).

2. Quoted from Marian Janssen, *The Kenyon Review, 1939–1970: A Critical History* (Baton Rouge: Louisiana State University Press, 1990), 185.

3. Fiedler also taught at one of Ransom's summer institutes, the Indiana School of Letters. For an appreciative account of his tenure during the summer of 1952, see James M. Cox, "Celebrating Leslie Fiedler," *South Carolina Review* 24 (Spring 1992): 108–16.

4. Philip Rahv and Mary McCarthy both published in the original series of the *Southern Review*, while Kenneth Burke, Delmore Schwartz, Sidney Hook, and James T. Farrell were frequent contributors with five or more appearances each. If anything, the *Kenyon Review* was even more cosmopolitan. In *What Was Literature?*, Fiedler notes that a shared commitment to modernism made "it possible after a while for some contributors to pass back and forth between, say, *Kenyon Review* and *Partisan Review*" (59).

5. In a letter to me dated 6 December 1993, the poet and critic Dana Gioia writes: "The three best selling college poetry textbooks of the past thirty years were probably *How Does a Poem Mean?* by John Ciardi, *Sound and Sense* by Laurence Perrine, and (probably the best selling of all) *An Introduction to Poetry* by X. J. Kennedy. All three are strictly New Critical as are the legions of their imitators. These are the books that are used by millions of students and tens of thousands of teachers in the classroom. New Criticism, even if it doesn't go by that name, remains virtually unchallenged as the method of choice in college classrooms."

6. Christopher Clausen, "Reading Closely Again," *Commentary*, February 1997, 54–57.

7. Ransom believed that art, manners, and religion all served as antidotes to the scientific mindset. As a consequence, he wrote an odd formalistic defense of fundamentalist Christianity in *God Without Thunder* (1930).

8. Cleanth Brooks, *The Well-Wrought Urn: Studies in the Structure of Poetry* (New York: Reynal and Hitchcock, 1947), 229.

9. In *What Was Literature?*, Fiedler argues that myth criticism provides a means of bridging the gap between popular and canonical literature without sacrificing standards of evaluation.

10. A connection between the New Criticism and deconstruction has been alleged by Gerald Graff in "Fear and Trembling at Yale" (*American Scholar* 46 [Autumn 1977]: 467–78) and Christopher Clausen in "Reading Closely Again." In point of fact, Richards's argument that literary language is non-referential has long bothered other New Critics because of its radical implications. In *Literary Criticism: A Short History* (New York: Knopf, 1957), Cleanth Brooks worries that Richards "seemed to be arguing that poetry was literally nonsense, though, for reasons bound up with his pscychologistic theory, a peculiarly valuable nonsense" (626).

11. See, for example, Wimsatt's "Northrop Frye: Criticism as Myth," *Northrop Frye in Modern Criticism: Selected Papers from the English Institute*, ed. Murray Krieger (New York: Columbia University Press, 1966), 75–107.

12. W. K. Wimsatt, *The Verbal Icon: Studies in the Meaning of Poetry* (Lexington: University Press of Kentucky, 1954), 50.

13. An even more radical experiment was conducted decades later by Stanley Fish. Coming into his class at Johns Hopkins one morning, Fish failed to erase the names of several prominent linguists that had been written on the black-

board in a previous class in linguistic theory. Instead, he drew a line around this list of six proper names and wrote at the top of the frame "p. 43." By convincing his class in seventeenth-century religious poetry that the list of six proper names constituted a poem of the type that they had been studying, Fish carried the denial of context and reference to ludicrous extremes.

14. Although no official distinction is made concerning the authorship of various parts of this book, we know that Brooks wrote the section on modern criticism.

15. Brooks and Wimsatt, *Literary Criticism: A Short History*, 713.

16. Making just such a point, Charles R. Larson writes: "Ultimately—and I feel that this is the crux of the problem with Fiedler—. . . everything becomes a myth, and what started as a serious attempt to define *mythos* and its relationship to poetry has grown into a gigantic tumor which Fiedler has used not as an appendage of literature but as literature itself." See Larson's "Leslie Fiedler: The Critic and the Myth, the Critic as Myth," *Literary Review* 14 (Winter 1970–71): 141.

17. Cleanth Brooks, "A Note on the Limits of 'History' and the Limits of 'Criticism,'" in *Seventeenth-Century English Poetry: Modern Essays in Criticism* (New York: Oxford University Press, 1962), 357.

18. Ibid., 358.

Leslie Fiedler As Leopold Bloom

Daniel Schwarz

I

Leslie Fiedler is one of the critics who have made a difference. In the guise of critical picaro, he has spent his life flouting the critical and scholarly establishment while publishing critical books and novels, lecturing worldwide, writing fiction and enjoying being Leslie Fiedler. And that enjoyment is on every page of *Fiedler on the Roof: Essays on Literature and Jewish Identity* (1991), an indexless and characteristically idiosyncratic collection of previously published talks and essays that contains his insights, musing, and rants on Jewish subjects.

In the 1960s every Jewish graduate student knew the fairy tale of Fiedler: exiled in Missoula, Montana, where he wrote and taught before returning to the East to SUNY Buffalo; in his life and work he thumbed his nose at the academic establishment and parochial historical criticism and what he saw as the narrow formalism of New Criticism, while making a very substantial reputation based primarily on one important book, *Love and Death in the American Novel* (1960).[1] Published when he was in his forties, the book was embraced by younger academics and graduate students as part of the generational battle that poses as a latter-day battle of the books.

At a time when the relevance of literary study was being increasingly called into question by rampant McCarthyism and, later, the Vietnam War, the antiwar protest movement, and the resulting fissures between university and society, Fiedler's book argued that literary study was central to our lives. Fiedler's bold discussion of psychosexual and political issues fulfilled the desire of younger academics for a lively and engaged critical discourse. For Fiedler literary criticism is, as he writes in an encomium to his mentor William Ellory Leonard, "an act of total moral engagement, in which tact, patience, insolence, and piety consort strangely but satisfactorily together; nor can anyone who once listened to him believe that the truth one tries to tell about literature is finally different from the truth one tries to tell about the indignities and rewards of being the kind of man one is—an American, let's say, in the second half of the twentieth century, learning to read his country's books" (*Love and Death,* preface, n.p.).

Some historical perspective is necessary, and my perspective is that of one who was in graduate school from 1963 until I came to teach at Cornell as an assistant professor in 1968. In a sense, the early 1960s were the Golden Age of graduate education in the humanities. Attracted by financial support, students flocked to graduate schools. Some of the fellowships were underwritten by the government, under the auspices of the National Defense Act, to fill a genuine need for college teachers. Generous fellowships and assistantships, rising salaries, and the breakdown of social barriers opened university teaching in the humanities to a more varied ethnic and economic mix, a mix that, for a variety of reasons, other fields had begun to achieve somewhat sooner. A plentiful job market fueled by rising enrollments and concomitant expansion, including the opening of new branches of state universities handsomely underwritten by state legislatures, provided ample job opportunities for all but the most unemployable. At times, universities recruited students finishing Ph.D.s in the humanities the way industry now recruits senior and Ph.D. engineering students. Graduate programs also offered an exemption from the draft, because university teaching had been among those jobs designated under the National Defense Act as crucial to the nation's welfare. Originally, this exemption merely relieved one from an inconvenient burden. However, with the involvement of American troops in Southeast Asia, the exemption provided not only a refuge from the strong possibility of being maimed or killed, but it also a free zone for those who did not wish to go underground or into exile. Studying literature became a way of joining this generation's version of the Abraham Lincoln Brigade without suffering, as did those idealists of the 1930s who fought in the Spanish Civil War, the inconvenience of disrupting one's life. Campus leaders of the antiwar movement often were graduate students and assistant professors in the humanities. In response, many local draft boards no longer recognized universities as inviolable sanctuaries and withdrew exemptions.

Given these circumstances, it is not surprising that English departments in the 1960s suffered from a kind of intellectual schizophrenia. On the one hand they were intensely political. On the other hand, as the original energy of the New Criticism lapsed, graduate programs seemed bogged down in what I call critical nominalism, the watchword of which was "A poem should not mean but be." All too often the study and teaching of literature were reduced to close reading of a work for its own sake without reference to either a theoretical or historical framework. Thus in the 1960s there was a powerful urge to discover a justification for literary study. Or, in Frank Kermode's terms, students of literature needed new fictions to make sense of their lives. Thus younger academics welcomed Fiedler's preface to his 1960 *Love and Death in the American Novel* where he wrote: "I have not, however, written what is most often meant these days by a 'critical' study, mere textual analysis, ahistorical, antibiographical: the kind of guide for courses in higher remedial reading which an age of lapsing literacy perhaps demands, but which it is somewhat craven to supply" (*Love and Death,* preface).

In many ways, the centerpiece of *Fiedler on the Roof*[2] is Fiedler's interest in Leopold Bloom, as seen in the two Joyce essays. Let us step back and consider Joyce's view of Jews and why he created Bloom. Although *Ulysses* demonstrates the strong kinship between differing cultures, and the possibility of reconciling apparent cultural differences in personal and historical terms, *Ulysses* is informed by Joyce's distinctions between Greek and Jewish civilizations, distinctions derived from his classical education but generally supported by modern scholarship. For the Greeks, mankind becomes important only when he achieves an heroic aspect. This occurs when an individual is a leader or major figure in great events—such as war or rebellion—that change history or when his deeds or words challenge the gods. Memories of legends of gods and prior heroes shape the decision-making and behavioral patterns of the classical Greek protagonists and their successors. In his obsession with the Christ story and the life of Shakespeare, isn't Stephen Dedalus in this Greek tradition? For the Jews, by contrast, human beings are the supreme beings on Earth; they do not share space or focus with Gods or mythical heroes. Human life itself is not only sacred, but the way humans live and behave is an important subject for study. It follows that personal experiences and memories give shape to the lives of individual Jews.

Thus the thoughts, feelings, and motives of Joyce's Irish Jewish hero, Leopold Bloom, are shaped by memories of his own and his family's past. But Leopold Bloom has never been bar-mitzvah or circumcised; nor is he the son of a Jewish mother, which by convention is the determinant of Jewish genealogy. Instead, he has been baptized *three* times. Yet he is considered a Jew by everyone in Dublin, and his identity as an ostracized outsider and the victim of anti-Semitism is crucial to his characterization.

By the time he wrote *Ulysses* in 1922, Joyce was fascinated with Jews. Joyce's embracing Jews had to do with his own rejection of Roman Catholicism. It also had to do with an incident when a man Joyce thought was a Jew named Alfred Hunter befriended him during a drinking spree on 22 June 1904. Joyce in exile identified with Bloom as an outcast in his own country. Joyce sees Bloom, like himself, as a threatening presence to traditional Irish cultural prejudices. Like Joyce, Bloom is a pacifist and internationalist who considers himself a patriot. By having innocuous, good-hearted Bloom also be a Mason, Joyce comically debunks the widely accepted notion that the Masons are in treacherous collusion with the Jews, or that the Masons or the Jews were a conspiratorial threat to Ireland or Europe. Nor did Joyce have much use for the often-voiced nonsensical view that considered the Irish to be the lost ten tribes of Israel. He not only saw the irony of the clichéd parallel that the anti-Semitic Irish were the Israelites to the British Egyptian Pharoahs, but specifically has Stephen mock that view in the "Aeolus" chapter of *Ulysses*.

In his Trieste years, Joyce was exposed to Jews, for Trieste, as Fiedler notes, had an influential Jewish population. In truth, probably there were more Jews than Irish in Joyce's Trieste: "Often, therefore, he must have felt himself (his name, after all, being James or Seamus, which is to say Jacob or Israel) not the Jews' martyr like Stephen, but the Jews' Jew: an ultimate exile in an unredeemably foreign-city, where he first imagined, then became, Bloom: a *yiddisher kopf* lost in the nightmare of goyish history, from which, as he wrote, we all strive vainly to awake" (57). Joyce was influenced by his friend Italo Svevo (whose real name was Ettore Schmitz), a non-practicing and non-matrilinear Jew whom Joyce met in Trieste, who conceived himself as a Jew. While Joyce was influenced by Otto Weininger's *Sex and Character* (1906) and Maurice Fishburg's *The Jews: A Study of Race and Enlightenment* (1911), Joyce wanted to reject racial stereotypes. Yet Joyce's Bloom, we need note, is not without Jewish racial stereotypes: he is guilt-ridden, family-oriented, compulsively curious, womanly, passive, and worried about money.

Both Fiedler's Joyce essays—"Bloom or Joyce, or *Jokey for Jacob*" (1976), "Joyce and the Jewish Consciousness" (1986)—were originally given as talks. Fiedler is interested in Joyce *because* Joyce alone of the "canonical modernists" has a place for Jews (xi). He compellingly argues that Bloom is Joyce's other self, the alternative to "the voice Stephen Dedalus, Ph.D." (31). Bloom represents the realist Joyce, the one who lived and breathed, not the artist paring his fingernails: "No, much, perhaps most, of what constitutes the authentic figure of Bloom comes, perhaps not entirely unbidden and unconsciously, but certainly less cerebrally, from deeper, darker, more visceral sources. The myth of Ulysses lives in the head of Christian Europe, but the myth of the Jew, which is Bloom's better half, resides in the guts of Europe: a pain in the dark innards of the gentile world, or better perhaps, an ache in the genitals, an ache in the loins of the gentiles" (39). Fiedler realizes that he writes as a Jew and thinks as a Jew; like Bloom— a Jew in spite of himself, not only because of his heritage but because his fellows think of him as a Jew, just as Joyce could not be anything else but an Irishman even in exile.

Fiedler is passionately drawn to *Ulysses:* "*Ulysses* was for my youth and has remained for my later years not a novel at all, but a conduct book, a guide to salvation through the mode of art, a kind of secular scripture" (33). As Fiedler sees it, "Joyce had created in Bloom the first archetypal modern Jew: not ghettoized Israelite or Hebrew, but emancipated, secularized *yid*, his knowledge of his own ancestral tradition approaching degree zero without diminishing his Jewish identity" (48). Fiedler finds in Bloom a character who was not "the property of an exclusive WASP critical establishment" (xi). For Fiedler, Bloom "turns out to be what can be adequately described only by another Yiddish word, a *mensch;* which is to say, a full male human being, as imagined by a tradition hostile to most of the qualities that the gentile world has thought of as being specifically macho" (50). Fiedler, who embraced the role of outsider, is using Joyce the exile and Bloom the marginal Jew—who valiantly and unsuccessfully tries to crossdress as a gentile—to define himself. Thus, Fiedler identifies with Bloom: "I have assumed and am assuming at this moment the voice of Bloom because it is the voice of the eternal amateur, the self-appointed prophet, the harassed Jew, the comic father; and that is a voice which I like to believe, for my own private reasons and some public ones too, is my own authentic voice" (31–32).

For Fiedler criticism is autobiography; books are what they mean to him. His idiosyncratic perspective enables him to make many splendid points about Joyce: "Many critics, including Hugh Kenner, fail to see, or are at any rate driven to deny, this 'womanly' mawkishness in Joyce, preferring to dwell on his antisentimental irony; but he tends to betray it whenever he enters Bloom's Jewish heart and head. Joyce himself seems to have grown ashamed of this weakness in himself after *Ulysses*, eschewing it completely in the goyish pages of *Finnegans Wake*, where, for that reason among others, I prefer not to follow him" (51). It is as if Fiedler sees himself as the Jewish anti-self of the high gentile priest of modernist studies, Hugh Kenner. Do we not feel that Fiedler still writes of himself as the Jewish outsider in the WASP establishment when he writes: "In any case, anti-Semitism is everywhere in *Ulysses* the chief, almost the sole mode of relating to Jews available to gentiles; and, indeed, it is only in response to it that Bloom can feel himself a Jew at all, since ritually and even ethnically he scarcely qualifies" (55). Readers of *Fiedler on the Roof* realize that Fiedler, too, feels himself both a Jew in response to a gentile world which defines him as Jew *and* a representative of his people to outsiders. At times, Fiedler writes as a Jew speaking to other Jews; at other times he writes as a stranger, an odd figure, like Bloom, among WASPs—academics and elsewhere. But Fiedler also acknowledges that he has benefited by being a Chosen person, "I have, that is to say, profited from a philo-Semitism as undiscriminating as the anti-Semitism in reaction to which it originated. And to make matters worse, I have shamelessly played the role in which I have been cast, becoming a literary Fiedler on the roof of academe" (177).

Fiedler enacts the ambiguity of us Jews in English studies who, on one hand, study a majority culture, accommodate to it, and are shaped by it but, on the other, arrogate that culture for our own understanding and professional ends. We conquer it and make it our instrument, *and* we are in turn conquered by it and are made its voice, and spokespeople. At its best, the tension works in Fiedler—and us. Perhaps Fiedler and other Jewish academics are in part attracted to *Ulysses* because it enacts how Joyce, the Irishman, was in a similar position of both accommodating to and arrogating English and Western literature.

That Fiedler has something of a larger-than-life ego, as we can see from his second sentence in the Preface to *Fiedler on the Roof,* will not surprise readers of his other works. "I no longer read their newest fiction with the sense of discovery and delight that led me to tout so extravagantly their earlier work, eventually helping to make it a part of the canon and to win for it an ever-growing audience both Jewish and goyish" (ix). He enjoys the vertical pronoun, but his sense of humor and self-realization that he is hyperbolically outrageous usually mitigates what otherwise might be Fiedlercentricism. In part because of the oral origin of these essays or talks, we can hear the biblical rhythm, prophetic, almost rabbinic, strain in Fiedler's voice, a strain that dissolves whatever irony was intended in spite of himself:

> Is there *nothing* left for me to celebrate on this night, in this place? I who believe that literature should be not *about* myth but living myth itself. I who have lost my taste for the ironic and have grown perhaps overfond of the comic and the pathetic. I who believe that criticism itself, which is a form of literature and not of science, should aim not at examination but at ecstasis. . . . But Bloom is Ulysses resurrected and transfigured, not merely recalled or commented on or explained. Bloom is Ulysses rescued from all those others who were neither Jew nor Greek, and who had kidnapped him, held him in alien captivity for too long. Bloom is Ulysses rescued from the great poets as well as the small ones, from Dante and from Tennyson, and—at the other end of the mythological spectrum from James Joyce—from that anti-Semite, Ezra Pound, who liked to think he was the only true Ulysses. (37–38)

Fiedler's comments on Joyce are lyrical and intuitive rather than logical and rigorous—and they are more exciting for their lack of rigor: "But in Joyce, and in him for the first time, the Jew, though he remains a father still, is no longer a dark, threatening, castrating father. He is no threat to anyone, because he is no longer Abraham, but Joseph: Joseph the carpenter, Joseph the joiner, which is to say, he is the cuckold, since for Joyce there is no Christian-Jewish God anymore" (40). Like so many of his generalizations, these are part of Fiedler's mythopoeic imagination. While criticizing Joyce for often allowing myth to take precedence over mimesis, Fiedler himself uses a mythopoeic imagination to propose his generalization: "In the novel, at any rate, the joke and the mystery become one: the sexual betrayal of Leopold by Molly in the arms of the supergoy, Blazes, is mythologically equated with that of Joseph by Mary—pregnant before he has ever bedded her, with a child sired, true believers say, by the Jewish God, but anti-Christian blasphemers insist by a wandering Roman soldier, not merely human but a goy" (53).

In the most brilliant essay in *Fiedler on the Roof,* "Why is the Grail Knight Jewish?," Fiedler interprets the Grail as a metonymy of the role he sees himself playing in academic life. For him, the Grail legend is "the oddly melancholy, the profoundly anti triumphal saga of Joseph of Arimathea and the long line of Jews who succeeded him as keepers of the Grail, right down to that oddly Jewish-non-Jewish son of a Jewish mother. . . . And the Grail it-

self—whether we understand it as the cup of the Passover benediction, the platter which held the paschal sacrifice, or the plate
in which the unleavened bread was displayed—I came to see was
a symbol for the role of Judaism in subverting the chivalric codes
and a way of life dependent on them" (92–93). While his analysis
on the Grail Legend is characteristically mythopoeic Fiedler—in
his role as literary anthropologist of ancient rituals and myths—
what is important is that Fiedler, Jewish *subversive*, sees that sub-
version as his role not only in this essay, but in the entire collection
and indeed his oeuvre. Fiedler sees himself as the keeper of the
Grail and for Fiedler, the Grail is the truth about books, Jews,
and himself. "I feel committed to an attempt to redream that
Passover dream as if it were my own; or to put it somewhat less
metaphorically, to try to relocate the myth that exists before, after,
outside all of the Christian texts that pretend to embody it, by
demonstrating the sense in which it is a Jewish myth. Or perhaps
I mean rather a myth about Jews: a reflection of the plight of my
own people at a particular historical moment—recorded first by
one who may have been a Jew converted to Christianity, and then
revised by a score of gentiles, some more, some less aware of what
in mythological terms they were doing" (86). Does not Bloom, too,
recuperate the Passover story in the terms Fiedler describes?

Is it not appropriate that I, as professor who have taught almost
thirty years at an Ivy League school and who still speaks with a
distinct Long Island intonation, should write about Leslie Fiedler?
Just as Bloom is his spiritual father, so Fiedler—as much as Lionel
Trilling, Irving Howe, Alfred Kazin, and M. H. Abrams—is as
spiritual father to a generation of Jewish scholars toiling in the
fields of English and American literature in American colleges
and universities. Like Fiedler, I have become more interested in
my Jewish heritage as I have become aware of how my Jewishness
defines me as a scholar. Like Fiedler, I am drawn to Joyce's Leopold Bloom because he enacts love of family, immersion and respect for the prosaics of life, the ability to take pleasure in small
things, imaginative and emotional resilience, and, yes, a sense of
being an outsider. I was always a little uncomfortable within the
world of mostly WASPish Ivy League English departments, a
world that prevailed in my early Cornell years beginning in 1968.
We might recall that just as women were excluded and marginalized by the academy, Jews were not welcome at the elite universities and particularly in the humanities. One will find no tenured
Jews on the rolls of Ivy League English faculties before World
War II, and few with Irish or Italian names.

I have been drawn to outsiders for my subjects since my Honors thesis and Ph.D. dissertation on Conrad:

• Conrad, a Polish émigré who felt himself an outsider in England, who in some of his major texts wrote of the process of a meditative surrogate narrator—Marlow, like himself, a merchant sea captain—coming to terms with his experience. I take into my writing and my teaching the Conradian process of sense-making;
• Disraeli, the unlikely converted Jew who became prime minister, a dominant political figure and widely read novelist, who thought of himself as a Jew, and (as his romance *Alroy* and his young England trilogy character Sidonia illustrate) maintained a strong if eccentric sense of Jewish identity notwithstanding his having been converted; and
• Joyce, who left his homeland to wander in exile and felt he lived in a country dominated by two imperial powers: the Roman Catholic Church and the British Crown.

My recent affiliation with Cornell's Jewish Studies and my current focus—on how novels and memoirs as diverse as Spiegelman's *Maus* books, Wiesel's *Night*, and Levi's *Periodic Table*, and Schwarz-Bart's *The Last of the Just* reconfigure the Holocaust—reflects an awakening that I describe as secularly spiritual but not religious. Moreover, many of the teachers who most influenced me were outsiders and oddities: gay or black men or pioneering academic women like Barbara Lewalski, or social pariahs who violated sexual or social conventions of their day—a day when bachelors and people living together out of wedlock were suspect. Perhaps they felt an empathy with a fellow outsider and took him under their wing.

II

Fiedler neglects such possibilities as Bloom's linkage to the Hasidic legend of the Just Man. Perhaps the best model for how Joyce regards Bloom can be found in the Jewish legend of the Lamed Vov. According to Schwarz-Bart in *The Last of the Just*, a novel based on this legend:

The world reposes on thirty-six just men, the Lamed Vov, indistinguishable from simple mortals; often they are unaware of their station. But if just one of them were lacking, the suffering of mankind would poison even the souls of the newborn, and humanity would suffocate with a single cry. For the Lamed Vov are the hearts of the world multiplied, and into them, as into one receptacle, pour all our griefs.[3]

In the legend of the Just Men, God manifests himself through individual deeds of human kindness and justice. The legend of the Just Men depends upon the Jewish concept that all men are equal before God and that divinity can be found within any man; a member of the Lamed Vov can as easily be a simple humble shepherd or a seller of advertisements as a king or prophet. The legend appears in some older texts of the Haggadah, the book of ritual prayer used on the Passover that reiterates the Zionist hope, "next year in Jerusalem," which Bloom is thinking of all day; as we learn in "Ithaca", he possesses an "ancient haggadah book" which he has been reading (*U* 17.1877–78). If one recalls Moses's words in Deuteronomy 10:18, one sees a crucial link not only between the legend of the Just Men and Moses, but also between Christ and Moses: "He doth execute justice for the fatherless and widow, and loveth the stranger, in giving him food and raiment. Love ye therefore the stranger; for ye were strangers in the land of Egypt." These words of Moses also remind the reader that the Jewish dream of a restored national destiny includes the dream of the family paradigm. When Bloom is anointed as leader of the "new Bloomusalem" in "Circe," he is at once Moses, Judas Maccabee, and the Messiah returned to rebuild the Temple (*U* 15.1544).

Within Joyce's fictional universe, Bloom is confirmed as "the new Messiah for Ireland" because it confirms him as a Lamed Vov (*U* 12.1642). Within Bloom's secular, humanistic universe, Bloom is the Just Man who, although unappreciated by his fellows, cares about them and feels for them, even as he thinks of how to improve their lot with his utopian plans. Gradually Bloom emerges as a vessel of humanistic values within the novel. Persecuted by his anti-Semitic audience, Bloom speaks eloquently against the use of force and for his credo of love, tolerance, respect, and justice: "Force, hatred, history, all that. That's not life for men and women, insult and hatred. And everybody knows that it's the very opposite of that that is really life" (*U* 12.1481–83). When Alf stupidly asks "What?" Bloom responds, "Love . . . I mean the opposite of hatred" (*U* 12.1484–85). For Joyce, Bloom's values represent possible redemption for man in a post-Christian world. To evoke other Jewish traditions, Bloom is, for the most part, less in the Jewish tradition of *schlemiel*, the kindly buffoon who is his own worst enemy, than of the gentle, well-meaning folk hero who can turn self-acceptance of his lot and even ostensible self-denigration into triumph. While Fiedler himself would hardly claim for himself a place among the Lamed Vov, one expects he would smile at the possible parallel between Bloom's integrity, courage, and resilience within a hostile environment, and Fiedler's own integrity, courage, and resilience within the academic milieu of late 1950s and early 1960s.

Does Fiedler not truly and commendably understand that the truth one tries to tell about books is the truth one tells of oneself? Once regarded as a kind of a mythopoetic interdisciplinary rebel fusing sociology, anthropology, and myth criticism, Fiedler now, in the very best sense, seems an old-fashioned humanist who believes books are written by humans for humans and about humans. He has no interest whatever in the theoretical revolution. What he said in the 1960 Preface to *Love and Death in the American Novel* then makes sense today: "The best criticism can hope to do is to set the work in as many illuminating contexts as possible: the context of the genre to which it belongs, of the whole body of work of its author, of the life of that author and of his times" (*Love and Death*, preface).

As readers of the entire book *Fiedler on the Roof* will see, Fiedler, like Bloom, is trying to rediscover the Jewish boy within the aging Jewish man: "The alphabet of his ancestors especially haunts him, suggesting perhaps that if only he could remember it all, he could reconstruct his lost tradition; but three letters is the best he can do when he tries once more in the Ithaca section to draw for Stephen the characters in which God's word was first written" (53–54). Doesn't Fiedler do the same thing with his own use of Yiddish words? The Jewish self that has reemerged in his later years, revealing a man not unlike a Bloom counterpart and alter ego, is *Leslie Fiedler, Ph.D.*, who writes, "I feel obliged to wrestle with the question of *why* the threat of annihilation and the promise of redemption have continued to be the pattern of our history" (162).

To be sure, Fiedler blithely ignores prior scholarship on Joyce, including the work on Bloom as a Jew in between when he gave the first talk in 1970 and when he published his book in 1991; even when he wrote the first talk, he ignored extant Joyce scholarship. Yet Fiedler is and remains an original voice. We might conclude by recalling what Stephen says of Shakespeare in the "Scylla and Charybidis" section of *Ulysses*, appropriate to both Bloom and

Fiedler: "All events brought grist to his mill" (*U* 204; IX.748), or, as Stephen says of Shakespeare: "His errors are volitional and are the portals of discovery" (*U* 190; IX.228–29).

NOTES

1. Leslie Fiedler, *Love and Death in the American Novel* (New revised edition. New York: Dell, 1969). References hereafter cited in the text.

2. Leslie Fiedler, *Fiedler on the Roof: Essays on Literature and Jewish Identity.* Boston: David R. Godine, 1991). References hereafter are cited in the text.

3. André Schwarz-Bart, *The Last of the Just,* trans. Stephen Becker (New York: Atheneum, 1961), 2–3.

4. James Joyce, *Ulysses.* The Corrected Text. Hans Walter Gabler, ed. New York: Vintage, 1986. References hereafter given in the text, with the abbreviation *U.*

"In [Mutant] Dreams Awake": Leslie Fiedler and Science Fiction

David Ketterer

Leslie Fiedler has published both critical reflections on, and works of, science fiction (sf). My survey of this output begins with his criticism, which came first and which remains his more influential, if not necessarily more valuable, contribution.

I

An appraisal of his most important essay bearing on sf—"The New Mutants" of 1965—is perhaps best approached by way of its 1985 near-equivalent—"The Cyborg Manifesto" by Donna Haraway.[1] Both essays gained a certain currency by exploring (and exaggerating?) the empowering relevance of an iconic sf image to an—at the time of publication—increasingly vocal segment of the population: the hippies in Fiedler's case, women in Haraway's. Haraway's essay highlights areas of both blindness and insight in Fiedler's analysis. What he was blind to—and what finally limits his conception of sf—was the rationalism that existed alongside the irrationalism of those 1960s hippies. Fiedler (like almost all of us) did not foresee that a significant percentage of them—and their younger brothers and sisters who inherited something of the same ethos—would mutate into the Masters of Silicon Valley. The imaginative stimulation provided by psychedelic drugs contributed to many of the computer advances of the 1970s and 1980s.

Like most things, the meld of natural and unnatural, the organic and the mechanical, represented by the cyborgs of sf, has been viewed negatively and positively. A number of examples from the movies come immediately to mind. Arnold Schwarzenegger as the Terminator of the 1984 and 1991 films has represented both the bad and the good cyborg. Against the bad Borgs

111

of *Star Trek: First Contact* (1996) may be opposed the good cyborg
of the *Robocop* films (1987, 1990). Haraway's innovation was to
appropriate the cyborg for its purely positive possibilities. The
world of computers, of cyberspace, is one that requires that we
fuse our identities with machines. Human beings, meaning
women in particular, should embrace the opportunities that this
new convergence opens up. Women should thus endeavour to
transform themselves into cyborgs not just to steal a march on
men but to eliminate the divide that separates male and female
(and in that regard, Fiedler's 1969 essay that I discuss below—
"Cross the Border—Close the Gap"—was genuinely prescient).

When Fiedler delivered "The New Mutants" at the *Partisan
Review*-sponsored Conference on the Idea of the Future at Rut-
gers University in June 1965, computers were not the omnipres-
ent desk accessory they are today, so it is not surprising that he
makes no reference to them. His concern was the emergence on
campuses across America of a representative portion of a "generation [of which now, at 55, I have to remind myself I was a
member] under twenty-five" (390) who dropped out, turned on,
and challenged the authorities of the day. He argues that "the
conjunction of homosexuality, drugs and civil rights" (396) accounts for the fact that those hippies, those "new mutants," wish
not only to be "more Black than White but more female than
male" (390). All of this is not so different from Haraway's program
or—given the end-of-[Humanism]-man rhetoric and the sympathy for madness—to the still-fashionable thought of Michel Fou-
cault. Where Fiedler departs from Haraway is in his claim that
the new mutants are the "new irrationalists" (384). The hippies
were drawn to the irrational and mystical but those who survived,
and their successors, did not abandon reason. They may have
abandoned some rational ideologies but those they eventually replaced with rational constructs of their own.

The account of sf that Fiedler aligns with his analysis of hip-
piedom likewise accentuates what Brian Aldiss has called the
"dreaming pole" of the genre to the virtual exclusion of its Enlightenment, rationalist roots.[2] For Fiedler, the apparent outer
space impulse of sf is a subterfuge—what is truly at issue is "the
conquest of inner space: by an adventure of the spirit, an exten-
sion of psychic possibility . . ." (399). This is a definition of the
genre that might be applied to the sf of J. G. Ballard, Kurt Vonnegut, and William Burroughs. But it does not particularly illuminate the sf of Arthur C. Clarke (to whom Fiedler refers), Isaac
Asimov, Gregory Benford, and many others.

All sf—whether directed towards inner or outer space—takes the future as its particular terrain, and "futurist literature" has moved, Fiedler notes, "from the periphery to the center of culture . . ." (381). It has done so, Fiedler wishes to claim, because the "mutant" counterculture of the 1960s can be related to the thematic goal of sf—the coming of an evolved, enhanced species that will replace present humanity, like the "slans" of A. E. van Vogt's 1946 novel of the same title. "Fans are slans" was and perhaps remains a rallying cry in the "fanspeak" of sf enthusiasts. But what Fiedler fails to consider is the likelihood that that slogan and any wider equation between hippies and mutants points rather to a sense of alienation and perhaps inadequacy on the part of those individuals (the Clark Kent syndrome) and not to their being, in actuality, evolved supermen or superwomen.

Nevertheless, Fiedler's version of what he calls "the myth . . . of Science Fiction" is sound enough, particularly if it is understood, more modestly, as *one of* the basic myths of sf:

> that myth is quite simply the myth of the end of man, of the transcendence or transformation of the human—a vision quite different from that of the extinction of our species by the Bomb, which seems stereotype rather than archetype and consequently the source of editorials rather than poems. More fruitful is the prospect of the radical transformation (under the impact of advanced technology, and the transfer of traditional human functions to machines) of *homo sapiens* into something else: the emergence—to use the language of Science Fiction itself—of "mutants" among us. (382)

Much sf *is* about our advancing to some new stage of existence—or new definition of humankind in my theorization of one of the three ways in which sf limns a "philosophical apocalypse."[3] But whatever metaphoric truth the mutant figure might have, the hippies were *not* that new stage of existence. (Fiedler is not averse to exaggerating for affect and his mutants—in spite of the reality of mutations caused by radiation—are essentially a rhetorical ploy.) Donna Haraway's cyborgs—a currently plausible image of a future species that has generated a good deal of feminist theory—might be dimly descried in Fiedler's parenthetical reference to "the transfer of traditional human functions to machines," except that his wording accentuates the division between humans and machines.

Fiedler's dream-born sf "based on hints in Poe" (381)—presumably the antirational rather than the analytic Poe—achieves its apotheosis in the work of William Burroughs. (Brian Aldiss's representative of sf's dream pole is Edgar Rice, rather than William, Burroughs.) "[William] Burroughs is the chief prophet of the post-male post heroic world" and his *Naked Lunch* (which, incidentally, "folds-in" passages from Edgar Rice Burroughs's *Thuvia, Maid of Mars*) is "a nightmare anticipation (in Science Fiction form) of post-Humanist sexuality" (392). Not surprisingly then, Fiedler concludes his essay by quoting from Burroughs, a passage about a war in the air of "Image Rays" to which the narrator contributes "My Silent Message" (400). As we shall see, this war of silent messages (to which Fiedler has contributed his writings) is not unlike the cosmic war at the back of the sf novel that Fiedler wrote in the next decade, *The Messengers Will Come No More*.

"The New Mutants" expands on ideas that Fiedler first floated in a paragraph of *Waiting for the End* published a year earlier in 1964. There William Burroughs is described as a "pioneer mutant" and mention is made of an sf future where "our unrecognizably mutant children will inherit the earth. . . ."[4] The mutant is one manifestation of what Fiedler informs doctoral candidate P. Marudanayagam is his favorite subject: "If I were to identify the single theme which has always possessed me it would be that of the stranger and the outsider."[5] Hence Fiedler's studies of freaks and of North American outsiders—"Red Indians," Blacks, and Jews. The other section of *Waiting for the End* about sf goes some way towards identifying sf as a Jewish genre: "The basic myths of science fiction reflect the urban outlook, the social consciousness, the utopian concern of the modern secularized Jew."[6] Waiting for the Messiah translates as sf's commitment to the future and the scientist-intellectual is a Jewish stereotype. Incidentally, this section of *Waiting for the End* demonstrates Fiedler's long-term interest in sf; it originates in Fiedler's 1959 monograph *The Jew In the American Novel*.[7]

It might seem contradictory that, when Fiedler interpolates some interesting ruminations in his 1966 revised edition of *Love and Death in the American Novel* (on what, in 1959, he describes as "in large part a Jewish product," or, in 1965, as "that largely Jewish product, science fiction") he refers to sf (the somewhat guilty, hypocritical, and pornographic "third wave of popular gothicism") as "primarily an Anglo-Saxon form. . . ."[8] Presumably he means that a *form* that is associated with England and America (having suppressed whatever Gallic claims might be ventured) has lent itself to the expression of Jewish *themes*. Or should one align the apparent confusion here with the ambiguous situation of a marginal genre promoted (with the Jews?) "from the periphery to the center of culture . . ." (381)?

Fiedler returns to the hippie-mutant-outsider in the final chapter of *Freaks* (1978), "The Myth of the Mutant and the Image of the Freak."[9] The freak, it is suggested, symbolizes the future possibilities of humankind. But the parallel drawn between physical freaks and drugged, hippie "freaks" is very hard to swallow. Fiedler wishes to claim the hippies as "*mental mutants*" (320) and relate them, once again, to the mutants of such sf cult books as *Slan,* Arthur C. Clarke's *Childhood's End,* and Robert Heinlein's *Stranger in a Strange Land.* The mutant savior of Heinlein's novel, Valentine Michael Smith, is described as "science-fiction's first mutant-turned-guru" (327).

In his doctoral-thesis-turned-book on Fiedler, P. Marudanayagam notes that Fiedler's "major concentration has always been on three themes: (1) eros and thanatos, the twin impulses toward life and death (2) the stranger in a White Anglo-Saxon Protestant Society and (3) Pop Culture."[10] Given these three foci, Fiedler's interest in sf was inevitable but, in terms of the chronological expression of that interest, the second (as we have seen) came first, and the third second. The role of sf as an important aspect of pop culture comes to the fore in an 1969 essay that appeared in the pop culture magazine *Playboy*—"Cross the Border—Close the Gap" (which is reprinted in, and provides the title for, the third section of volume two of *The Collected Essays of Leslie Fiedler*)—and in a 1973 essay on Kurt Vonnegut.

The title of the *Playboy* essay refers primarily to the border or gap between high and low literature, and its alignment with the class hierarchy (the border between male and female is not mentioned, but that between human being and machines makes an appearance at the essay's conclusion).[11] We require, Fiedler claims, a literature and a criticism "adequate to Postmodernism" (462), which he characterizes as "an age of Myth and passion, sentimentality and fantasy" (463). Because literature as "art," as elite Church "scripture," is dead, "the truly new New Novel must be anti-art as well as antiserious" (467). The genres that cross the border are "the Western, Science Fiction, and Pornography" (469). I shall confine myself here to what Fiedler says about the contribution of sf, "a common 'Anglo-Saxon' form" whose "proper subjects" are "the Present Future [an addition to his earlier definition] and the End of Man—not time travel or the penetration of outer space, except as the latter somehow symbolize the former" (474). Once again Fiedler is downplaying the rational materiality of sf—it is the mythic dream of sf that matters. Kurt Vonnegut, Jr., is singled out as "a writer of the first rank whose preferred mode" is sf (474). The goal of the effectively religious sf text (and that of the new western and the new pornography) is the creation of a new mass scripture and the realization of *ekstasis,* the realm of Vision, Dream, Wonder. (Wonder is, in fact, the name of one of Fiedler's daughters). Thus may be created "a thousand little Wests in the interstices of a machine civilization," and lived "the tribal life among and with the support of machines . . ." (484). The gap between humans and machines is here significantly narrowed but it is not breached. Haraway's cyborg has not arrived.

Vonnegut's achievement as a border-crossing sf writer anticipated in the 1969 article is analyzed the following year in "The Divine Stupidity of Kurt Vonnegut" (an essay that Fiedler apparently did not think well enough of to include in his *Collected Essays*).[12] Vonnegut is celebrated for bridging the High Art of Modernism and the Pop Art of Postmodernism. Of his various works, which seem "more like scriptures than commodities" (195), Fiedler focuses attention on top of his sf novels, *The Sirens of Titan* (1959), "his best book, I think" (and so does the present author) (202), and *Cat's Cradle* (1963), his second best.

Between 1972 and 1975 Fiedler's commitment to sf intensified; he wrote an article on the work of an sf "hack," Philip José Farmer (rather than a mainstream, crossover writer like Vonnegut), he wrote an sf novel and an sf short story, and he edited an sf anthology. Since I am delaying my discussion of Fiedler's own sf until the end of this essay, only the Farmer article and the anthology are presently relevant.

An editorially emended version of "Thanks for the Feast: Notes on Philip José Farmer" first appeared in the Book Review section of the *Los Angeles Times* for 23 April 1972 under the editor's gauche title "Getting into the Task of the Now Pornography." The original version with Fiedler's title was published in the fanzine *Moebius Trip* and was reprinted in 1976 as an afterword in *The Book of Philip José Farmer*.[13] The "wonder and ecstasy" to be found in sf "is ultimately rooted in our sexuality" (a debatable explanation of everything that might be accounted the sf sublime), but the orally obsessed Farmer is notable as, "During the 50s, the only major writer of Science Fiction to deal *explicitly* with sex" (234). Taking an explicitly Freudian approach, Fiedler finds in Farmer's sf, beginning with the story "Mother," "the vision of a cloying and destructive relationship between Mothers and Sons . . ." (236), with the Sons achieving a phallic apotheosis in Farmer's re-creation of Tarzan. More broadly what Fiedler discovers is that conflict between matriarchal and patriarchal religions that is at the center of the sf novel Fiedler himself was about to write (or perhaps already writing)—an indebtedness to which I shall return.

Fiedler's 1975 sf anthology (which includes Farmer's "Mother" and twenty other too-often reprinted "classics") is entitled *In Dreams Awake*. He earlier used the same phrase as the chapter title for the discussion of the fourth and last of his basic myths of the West in *The Return of the Vanishing American* (1968)—the myth of the runaway male as represented by Rip Van Winkle. Altogether these myths tell the story of the white male who runs away from the white female and replaces her with a colored male. Presumably the reapplication of the same title to sf implies that sf, like the Western, like American literature generally, basically tells the same story, a story that, looked at most positively, expresses the dream of interracial love and reconciliation. The title is taken from a passage in Henry David Thoreau's *A Week on the Concord and Merrimac Rivers* (1849) that appears in abbreviated form as one of the epigraphs to the sf anthology (the other is Mary Shelley's 1831 description of her waking dream of Frankenstein's monster):

> In dreams we see ourselves naked and acting out our real characters, even more clearly than we see others awake. . . . Our truest life is when we are in dreams awake.

There are many references, literal and metaphoric, to dreams and awakenings in Fiedler's critical and creative works. Beyond the inevitable importance of dreams to a Freudian "literary anthropologist,"[14] the word "dream" for Fiedler signifies a romantic Vision of Utopian Truth. Clearly Fiedler is drawn to sf because sf is drawn towards the realization of our utopian potential.

Fiedler provides a useful historical introduction for *In Dreams Awake* and capsule explanations for his three sections: "The Beginnings," "The Golden Age," and "New Directions."[15] Mary Shelley is credited with inventing in *Frankenstein* "the first myth of the Age of Technology: man seeking through science to become the creator of the species after himself—and failing" (12). Because sf creates "technologically oriented mythologies to replace the older ones made obsolete by science," it "is a religious literature . . ." (15) and was so exploited by Charles Manson's reading of *A Stranger in a Strange Land* and by sf writer L. Ron Hubbard, the inventor of Scientology. As Fiedler conceives it, sf derives from two arche-types, that of (A) the "Extraordinary Voyage" (developed by Wells as time travel and space travel), and (B) "the End of Man" (16), which led, it is claimed, to five variants. When "Man" means spe-cifically the male of the species, the variant threat number 4 is women. In terms of this topology, then, Fiedler's *The Messengers Will Come No More* is a category B4 sf novel. The point about "eroticized technology" (19) was previously made in the essay on Farmer; it is well represented in this anthology by Fiedler's most original selection—Melville's "The Tartarus of Maids" (if it is in-deed sf).

By the late 1970s and into the 1980s the academic sf research industry was in high gear and, now that he had established himself as critic, theorist, and author of sf, Fiedler's services were called on at least four times. The sf writer Harry Harrison persuaded him to write an introduction to Olaf Stapledon's *Odd John* (1935) for that work's appearance in 1978 in the SF Masters series that Harrison and Brian Aldiss were editing.[16] Fiedler's introduction seeks to "rescue" this early mutant superman story "from the context of" such similarly themed works as Philp Wylie's *Gladiator* (1930), van Vogt's *Slan* (1940), Theodore Sturgeon's *More than Human* (1953), and Clarke's *Childhood's End* (1953) "and return it to the centre of Stapledon's unique vision of man and his fictions, where it properly belongs" (11). Subsequently, Robert Scholes per-suaded Fiedler to contribute a book on Stapledon to the Science-Fiction writers series he was editing for Oxford University Press. Clearly a writer who also favored imagery of sleeping and waking, who theorized philosophically about "ecstasy," and who envi-sioned the successive mutations of humankind over aeons in *Last and First Men* (1930)—a matter of vanishingly small import in the staggering context of Stapledon's second masterpiece *Star Maker* (1937)—was of interest to Fiedler.[17] His *Olaf Stapledon: A Man Divided* was published in 1983. A sadomasochist who "suffered from an Oedipus complex" (12), Fiedler's Stapledon, whether an optimist or a pessimist, sane or mad, is divided about the existence or nonexistence of God. But that is not all. "On the conscious level, he is the heir to socialist humanism . . . but on the deeper psychic levels . . . he is a shameless elitist . . ." (117). His "bipolar titles" (222) reflect these divisions; Fiedler's own bipolar favourite, eros and thanatos (the first of his three thematic obsessions but the third to fully manifest itself in the sf context) is also germane to judge from the title of the book's last chapter (which deals with the love stories *Sirius* [1944] and *A Man Divided* [1950]): "Love Against Death, or Beauty and the Beast." ("Love" also figures in the titles of chapters 3 and 5, and "death" in the titles of chapters 3, 8, and 9.) All told, Stapledon offers "a unique vision of the breadth of the physical universe and the depth of the human psyche as revealed by modern science" (5). But there is a sense of Fiedler gabbling, crudely throwing in everything including the kitchen sink, and Brian Aldiss is justified in preferring the introduction to *Odd John* to the rather wilder full-length study.[18]

Since 1979 George Slusser and others have organized the small, rather elitist annual J. Lloyd Eaton Conference on Science Fiction and Fantasy, usually held at the University of California, Riverside. For the third such conference (February 21–22, 1981) Fiedler was invited to be the guest speaker. Published in 1983, his speech, entitled "The Criticism of Science Fiction," provides a history of that criticism and returns to the problem of elite culture versus popular culture.[19] The academic criticism of sf is attuned to the demands of high literature rather than those of a popular genre. A. E. van Vogt is Fiedler's "test case . . . since any apology for or analysis of science fiction which fails to come to terms with his appeal and major importance, defends or defines the genre by falsifying it" (10). Van Vogt (like Farmer), operates at Aldiss's "dream pole" of sf and what is required to truly appreciate his work turns out to be a critic much like Fiedler who can "identify his mythopoeic power, his ability to evoke primordial images, his gift for redeeming the marvellous in a world in which technology has preempted the province of magic and God is dead" (10–11). Fiedler moves on to a discussion of Stapledon (a non-genre and much more cerebral writer) "who represents . . . a complementary test case" (11). Mainstream and sf critics have likewise not been able to come to terms with his work and, although Fiedler points usefully enough to Stapledon's masterpiece *Star Maker* as "Scripture," a "mythological statement" that triggers "transport" and "ecstasy" (12) in its readers, there is considerable doubt that his own book on Stapledon does much better. But Fiedler's essential point, his restatement of the familiar assumption that sf be evaluated for its ability to convey a "sense of wonder," is well taken.

Fiedler's fourth commission was to give the academic Guest-of-Honor speech at the Fifth International Conference on the Fantastic in Boca Raton, Florida (March 22–25, 1984), always a large and somewhat populist gathering. It was published in the now-defunct *Fantasy Review* under the title "Fantasy as Commodity, Pornography."[20] Describing fantasy as "the reigning genre of the moment", especially its "sub varieties . . . Horror and Science Fiction" (6), Fiedler sketches the history of Horror (which combines the *frisson* of fear with the kind of taboo-breaking guilt associated with pornography) from gothic fiction to Michael Jackson's *Thriller* album and the accompanying "camp" video. As a member of Fiedler's audience at the time, I recall that it was his description of the "palpably hybrid" Michael Jackson in relation to his video portrayal of a werewolf that made the most impact:

> neither quite black or white, male or female, straight or gay, child or adult; and, therefore, himself a genuine weirdo, a freak—though one, to be sure, benign and sympathetic, like Peter Pan or E. T. "I've got something I want to tell ya . . . I'm not like other guys," the words of the song go, to make the point quite clear. (8)

Today Fiedler might wish to remove the clause containing the adjectives "benign" and "sympathetic" in view of allegations about Michael Jackson's own taboo-breaking sexual activities. Fiedler moves on to deal with sf as a form that lets "us have our cake and eat it, too: a fictional genre able to evoke 'other worlds and other times,' and to imagine 'supernatural or unnatural beings' compatible with, explicable in terms of the 'laws' of Physics, Chemistry, Astronomy and Biology" (8). In fact, and this is Fiedler's concluding point, the four "classic works of weird fiction"—*Frankenstein, Dracula, Dr. Jekyll and Mr. Hyde,* and *The Island of Dr. Moreau*—are "inter-generic works" that meld gothic romance, horror, and sf, and in so doing they have created the "Myths and Archetypes" that seem increasingly relevant today. They reveal science to be "the ultimate horror in a universe it had promised to deliver from horror forever" (9). And there, in 1984, Fiedler's speech, and his critical commentary on sf apparently begun around 1959, concludes.[21]

II

Fiedler's career as an sf writer seems to have been confined to about three years in the early 1970s. Certainly the response to his sf novel, *The Messengers Will Come No More* (1974), was not encouraging. Robert Alter's negative review opens with this elegant put-down: "Leslie Fiedler is, of course, better known as a critic than as a writer of fiction, and criticism has in fact been the more congenial medium for the exercise of his most engaging qualities of fictional invention."[22] Mark Winchell ends his account of the novel by quoting Fiedler's description of *Messengers* as "the most unread of all my work," and commenting, "It is doubtful that his reputation will suffer for its remaining so."[23] The novel's reception within the sf ghetto was similarly dismissive. Was this reception justified? In part, yes. Many of the novel's futurist touches seem clunky and too much of the narrative consists of explanation; there is not much in the way of characterization and dramatic interest. But the basic idea is intriguing and its playful implications for our understanding of human history are inventively developed. And sf, it should be emphasized, remains a literature of ideas (as well as a literature that aims at wonder or *ekstasis*).

Messengers belongs to that "philosophical apocalypse" category of sf that revolutionizes our understanding of present (and past) human reality by supposing the intervention of unsuspected alien manipulators. Consequently, as put at one point in the novel, "the future is no more than the present actualized, i.e., fully known" (115).[24] It is eventually revealed that at the back of human history is a cosmic conflict between female and male principles or powers (a conflict related to the *agon* of eros and thanatos). Unknown to humankind, these "entities" have interfered in our history and culture—particularly by way of the world's religions—to bring about either male or female predominance. Presumably, they have interfered with civilizations on other planets for the same purpose. The one-time hold (from the novel's twenty-fifth century perspective) of the major patriarchal religions—Judaism, Christianity, and Islam—over a significant portion of the world's peoples was due to the *temporary* victory of the male cosmic force. However, there have been and are matriarchal religions, and *Messengers* is set in a "dying twenty-fifth century" (7) when the matriarchal principal is dominant. Various pagan female deities; the important role given to the Virgin Mary in Christianity (particularly the Catholic version); in Exodus, the struggle between Miriam and her brother Moses, and the exiled Israelites turning to worship a "Golden Cow" (the more familiar word "Calf" suppresses its gender); and the woman's movement that reignited in the 1960s are all but steps in a cosmic struggle that has led to the establishment of the twenty-fifth-century matriarchy on Earth. In retrospect, it would, then, appear that the mutants—the eccentrically evolved offshoot that Fiedler identified in the sixties—were (in fictional actuality) predominantly female (or homosexual).

The gradual revelation of this back plot dates from the late twenty-fifth century, when the emissaries of (it may be assumed)

that the masculine cosmic power, the "Messengers" of Fiedler's
title, mysteriously communicate to some members of a presumably all-male group known as "Meta-Technicians of the Para-
Space Program" (21), the image of an aged, skullcapped, shawled
figure from a bygone age concealing what turns out to be two
scrolls at the mouth of a cave in the Negev Desert. Three aging
Meta-Physicians contact Mindyson, a soon-to-turn-fifty-year-old
archaeologist and Hebrew specialist, whose first name is Jacob
(like Fiedler's father and like the protagonist of his 1966 novella
"The Last Jew in America"), and persuade him to attempt to
locate the buried scrolls and then translate them. It transpires
that the scrolls were written and hidden in A.D. 4 by "the Arch-
Priest of Israel" (144), Eliezar ben Yaakov (i.e., also the son of
Jacob). Eliezar's scrolls contain an account of what he learned
from the communications of cosmic Messengers presumably
working, like the twenty-fifty century ones, for the masculine cosmic power. And what he learned and recorded was the cosmic
back plot that I have briefly summarized. As for matters of detail,
Jesus, apparently was the consequence of the "Virgin" Mary's being inseminated by an extraterrestrial Messenger, presumably one
working for the female power since Mary's role in the New Testa-
ment story would lead to Mariolatry. The Star of Bethlehem was
a spaceship. Of course, the unusual spelling of the name Eliezar
implies the possibility that this whole back plot was a deliberate
lie or the result of delusions. Whether or not one wishes to emphasize this ambiguity, Fiedler has contrived an sf story that quite
literally bears out his claim that "Imagining the future . . . is for
me finally just another way of discovering or inventing a usable
past. . . ."[25]

The first part of the novel fills in the late twenty-fifth-century
setting and provides something of Jacob's personal history. The
"when-women-rule" society is a familiar sf gambit and Fiedler's
main innovation is to align this with a second reversal, that of the
power relations between blacks and whites. It is black women who
are at the human apex of this matriarchy controlled by "the Great
Computer we call Mother" (160).

As if to reflect the cosmic yin-yang struggle, *Messengers* is dedi-
cated to a woman and man—"To [Fiedler's wife] Sally who broke
the [writer's] block" and "To Phil who showed the way. . . ." In
response to my inquiry, Fiedler confirmed that "Phil" is Philip
José Farmer.[26] The matriarchal set-up in *Messengers* is similar in
some ways to that elaborated in Farmer's *Flesh* (1961). In both
future societies, North America (or part of it) is called Columbia

(a mythic female identification derived from [Christopher] Columbus), male body hair is removed, and men are at the sexual service of women. Farmer has published three erotic fantasy novels and his sf regularly includes explicitly described sexual material, something that Fiedler emulates in *Messengers* (to the distaste of some reviewers). In "Thanks for the Fast," Fiedler observes that

> the Cults of the Great Goddess have always obsessed Farmer; and, indeed, there seems something deep within him that yearns for a time, real or imagined, in which the male was not the Hero but a Servant of that great principle of fertility, as in the bawdiest of his sub-pornographic novels, *Flesh.* Yet Farmer's third obsessive theme comes into direct (and perhaps irreconcilable) conflict with this fearful nostalgia for the matriarchal security each of us has known in infancy. (236)

Farmer's first obsessive theme is "Mother as a threat to freedom" and his second, "the discovery of new religions in a new world" that "always turn out to be matriarchal and are presented as an overwhelming challenge to the patriarchal faith of Christianity" (236).

Fiedler writes "that a special favorite of mine has been Phil Farmer" and "that any evidence you suspect he has had on me is real."[27] Fiedler and Farmer are close in age (they were born in 1917 and 1918 respectively) and both are iconoclasts whose slogan might well be: *épater la bourgeoisie.* The mysterious godlike aliens who control events in Farmer's *Riverworld* series are akin to Fiedler's Messengers. (At the same time, Fiedler's interest in mutant superiority would no doubt have drawn him to Farmer's *Wold Newton Family* series, which reveals that Tarzan and other mutant supermen were born because a meteorite that landed in eighteenth-century Yorkshire irradiated a number of pregnant women.)

As for Jacob's personal history, we learn of his past relations with Marcia and Megan—the latter "expelled" him because he secretly had their son circumcised—and his present sexual relations with the young Melissa-Melinda. (We are informed that all women in "Upper Columbia" have names beginning with the letter "M"—standing ultimately it seems for Mother, Mary, or Mistress, or perhaps Marilyn Monroe.) Melissa-Melinda is a "Hypsie" (19)—a combination of "gypsy" plus "hippie—who speaks the argot of the sixties hippies. This aspect of the first part of the book does not work particularly well; it badly dates the novel and undermines the credibility of its far future setting. But the ac-

count in Chapter 7 of Jacob's journey to the cave in the Negev
Desert imaged by the Messengers and his locating the scrolls is
effective. And, although many of the futurist touches are clumsy,
remarks about the breakup of the Soviet Union (13, 95) are
prescient.

The second part of the novel is Eliezar's story as conveyed by
Jacob's translation (made in the new century A.D. 2501) of Eliezar's
two scrolls. It is something of a problem that, although there are
supposedly two narrators, there is not much discernable distinction between Jacob's voice and Eliezar's. As for Eliezar's tale of
alien transmission and interference, it need not only be indebted
to Farmer's *Riverworld* set-up. Fiedler's favorite Vonnegut novel,
The Sirens of Titan, which features a robot messenger from space
and in which we learn that human history has been manipulated
by the alien, time-transcendent Tralfamadorians is also a likely
influence. So too is Erich von Daniken's *Chariots of the Gods?* (trans-
lated by Michael Heron, 1968); the popularity of this work (and
its successors) had the unfortunate effect of making the alien-
explanation-of-history plot an sf cliché. Jacob finds it necessary
to append "A Glossary of Unfamiliar Names and Terms" to his
translation—something that further accentuates the over-
explanatory tenor of this novel. But for non-Jewish readers—like
myself—the glossary is very useful and adds a variety of dimen-
sions that would be overlooked without it.

In the third and last part of the novel, Jacob repeats Eliezar's
action of hiding the scrolls (together with his translation of them),
since geological disturbances (brought about no doubt by those
pesky Messengers—presumably this time the servants of the matriarchal power) are about to cause his death. At some point in
the far future, it is assumed, they will be rediscovered (perhaps
when a second time Eliezar's prediction that "The Messengers
will come no more" [183] will be disconfirmed).

One of the more artful aspects of the novel is the alternation
of sleeping and dreaming and then awakening. This alternation
of dark and light parallels that between fictional past and fictional
future/present, and that between male domination in the cosmic
war and then female. In the second part of the novel, Eliezar's
past present gives way to the still deeper past revealed by the
Messengers. And in the third part of the novel, the further future
discoverers and readers of the scrolls and their translation that
Jacob hides are actually in the past—the few readers of today
(with whom they form a loop) who have actually read *Messengers.*
The structural effect is of three zigzags or pendulum swings. Both

Eliezar and Jacob are vouchsafed "in dreams awake" style, *sktasis*, symbolic visions of Fiedler's alternating view of history. Eliezar experiences the water wheel (or perhaps washing machine?) of time and history via the pool outside the cave where he buries the scrolls:

> And now the pool no longer circled round and round within its own perimeter. But it heaved over and over, bottom becoming top and top bottom, in almost instantaneous reversal, as I revolved with the revolving waters like one lashed to a wheel. I had, and indeed still have, no way of telling how long I was whirled about, turning head over heels within the large cycling of the pool. (154)

Jacob receives the same message via the magical energy stone— "a Power-Source-Solid-State" (82), one of a number of such rare ancient alien artifacts—that he stole from Melissa-Melinda:

> My only clock is the Stone, which continues to grow dim, as it blinks off and on faster and faster; the rhythm of alternating light and dark synchronized now with its scarcely perceptible pulse. I have the sense that its pulse has meaning—even a specific meaning for *me*. But what is it saying, faithful still to its Makers, who coded into it aeons ago a message in search of a listener?

It is telling Jacob that, although the cosmic feminine power is currently on top, the turn of the cosmic masculine principle and patriarchal power on Earth will come once more.

And what of the novel itself? To my mind, *Messengers* is a clever but flawed sf novel that alternates patches of not-so-subtle satire[28] and patches of visionary intensity with much that is tiresome, awkward, and crude. Nevertheless, Alter, Winchell, and others to the contrary, it deserves to be more widely read.

In his 1981 Eaton Conference presentation, "The Criticism of Science Fiction," Fiedler refers to "the fact that I have recently become a writer of science fiction, proud that my most recent effort is to be included in Harlan Ellison's *Last Dangerous Visions*" (7). That "most recent effort" in fact dates back to 1972 or '73. In the 7 January 1974 issue of his fanzine *The Alien Critic*, Richard E. Geis prints a letter from Ellison with a projected Contents listing for *The Last Dangerous Visions* as of 13 September 1973; Fiedler's "What Used to be Called Dead" is among the sixty-eight titles.[29] Since the now-legendary *Last Dangerous Visions* has not yet (as of 1996) been published and may never be, I wrote to Fiedler about the possibility of seeing a photocopy of the manuscript (if

126   DAVID KETTERER

it had not already been published elsewhere). Fiedler replied (5 February 1997) that the "story . . . was published in the Kenyon Review . . . for the Winter of 1990."

"What Used to be Called Dead" begins as what appears to be symbolic realism (except perhaps for the italicized opening and two subsequent italicized, similarly choral, passages) and gradually comes to make sense only in sf terms.[30] The group-mind "voice" in the opening italicized section introduces "the Speaker" (104) who begins "the Ritual" (106), presumably of "resurrection," and refers to the death of an Old Man who first appears (in his symbolic reality?) as a beggar living in what turns out to be the symbolic cave of his heart. Literalized, this setting links the Old Man with both Jacob and Eliezar in *Messengers*. The longer sections of the story, which are in regular type, deal with the life of the Old Man (Fiedler himself as Rip Van Winkle, one wonders?) in terms of his going to sleep and then awakening at seemingly greater intervals. That life includes a wife and daughters, working in a shoe store, and the experience of taking refuge, with his fellow workers, from a destroyed, burning city in a concrete shelter.

When he awakes a final time, he finds himself lying naked on a pallet "in the heart of" of a strange city under "a translucent vault . . . (107)." An italicized comment notes, "*its* schlang *stood erect, swollen and purple*" (105), and later "*that its* schlang *had fallen . . .*" (106). The Old Man

felt like a chill at the core of his bones a sense of the aeons that must have passed between the time out of which he had fallen asleep and the time into which he awoke: an endless desert of time, more like the vacuum of space than the small crowded cycle of life he had grown up expecting to live. (107)

Apparently a vast time period has elapsed since his death, and now, somehow conscious, he is attended by three Doctors and surrounded by a multitude of men who are also impotent, naked, and hairless—the source of the group "voice." It is that voice that concludes: "He is *dead*. We remember now, he is what used to be called *dead*" (108). The naked men of this far future are presumably immortals.

This genuinely disturbing meditation on life and mortality (in which thanatos has seemingly irrevocably replaced eros) might owe something to the alien-controlled artificial resurrections of Farmer's *Riverworld* series (and something to Huxley's *Brave New World*) but the story makes most sense in the context of Fiedler's own work. It appears to be a coda to *Messengers*—and also a not-inappropriate coda to all of Fiedler's work. At one point the war between male and female has heated up to the extent that the Old Man's wife attempts to kill him with a knife. But in the alien future wheel of time and history has turned once more and the patriarchy seems finally dominant. But at what cost? Women, it seems, are no more. The domed remnant of male humanity endures what appears to be an eternal, sterile, living hell. Is this the final consequence of the homoerotic flight from women that Fiedler discovered in the classic works of American literature and so famously described in *Love and Death in the American Novel?* Are the all-male mutants of Fiedler's forlorn future what used to be called alive?

NOTES

1. Fiedler, "The New Mutants," *Partisan Review* 32 (Fall 1965): 505–25; reprinted in *The Collected Essays of Leslie Fiedler*, 2 vols. (New York: Stein and Day, 1971), 2:379–400 (the source of my in-text parenthetical page references). Haraway, "A Cyborg Manifesto: Science, Technology, and Socialist Feminism in the 1980s," *Socialist Review* 15 (1985): 65–108; reprinted as "A Cyborg Manifesto: Science, Technology, and Socialist-Feminism in the Late Twentieth Century" in *Simians, Cyborgs, and Women: The Reinvention of Nature* (New York: Routledge, 1991), 149–81.

2. Aldiss (with Brian Wingrove), *Trillion Year Spree: The History of Science Fiction* (London: Victor Gollancz, 1986), 163–65. As in the original version (1973's *Billion Year Spree*), Aldiss distinguishes "two sorts of vision, the Wellsian and the Burroughsian, or the analytic and the fantastic" (163); or "the thinking pole" and "the dreaming pole" (165).

3. Ketterer, *New Worlds for Old: The Apocalyptic Imagination, Science Fiction, and American Literature* (New York: Anchor Books, 1974; Bloomington: Indiana University Press, 1974). The second and third kinds of "philosophical apocalypse" provide reality transforming conceptual breakthroughs by positing the existence of an unsuspected outside manipulator, or by redefining (as, for example, postmodernism does) reality itself.

4. Fiedler, *Waiting for the End: The American Literary Scene from Hemingway to Baldwin* (New York: Stein & Day, 1964), 169.

5. For this quotation from a letter to Marudanayagam dated 18 August 1978, see Marudanayagam, *Quest for Myth: Leslie Fiedler's Critical Theory and Practice* (New Delhi: Reliance Publishing House, 1994), 101, 133 n.2.

6. *Waiting for the End*, 68.

7. Fiedler, *The Jew in the American Novel* (New York: Herzl Press, 1959); as reprinted in Fiedler's *Collected Essays*, the passage appears on pages 102–3.

8. *Collected Essays*, 2:102; *Waiting for the End*, 68; *Love and Death in the American Novel* (New York: Stein & Day, 1966), 463. Brian Aldiss, in an essay about the importance of Mary Shelley in *Billion Year Spree* (see note 2 above)—"Science Fiction's Mother Figure"—explains the partial indebtedness of his conception of sf to Fiedler. Quoting the last part of his later-to-be-slightly-revised definition

of sf in *Billion Year Spree*—"characteristically cast in the Gothic or post-Gothic mould"—Aldiss comments "I got it from Leslie Fiedler." He goes on to explain that it was Fiedler's description of the gothic mode in the 1960 *Love and Death in the American Novel* that made him realize that sf was a largely a gothic form. See Aldiss, *The Detached Retina: Aspects of SF and Fantasy* (Liverpool: Liverpool University Press, 1995), 72–73.

9. Fiedler, *Freaks: Myths and Images of the Sacred Self* (New York: Simon and Schuster, 1978), 320–47 (the source of my in-text parenthetical page references).

10. Marudanayagam, *Quest for Myth*, 80. Marudanayagam's central chapters 3 to 5 (out of six) are entitled "Eros and Thanatos" (devoted to *Love and Death in the American Novel* and *Waiting for the End*), "The Stranger Theme" (mainly about *The Return of the Vanishing American*, *The Stranger in Shakespeare*, and *Freaks*), and "In Defense of Pop Culture." Although mainly written in 1978 and 1979, *Quest for Myth* was not published until 1994; Mary Royden Winchell could not, then, have read Marudanayagam's earlier written book when he wrote his fourteen-chapter study *Leslie Fiedler* (Boston: Twayne Publishers, 1985), but Winchell focuses on the same three themes in his chapters 5 ("Eros and Thanatos" on Fiedler's masterpiece *Love and Death in the American Novel*); 6, 7, and the last half of 11 (which cover Fiedler's treatment of Indians ["The American Other"], Jews ["Next Year in Jerusalem"], and "The Shakespearean Other"); and 8, 9, and 10 (which deal with Fiedler's account of the opening of the literary canon to popular culture).

11. "Cross the Border—Close the Gap," *Playboy* 16 (December 1969): 151, 230, 252–54; reprinted in *The Collected Essays of Leslie Fiedler*, 2:461–485 (the source of my in-text parenthetical page references).

12. Fiedler, "The Divine Stupidity of Kurt Vonnegut: Portrait of the novelist as bridge over troubled water," *Esquire* 74 (September 1970): 195–97, 199–200, 202–4 (the source of my in-text parenthetical page references).

13. Fiedler, "Thanks for the Feast: Notes on Philip José Farmer," in *The Book of Philip José Farmer* (New York: Daw Books, 1973), 233–39 (the source of my in-text parenthetical page references).

14. In a letter to P. Marudanayagam dated 6 December 1978, Fiedler writes: "I . . . think of myself as a Literary Anthropologist." Quoted in *Quest for Myth*, 133 n.1.

15. *In Dreams Awake: A Historical-Critical Anthology of Science Fiction* (New York: Dell/Laurel, 1975), 11–23, 25–26, 119–20, 287–88 (the source of my in-text parenthetical page references).

16. Brian Aldiss, "The Immanent Will Returns—2," in Aldiss, *The Detached Retina: Aspects of SF and Fantasy* (Liverpool: Liverpool University Press, 1995), 40. Fiedler, Introduction to Olaf Stapledon, *Odd John* (London: Eyre Methuen, 1978), 7–13 (the source of my in-text parenthetical page reference).

17. In what is surely the definitive biography, Robert Crossley observes of Stapledon that "the old tale of the Sleeping Beauty, with the beloved's sleeping and waking used as figures for states of spiritual consciousness, underlies all his later [i.e., post-1921] utopian thinking." A "climactic discussion of the relation of moral theory to ecstasy" appears in Stapledon's *A Modern Theory of Ethics* (1929). See Crossley, *Olaf Stapledon: Speaking for the Future* (Syracuse, N.Y.: Syracuse University Press, 1994), 155. Fiedler comments on Stapledon's theory of "ecstasy" in his *Odd John* introduction (7) and in his extended study, *Olaf Stapledon: A Man Divided* (New York: Oxford University Press, 1983), 48–49. Subsequent in-text parenthetical page references are to this book.

18. Aldiss, "The Immanent Will Returns—2," 40. In his review of *Olaf Stapledon*, Aldiss notes that Fiedler's account of *Last and First Men* is based on the abridged American edition and objects to Fiedler's "pop psychology." See "In Orbit With the Star Maker," *Times Literary Supplement* 199, no. 4, (23 September 1983): 1007–8; revised as "The Immanent Will Returns" in Aldiss, *The Pale Shadow of Science* (Seattle: Serconia, 1985), 51–60. In his surely definitive biography, Robert Crossley draws attention to a number of faults in Fiedler's study (8, 408 n.1, 418 n.67, 432 n.33, 448 n.18).

19. Fiedler, "The Criticism of Science Fiction," in *Coordinates: Placing Science Fiction and Fantasy*, ed. George E. Slusser, Eric S. Rabkin, and Robert Scholes (Carbondale and Edwardsville: Southern Illnois University Press, 1983), 1–13 (the source of my in-text parenthetical page references).

20. Fiedler, "Fantasy as Commodity, Pornography," *Fantasy Review* (June 1984): 6–9, 42 (the source of my in-text parenthetical page references).

21. Fiedler's interest in sf, however, has clearly continued. His entry in *Who's Who in America, 1996* (New Providence, N.J.: Marquis, 1995) includes the "ghost" title *Stranger in a Strange Land* (a direct appropriation of the title of Heinlein's 1961 cult sf novel) for a collection of essays supposedly published in 1994. Fiedler writes (letter to Ketterer, March 3, 1997): "I think it is one of the provisional titles I gave at one point to the book which eventually became *Tyranny of the Normal* [*: Essays on Bioethics, Theology, and Myth* (1996)]." That provisional title (and the actual title for that matter) could imply that Fiedler considers himself an sf mutant, a "mental mutant" like the protagonist of Heinlein's novel and like the hippies. Certainly, what might be regarded as an estranging "science-fictional perspective" is important to Fiedler's work. He might be described as "an anthropologist on Mars" (the title of Oliver Sack's 1995 book).

22. *New York Times Book Review,* 29 September 1974, 5.

23. Fiedler, *What Was Literature? Class Society and Mass Culture* (New York: Simon and Schuster, 1982), 16–17; Winchell, *Leslie Fiedler,* 131.

24. Subsequent in-text parenthetical page references are to Fiedler, *The Messengers Will Come No More* (New York: Stein and Day, 1974).

25. Fiedler, *What Was Literature? Class Society and Mass Culture,* 17. His preceding comments about sf should also be noted: "the expectation of apocalypse . . has always possessed the American imagination. . . . I had long read futurist fantasy, but only since realizing its connections with our chiliast view of history have I explored it in depth . . ." (16).

26. "You are indeed right in believing that the Phil I refer to . . . is Philip José Farmer. . . ." Letter to Ketterer, 3 March 1997.

27. Letters to Ketterer, 5 February and 3 March 1997.

28. A representative example of such satire is the reference to "the great Book-Burning of 2069" that "began with the firing of the Library at [t]he Marilyn Monroe School of Women's Studies (formerly Yale University) by an Assistant Professor of Witchcraft. Refused tenure for her failure to 'publish,' she first kindled the flames, then flung herself into them from the rooftop solarium of the 125-story Parapsychology Building" (149).

29. *The Alien Critic* 7 (January 1974): 23 (complete Ellison letter: 22–24). Ellison's list is referred to and repeated in Christopher Priest's personal publication, *The Last Deadloss Visions* (1987), 3, 25.

30. Fiedler, "What Used to be Called Dead," *Kenyon Review* 12 (Winter 1990): 104–8 (the sources of my in-text parenthetical page references).

Myth, Archetype, and *Chopper Chicks in Zombietown:* What We've Learned from Leslie

Harold Schechter

In addition to my academic labors, I have managed to forge a fairly successful career as a writer of true-crime books about America's most infamous sociopaths. This is just one of the many aspects of my creative life I owe, in one way or another, to the influence of Leslie Fiedler, who—as a mentor to graduate students like me at SUNY–Buffalo back in the Golden Age of the early 1970s—inspired us to pursue our obsessions wherever they led. Given the nature of my own obsessions—violent death, pornographic horror, aberrant sex—following the Fiedlerian way has meant periodic, extended sojourns into the warped lives, sadistic dreams, and unspeakable deeds of assorted necrophiles, cannibals, and lust-killers.

To date, I've published three of these volumes: *Deviant, Deranged,* and *Depraved* (a trio of titles that sounds—so I've been told—like the name of a really sick Cole Porter tune). These deal respectively with: Ed Gein, the real-life model for *Psycho's* Norman Bates; Albert Fish, a grandfatherly gent whose deepest pleasure was torturing, dismembering, and feasting on the flesh of young children; and Dr. H. H. Holmes, America's first officially recorded serial murderer, who racked up a total of twenty-seven victims (at a conservative estimate) at the height of the Gilded Age.

I have also just published a handsome trade paperback called *The A to Z Encyclopedia of Serial Killers,* which I like to think of as the first truly *fun* coffee-table book about psychopathic sex-murder and which has recently landed me guest appearances on a number of America's trashiest TV talk shows, including *Montel* and *Jerry Springer.* Though I blush (with pride) to admit it, it has also earned me a citation in *Esquire* magazine's "Dubious Achievements Awards of 1996"—and I think I'm safe in saying that I'm the only member of the Queens College Department of English who can make such a claim.

I mention these accomplishments for several reasons besides the obvious one of shameless self-promotion. First, because it was, by and large, Leslie's example that emboldened me to break out of the increasingly constricted world of academic "discourse" and attempt to address the larger, "mass" audience. Second, because Leslie's work—especially his brilliant, scandalously undervalued book, *What Was Literature?*—taught me that, to be true to the essential nature of his or her chosen material, a pop culture critic ought to write—ought to *perform*—in a pop culture mode. And finally, because my career as a "commercial" author recently led to an experience that struck me as marvelously revealing of Leslie's impact on contemporary American culture.

This incident occurred about a month ago (I'm writing this in February 1997), when a book editor approached me about the possibility of writing a history of Troma Entertainment, Inc., the spunky, independent film company responsible for such cinematic classics as *Zombie Island Massacre, Surf Nazis Must Die,* and *A Nymphoid Barbarian in Dinosaur Hell*—unspeakably cheesy, sex-and-violence schlock movies whose sheer, exuberant tackiness has won them a fervent cult following. Naturally, I was keenly interested. Shortly thereafter, I was summoned to an interview with Troma's founder, creative mastermind, and visionary auteur, Lloyd Kaufman. This meeting took place at the company's New York City headquarters, the grandly named "Troma Building," which—perhaps not surprisingly—turned out to be a hole-in-the-wall rat-trap wedged between a greasy-spoon diner and a rather garish emporium called Sex World.

Naturally, Lloyd Kaufman wasn't about to bestow such a plum assignment on just *anyone,* so I proceeded to establish my qualifications by impressing him with both my knowledge of and admiration for such Troma masterworks as *The Good, the Bad, and the Subhumanoid, Chopper Chicks in Zombietown,* and *Sgt. Kabukiman, N.Y.P.D.* (an edge-of-the-seat thriller about a New York City cop who is possessed by the spirit of a Japanese kabuki actor and who defeats his enemies by impaling them on chopsticks and using oversized sheets of seaweed to turn them into human sushi). None of this fawning, however, appeared to make the slightest impression on Lloyd, who maintained a polite but distinctly noncommittal mien throughout our interview.

Finally, he asked (in effect) what a nice literature prof. like me was doing in a place like Troma. I gave him a brief run-down of

the formative life-experiences that had shaped my lurid sensibility: my baby-boomer boyhood, steeped in the delights of E. C.
horror comics, *Famous Monsters of Filmland* magazine, and movies
like *The Blob* and *I Was a Teenage Werewolf;* my subsequent countercultural fascination with the horror-porn fantasies of S. Clay Wilson and other "underground" cartoonists; my years at
SUNY–Buffalo, where I was encouraged to explore my most dis-
reputable interests by my Ph.D. advisor, Leslie Fiedler—

"Leslie Fiedler?" Lloyd interrupted. "You studied with Leslie
Fiedler?" In an instant, his expression had shifted from utter
indifference to serious respect. "That's really something."

That the filmmaker responsible for giving the world movies like
Bloodsucking Freaks, Blondes Have More Guns, and *Femme Fontaine:
Killer Babe for the CIA.* was an ardent Fiedler-fan should have come
as no surprise to me, since Leslie is, after all, the original champion of American trash cinema—the first critic to recognize the
outlandish genius of pioneering sleazemeister Russ Meyer. (Typically, it's taken the rest of the world several decades to catch up
with Leslie. In the fall of 1995—thirty-plus years after Leslie's
groundbreaking celebration of *The Immoral Mr. Teas*—Meyer's
work was being honored with showings at Manhattan's prestigious
Film Forum theater and touted in such tony publications as the
New Yorker).

Moreover, I had encountered this phenomenon before. A couple of years ago, I became friends with a brilliantly eccentric artist
named Joe Coleman, whose work is rapidly gaining the international attention it so richly deserves (Coleman's life and art are
the subject of a feature-length documentary, *Rest in Pieces,* which
has just had its world premiere at the Rotterdam Film Festival,
where it is reportedly making quite a splash). Largely because of
his "naif" style and disquieting subject matter (which tends to
dwell on disfiguring disease, grotesque bodily deformity, and an
astonishing range of deviant behavior), Coleman is generally classified under the currently trendy label of "Outsider Artist."
(Imagine some unholy blend of American folk art, medieval altar
painting, and the infernal fantasies of Hieronymus Bosch and
you'll get a sense of Coleman's work.) Not so incidentally, Coleman
is also the only major American painter—so far as I know—to
perform as an actual *geek,* having once been sued by TV game-
show host and animal rights activist Bob Barker after biting off
and swallowing the head of a live rat during a public exhibition.

Anyway, shortly after meeting Joe, I happened to mention—in
the course of a conversation about sideshow freaks—that Fiedler

had been my dissertation director at SUNY–Buffalo. Joe's response was identical to Lloyd Kaufman's—i.e., he regarded me with new-found respect. He also insisted that I immediately provide him with Leslie's home address, so that he could send Leslie—whose bestseller *Freaks* was one of Joe's favorite books—a letter of admiration.

In short, on these and several similar occasions, I have encountered striking proof of Leslie's enduring, inspiring influence on those artists, writers, and thinkers who—like Lloyd and Joe—are all (in the sense that Fiedler himself has always been) "outsiders": creators who look to the taboo, the transgressive, the freakish, and forbidden for those vital (even redemptive) energies that are the swellspring of art. At the present moment, such creators are under relentless assault not only by the usual forces of bluenose repression but—perhaps even more insidiously—by the bland corporate homogenization of our popular culture, represented most depressingly for many of us by the wholesale Disneyfication of New York City's Times Square (where such gloriously seedy shrines as Hubert's Museum and Flea Circus and the Melody Burlesk have been supplanted by an indistinguishable array of shiny, "family-oriented" theme-stores, restaurants, and theaters).

At least as significant as Leslie's direct, acknowledged impact on a new generation of artists and thinkers is the pervasive way his insights have been assimilated into our popular culture—the way (as Buffalo newspaper critic Jeff Simon has put it) "his ideas and concerns have become common currency among people who haven't the foggiest notion where they came from." The most obvious example of this can be found in Hollywood, where every second action movie is a pumped-up version of Leslie's myth of interracial male bonding—Huck and Jim on steroids and armed with semiautomatic weapons. And Leslie's radically original insights into the essentially religious function of pop entertainment have become so endemic to our cultural discourse that the Internet is crammed with Websites where fans can hold forth on the "X-Files mythos," "Trekkie religion," and the "Elvis cult."

To those of us who recognize the source of these ideas, it's frustrating to see them go largely uncredited. Still, I can't help thinking that Leslie himself must take some wry satisfaction from the situation, since it exactly parallels that of those pop artists like Bram Stoker and Edgar Rice Burroughs whose work he so loves: originators of some of our culture's most enduring myths, whose creations are familiar to everyone, even while the authors themselves remain mostly unknown.

I have to confess that there are other frustrations involved in being—as I consider myself—a disciple of Fiedler: mainly, the uncanny way in which he seems to have anticipated every significant development in the realm of pop culture studies, leaving his followers very little to say that's especially new. I've experienced this directly on a number of occasions, when—having been struck with what I consider a staggeringly original insight and struggled to find the perfect way to phrase it—I happen to pick up some twenty-year-old essay by Leslie and discover that he not only said it first but said it better. The extent to which he's been ahead of the curve has never ceased to amaze me. In February 1995, for example, *The New York Times* ran an essay called "Rhett and Scarlett: Rough Sex or Rape?" The gist of the piece was that certain "feminist philosophies," having focused their attention on *Gone With the Wind*, had noticed—much to their outrage—that the book was built around rape fantasies. No less than nine years earlier, however—in the spring of 1986—Leslie and I appeared together on a popular culture panel as part of a "C. G. Jung and the Humanities" conference held at Hofstra University. In the course of his remarks, Leslie—who spoke at length about *Gone With the Wind*—declared (I'm quoting from the transcript, published in book form by Princeton University Press): "Clearly, the basic myth and controlling metaphor, the very leitmotif of Margaret Mitchell's book, is rape."

And here's one final example. At this very moment, I am looking at a handsome brochure I just received in the mail announcing a major conference on *Dracula*, scheduled for March 1997, and featuring such luminaries as Joyce Carol Oates, Stephen Jay Gould, and the undisputed king of the Grade-Z movie, Roger Corman. I can't help recalling, as I marvel at the extent to which Stoker's creation has become such a hot academic subject, that Leslie was already mulling over the archetypal meaning of the vampire king at least twenty years ago—back in the halcyon days of the early 1970s, when I would drop by his office for periodic chats about things like necrophagy, devouring mothers, the *vagina dentata* myth, and the films of Todd Browning and Bruce Lee.

I see that I have spent almost as much time talking about myself in this tribute as about Leslie. But this strikes me as apt, since speaking in the first person is a particularly Emersonian notion, and I've always considered Leslie the most Emersonian of our critics. In *What Was Literature?* Fiedler writes that "it is a major mystery of my career that I have come to be regarded as a 'seminal' . . . critic even though almost every one of my books has been more scorned than praised in academic and literary reviews." The solution to that mystery, I believe, can be located in Emerson's "The American Scholar," which portrays an intellectual ideal that Leslie has come closer to fulfilling than any other contemporary critic I know:

"If a single man plant himself indomitably on his instincts, and there abide, the huge world will come round to him."

Prometheus at 14

Irving Feldman

Three kids shove one another across
the lawn toward the pool, hotfoot the cool
sharp turf, feeling, dropped among elders,
unfamiliar and small. Embarrassment flies
before and points behind, accusing
and knocking their naive manhood.
Constricted and pale, their bodies tremble,
"What am I showing? What do you see?"

But three geysers smack up suddenly.
They—their escape made good, their cheap
stupendous laughter, their heroic gabble
—honk in triumph at the plundered shore
from safety where perilously they tread,
"A god's nuts! Fire!—that's what you saw, my friend!"

Poolside, chez *Fiedler*
Buffalo, New York
July 4, 1967

Part III

The Accidental Mentor

John Barth

In 1956, a certain American first novel was blessed by a prevailingly favorable review from a certain noted American critic, who characterized it as a specimen of "provincial American existentialism" that committed its author to nothing and left him free to do whatever next thing he might choose. At the time, fresh out of graduate school, this interested reader of that review had no very expert notion of what existentialism was. Intrigued by that critic's remark, like a good provincial American Johns Hopkins alumnus, I set about re-reading Sartre and Camus (Heidegger was beyond me) and soon decided that both parts of the proposition applied: The book *was* provincial, American, and existentialist, and its author was free to sing whatever next tunes his muse might call. Which I did. Forty years later, I'm gratified to report, that novel, that novelist, and that noted critic are still all actively with us, and Leslie Fiedler's instructive characterization of my *Floating Opera* still strikes me as altogether valid.

Not long after writing that review, the author of *Love and Death in the American Novel* and other notorious iconoclasms made a lecture-visit to Penn State, where I was then employed, and there began an acquaintanceship that over the years ripened into friendship and colleaguehood; that affected in large and small ways my professional trajectory; and that I remain the ongoing beneficiary of. I have counted those ways elsewhere and will gratefully here recount just a few of them:

In the mid-1960s, Fiedler recruited me to join Albert Cook's bustling new English department at SUNY–Buffalo, whereto he himself had lately shifted after his long tenure in Montana. More than any other single factor, it was Leslie's presence there that tipped my scales Buffaloward, and for the seven years following we were near-neighbors. In retrospect, the lively intellectual/artistic/political atmosphere of that place in that turbulent time seems to me as much centered at the *Fiedlerhaus* as at the rambunctious university campus and the pop-artful Albright-Knox Museum, both nearby. A Buffalo book-reviewer recently opined, in the course of noticing a new book of mine, that its author had done "his most lasting work at Penn State, his most interesting work at Buffalo, and his most fatuous work since returning to Johns Hopkins." While I don't necessarily agree with any of those three propositions and would heatedly contest the last of them, I know what the chap means by that second one. It is the High-Sixties Buffalo Zeitgeist that I associate with the story-series *Lost in the Funhouse,* the novella-triad *Chimera,* and the intricated ground-plan of the novel *LETTERS;* and it is Leslie Fiedler, more than any other single figure, who for me embodies that so-spirited place and time.

From whom if not him did I learn, back then, that the USA had changed "from a whiskey culture into a drug culture"—just when I was learning to appreciate good wine? Who first alarmed me with the prophecy that "if narrative has any future at all, it's up there on the big screen, not down here on the page"? (This was before videocassettes and the Internet, when folks still "went to the movies.") In those pioneer days of Black Studies and Women's Studies, who puckishly (and illuminatingly, as always) offered counter-courses in White Studies and Male Studies? Whose prevailingly apocalyptic prognosis for literature *(What Was Literature?)* would one take only half seriously, had one not seen heresy after heresy of Fiedler's turn into prescience? The list goes on: He is a mentor from whom this incidental, often skeptical, sometimes reluctant mentee has never failed to learn, most frequently in that period of our closest association.

Toward the end whereof—while I was visiting-professoring in Boston and deciding to return to Baltimore (if not to blissful literary fatuity)—the fellow did me another significant service, a sort of bookend to his having recruited me to Buffalo in the first place. One would prefer to imagine that whatever official recognition one's writings earn, they earn purely on their literary merits. The world, however, is what it is, and so it did not escape my notice that the five National Book Award jurors in fiction for 1972 included two (Leslie Fiedler and William H. Gass) who had not only spoken favorably of my fiction but had become personal friends of mine as well; one (Jonathan Yardley of the *Washington Post*) who had consistently trashed me; and two with whose literary-critical opinions I was unacquainted (the novelists Evan Connell and Walker Percy). I readily and thankfully assumed that it was owing to Fiedler and/or Gass that my *Chimera*-book was among that year's nominees; with equal readiness I assumed that that would be that: victory enough to have been a finalist, as had been my bridesmaid fortune twice before. Leslie even telephoned me in Boston from New York to assure me that I hadn't a prayer, inasmuch as "the other three" judges had favorite candidates of their own. Not long after, news came that *Chimera* had won the thing after all (more precisely, a divided jury divided the prize).

How so?

"You had two for you and two against you," Leslie cheerfully confided to me later, "and I drank the swing-vote under the table."

Owe you one, pal. Owe, you, rather, yet another.

Celebrating Leslie Fiedler

James M. Cox

I cannot think of Leslie Fiedler without remembering when I encountered him at the Indiana School of Letters in 1952. Having graduated from the University of Michigan in 1950 and stayed on for an M.A. in English, I had, at the urging of Austin Warren, applied for admission for the 1950 summer term to the Kenyon School of English. But I had also sent out fifteen letters to small colleges offering my services as a teacher if any of them would have me. Emory and Henry College offered me a position beginning not in the fall but in the summer session at almost the same time the School of English accepted my application. So there I was, a very green student, facing a conflict I didn't know how to resolve, yet inclined to submit to the terms of the Emory and Henry offer. When I went to Austin Warren to tell him of my dilemma, he suggested that I write to Emory and Henry requesting permission to delay my appearance there until September in order to advance my education by attending Kenyon. I can't forget his confident assurance that, if Emory and Henry were a sound institution, it wouldn't hesitate to comply with my request. It was sound and it did. So I went to Kenyon and took classes from Kenneth Burke and Philip Blair Rice. Burke was a metacritic long before that term came into vogue, and, though I really didn't understand more than a third of the operation of his rhetorical machine—his pentad of terms, his scene-act and act-agent ratios—I learned from him more than I knew. Looking like Groucho Marx taking flight through metaphysics, he was a great teacher. His example proved to me then and forever after that a student doesn't have to understand a teacher in order to learn.

After the summer at Kenyon I went on to Emory and Henry, where I taught a five-course load (in addition to coaching the debate team and advising the student paper) at a salary of $2500, only to get fired at the end of the academic year because of the college's projection of shrinking enrollments in face of the Korean War. Yet when September came, enrollments held up enough for the college to want me to return for another year at the same salary. I was glad enough to be asked back. I learned in my two years at Emory and Henry that I wanted to be a college teacher, but, as I looked over the prospect of teaching another year at the same salary, I decided that I had better seek the Ph.D. But where? I really didn't know, though I looked at Virginia, North Carolina, and Duke. Knowing that John Ransom had moved the School of English from Kenyon to Indiana University in Bloomington and renamed it the School of Letters, I determined to go there in the summer of 1952.

It was there that I signed up for two courses, "Myth in American Fiction and Verse," taught by Leslie Fiedler, and "Auden and Frost" taught by Randal Jarrell. Looking back across the all but forty years separating me from the moment I entered those classes, I am still astonished at the freshness of impressions of both Jarrell and Fiedler. Jarrell was manic in class, displaying astonishing insight and at the same time delighted with his perceptions. He liked to read the poems of his chosen poets, exulting all the while in providing a running commentary, congratulating himself on having finally understood this or that poet, and gloating over the many critical misreadings that were finding their way into print. In that age of Eliot, he took malicious pleasure in challenging the low esteem in which most of his class held Frost. He also loved to shock the class with extravagant claims, contending that Rilke was without question the preeminent modern poet, and wondering what would become of us if we didn't realize that Beatrix Potter was probably the greatest writer of the twentieth century.

It was Fiedler's class, however, that was for me a turning point. When I think of how ignorant I was, and especially when I think of how ignorant I still am after all these forty years, I look back upon that class as a beacon—a Drummond light—illuminating the landscape in all directions. The classes of the School of Letters met in the English building, a former U.S. Navy sick bay that had been moved to the Indiana campus at the end of World War II. It had no air conditioning, and was situated in a vale where no air could circulate. As anyone knows who has ever been in southern Indiana in the summer, the weather can be as sweltering as it can be in the lowlands of Alabama. It was particularly so in the summer of 1952. Since the School of Letters ran only six weeks, as opposed to the regular eight-week summer session, its class periods were longer, meeting for two full hours three times a week. These, then, were the conditions—as hard and hot and humid as

I had then known or have known since. Day after day, it seemed to me the temperature hovered between ninety and ninety-five outside, and surely over a hundred inside, with the humidity always over eighty.

Into these conditions came Leslie Fiedler. Coming from the University of Montana, where he was then teaching, he had already begun to make his name with his publication of "Come Back to the Raft Ag'in, Huck Honey!" and "Montana; or the End of Jean-Jacques Rousseau" in *Partisan Review*. I had read the second essay, having subscribed to *Partisan* in 1949, but I did not read the first until years later. Short in stature but barrel chested, Fiedler faced the class with a compact force. Once he started to speak, his whole presence radiated intensity and energy, all concentrated in his voice. He had notes, written in such a minuscule hand that he could contain a two hour lecture in remarkably few pages. Though his notes were in front of him, he did not seem to read from them, but I felt that they were actually manuscript rather than mere headings. His voice had a fierce urgency, often rising in intensity to the threshold of something between a cry of agony and a painful laugh, before descending on a line of measured and periodic finality.

Even to try to describe his "delivery" may make it seem that he was histrionic. He never seemed so to me. Intense, yes; even a performer, yes; but his lectures were never staged or stagey. They were urgent, gripping in their concentration, and explosive in their insights. Their substance for me always outweighed their rhetoric. Both their form and content were the spine of *Love and Death in the American Novel*, published eight years later. Anyone hearing those lectures would have had to wonder why Fiedler waited so long to publish the book, yet that length of time is surely but a measure of the care and responsibility—the long preparation—that went into the book. felt the same kind of preparation had gone into the lectures, felt indeed that I was a privileged auditor of a wonderful book that absolutely had to be published. When the actual book appeared, I felt that I did not really need to read it, and I never did read it consecutively at the time it appeared, though I consulted it over the years, but even in these engagements its text was always entangled with my memory of the remarkable lectures I had heard in 1952.

And they were remarkable. Fiedler brought all his learning and passion to bear on his subject, a subject that was at once large and vital. He intended nothing less than to relate the American novel to the core of myths that ran like an underground water course beneath their surface texts. Books that loomed large in his context were Robert Graves's *The White Goddess,* Denis de Rougemont's *Love in the Western World,* and, of course, D. H. Lawrence's *Studies in Classic American Literature.* Yet for all his larger range of reference, Fiedler pursued the contextual substratum of myths toward American literature rather than referring it back to them. It was as if all the myths were but tending toward America. For me the course did what Emerson said college should do—"set the hearts of their youth on flame." I have taken many courses and have heard hundreds of lectures, yet no course and no lecturer has ever inspired me as Fiedler did. The heat of that summer, the discomfort of the classroom, and the inevitable distractions of student life were forgotten in the face of the illumination I felt at every moment of the class. I could have listened to Fiedler for three hours without a break.

I have deliberately refrained from rehearsing Fiedler's ideas in this memory of his influence precisely because influence is so much more than mere "ideas" or "methodology" or "scholarship," just as literature is so much more than mere text—so much more than, as William Spengemann would have it, "words on a page." Like teaching itself, literature is a *presence* having to do with passion, charged emotion, narrative intensity, poetic rhythm and images, all of which engage us at a proverbial depth where both freedom and tyranny are at primordial play. That play is nothing less than *inspiration,* a freedom to touch, release, and experience in forms of pleasure the pain and agony through which we enter this world. The creative *feeling* at the heart of inspiration is surely a recovering of the pleasure of conception lying behind the pangs of birth that attended our emergence in material form. How right Emerson was in saying that the function of teaching was to set not the mind but the heart on flame.

In just that sense, Fiedler's lectures were for me inspiring. In the presence of those lectures I felt that I too could be an interpreter, that I too would be able to speak and write, and that American literature (I had had but one course on the subject in all my years in college) would be the subject of my being and endeavour. The feeling had much less to do with following Fiedler than with coming into touch with what seemed my deepest self. In my final paper for the course I wrote on *Adventures of Huckleberry Finn,* and I shall never forget the first sentence of Fiedler's comment: "I feel almost ashamed to give this paper a grade." He went on to praise the paper and made suggestions for strengthening it. It wasn't the praise that mattered so much as his confirmation of my own feeling, in writing the paper, that I was no longer fulfilling requirements but was reaching the ground of independent perception.

All that was forty years ago. In those years I taught, wrote, and, in 1990, officially retired. I had actually taken early retirement in 1985 and moved back to the Virginia farm I was raised on and the house I was born in. One of the things that being on the farm does is to provide a different perspective. Old colleagues foolishly congratulate me for having both place and time to write. How little they know. *The farm is against writing.* It draws me out of my study into it to patch fences, grub bushes, clear briars, and cut up fallen trees for firewood. It asks most of all for illiteracy, and I more and more yield to its demands. In such submission, I am all but frozen—particularly in these winter months—with one foot forward onto the firm footing of the land, the other just lifted to follow yet lingering within the border of the life I can't quite leave, the life of literature and literary criticism.

Recent critical movements—I shan't say contemporary criticism because I no longer know what the latest criticism may be—are at the threshold of losing their gravitational force. Even their attraction no doubt possessed a strong enough element of repulsion to drive me toward the farm. Merely to mention them is to implicate the whole sequence of criticisms I have lived through. How quickly they have spent themselves in succeeding the New Criticism in which I began. Affectivism, phenomenology, reader response, structuralism, post-structuralism, deconstruction, and the new historicism all formed the accelerating current that carried me to early retirement. It took younger colleagues not merely familiar with but actually living through—which, heaven help me, is not merely enduring but being given life by—the newer criticism to bring me to my present shore. They embodied the force of structuralism and deconstruction and so were a living presence of its existence to the extent that I didn't have to read it all. Then I understood that I couldn't read it all and finally realized that I could hardly read it at all. There comes a time when one's outsetting determination to "keep up" with current scholarship and criticism proves to be an illusion or, worse, becomes a delusion. Hawthorne put it well when he observed in a notebook entry that he no longer sought the newer fashions in clothes but was content with the old fashions that had become comfortable. He had, of course, taken retirement upon graduating from Bowdoin, and so had time to be an excellent observer. It took me much longer, but I have had time to reach his conclusion.

Yet for all my retirement, I am sometimes called back, and when, two years ago, Leo Lemay asked me to speak on his MLA program devoted to criticism since World War II and suggested that I choose a single book of criticism to emphasize if that suited me, I resolved to address myself to *Love and Death in the American Novel*. And so I returned to it after long absence. Here were, and are, my conclusions. First of all, it is a truly learned book. When I think of the immense reading that went into it, I am sorely humbled. There was a moment when I must have thought that I might, given time, read so much, but when I took the book up once more I was as astonished as ever at the sheer number of books that Fiedler incorporates into his narrative. And they are incorporated, which is to say that they are fully brought to bear in and upon the argument. I know that there are mistakes in some of Fiedler's accounts of these resources. I once lent the book to a colleague who took pleasure in pointing to the discrepancies in Fiedler's treatment of *Clarissa*. Yet in light of the enormous inclusiveness of the book, these mistakes actually seem to me a happy rather than an annoying presence. Far from being the result of mere carelessness, they are a testimony of the author's genuine life—his impulse from time to time to take over an author. When I see, at my late age, how Fiedler again and again hits the mark in his treatment of work that I do know, I would feel like a pedant to gloat over his infrequent misrememberings. The finest thing about Fiedler's learning is precisely its lack of pedantry. I do not mean that Fiedler is modest. On the contrary, his ego is very much in evidence at almost every turn. If his learning is very much in the service of his argument, he remains a sufficient presence in his text to be argumentative. He doesn't gloat over the failures of his competitors or try to put them down, but he nonetheless establishes a perspective that exposes their limitations. Then too he has a bad boy in him, and he doesn't want to be a good bad boy, nor would I wish my praise to cast him in that role. When he refers to the work of Diderot and Richardson as constituting a breakthrough of the submerged nightmare into the light of the Enlightenment, his term for their achievement is also a naming of his own ambition to break through and out of the placidity of the academy.

Breaking through brings me to the second point of Fiedler's strength—his freedom with his material. He follows, as much as he can, the spirit of D. H. Lawrence, whose slender book on classic American literature is for me the best thing ever done in the "field." Even to hear that word "field" is to be reminded of the stifling connotations that the academy has put on it, as if it were an enclosed and deadened space fending off the wild life that might creep into it. Why is it, we must surely ask ourselves, that the very form of the official periodicals of our world—*PMLA* and *American Literature*—carries with them on their covers a blight sufficient to kill whatever life that may have gone into them. At least I, who have been at one time on the board of editors of both these periodicals and have read good essays that were accepted, have asked myself that question. Glossing *PMLA's* cover with pictures, as the editors have recently decided to do, is of no avail. The sterility conditions everything that touches it. If these magazines represent the profession, one can begin to understand why R. P. Blackmur insisted that he was an amateur. One of the most remarkable things about Leslie Fiedler is that he has stayed in the profession without ever becoming merely professional. He has served as chairman of his department without suffering seeming loss of life. If his writing lacks the quick elegance of Blackmur's, it nonetheless retains a sense of wonder and surprise that drives him in his book toward the exclamation point, as if he were both pleased and surprised at his own insights. Half his interest in the old authors is to bring them in abrupt relation to contemporary authors. His readiness for these relationships is a mark of how much the archetypes with which he deals are for him living myths. Yet—and here is a great part of his strength—the archetypes never dominate his wonder at the writers themselves. He not only knows the story of their stories; he knows the story of their lives and delights in reminding his readers of their weaknesses and struggles. Their lives are for him an inescapable part of the drama of their form; that is precisely why they retain life for him. Through all his argument Fiedler never loses his feeling for the experience of reading his authors. Again and again his observations tally with our sense of what it is to read the work he is discussing. He knows, for example, exactly where Cooper is insufferable and can bring his criticism fully into play as a means of discovering Cooper's ultimate vitality. This constant awareness frees him from assuming the depressing academic posture of defending his writers.

Fiedler is different from American literature specialists and Cooper scholars because his visionary relation to Cooper and all his other writers puts them in a configuration that relates them yet never reduces their individual achievement. Thus he can see just how Dreiser revives the sentimental novel of seduction that had been all but moribund in this country; he sees that Lardner is able, for almost the first time in American literature, to realize the possibilities of the epistolary novel; he sees how the gothic impulse came to dominate the novel of sentiment in the career of Charles Brockden Brown and how that impulse—running through Hawthorne, Poe, Melville, Twain, and Faulkner—kept the Richardsonian novel of sentiment in a secondary position. He can do all this without ever letting his book descend into *The Gothic Novel in American Literature*. Finally, of all the truly influential books on *American literature*—I am thinking of Matthiessen's *American Renaissance*, Perry Miller's *The New England Mind*, and Henry Smith's *Virgin Land*—only *Love and Death* establishes a vital relation between American and continental literature. Fiedler has thus seen America as itself a continent and not a colony and so has fully escaped the iron grip that Harvard and New England have exerted on American literature.

If these were my essential conclusions on *Love and Death* two years ago, I determined to read more Fiedler in preparation for my celebration of his work. I felt no compulsion to read all his work; haven't read it all and probably won't, but I did read *The Return of the Vanishing American, What Was Literature?*, and his latest book, *Fiedler on the Roof*. Having returned to the first two of those books, having read in the past most of Fiedler's previous work, and now having seen his latest work, I believe that I can begin to estimate his achievement.

He has established, in a way no other critic has, the full relation between American and European literature. His knowledge of both literatures makes a reader—or this one at least—feel with almost every sentence that he has literally read his way across the Atlantic in an arduous voyage to reach these shores. The result is a mental bridge between the two continents allowing Fiedler to negotiate instant connections in either direction yet remain always here in America, an unmistakably *American* critic. He is here because he has spent his imaginative life struggling to reach America. If he knows he is at once a Jewish and academic American, he nonetheless has striven with all his might to free himself from the confinements of that identity. If the academy has been his profession, the Jewishness is not merely in but is his blood. Yet he still wants to live imaginatively in America. Thus he has sought to break the barriers that the academic community has erected to separate "true" literature from popular literature, or, to put it another way, the imagination from the marketplace. And, much as he has recognized, and even taken pride in, the achievements of the "Jewish novel," he has been disappointed in the movement that Saul Bellow and others have taken toward either (or both) conservative ideology or form.

The drama of Fiedler's life, as he presents himself in his books and essays (and he irrepressibly presents himself!), is one of sloughing off the old skin of past enthusiasms and ambitions, of breaking out and down, not toward liberal politics but toward the raw energy, the myths, the chaos that unsettle the distinctions of class and identity that the settlement helplessly erects. The rhetoric accompanying this vision of breaking away tends always to exaggerate the distance Fiedler has come since *Love and Death*. It would have us believe that the old identity was deluded in its ambitious effort to get into the academy and the New Criticism, whereas, it seems to me, the spirit of that book was already and always breaking away, that Fiedler's end was very much in his beginning, just as, in his vision of Joyce's *Ulysses*, Bloom the comic Jew was always there against the artist Stephen Dedalus, who would invariably attract the learned commentary of the academy in the project of creating the myth of the artist. Leslie Fiedler has always been there, able to see, surely from the beginning, that Joyce's achievement is also to have created (or recovered or released) the myth of the Jew.

If it took the exiled Irishman to imagine in resolutely modern form the mythic Jew, Fiedler has tried all his life to reach and realize the mythic American who is somehow exiled from civilization on a frontier where the ancient myths refigure themselves, or are refigured, along American lines of force.

That refiguration takes its shape on the primal lines of race, which dominate even the ancient battle of gender. Fiedler knows, in the depth of his Jewish identity, the meaning of race and blood identity, yet he also knows that in America it has been Indians and blacks who have displaced the Jew as the primordial other, and that the feminine forces have—or may have—been subsumed under the "cover" of race. That it is Pocahontas who figures as the Indian maiden who saves Captain Smith, and it is Harriet Beecher Stowe who projects herself into the slave Uncle Tom, the ultimate mother figure who carries little Eva about the plantation. The male counterpart of this dream of gender reconciliation between the white and dark races is to be found in Cooper's Natty and Chingachgook (who Mark Twain suggested was pronounced "Chicago"—he thought!) as they meet in transcendent friendship over the grave of the slain Uncas, the last of the Mohicans; or it is to be found again in the drifting river journey of Huck and Jim on the raft. The power of these dreams to move us is but a signal of the nightmare force of fear that is wedded to the dream—the sense of some irreconcilable fright at the heart of the European mind as it confronted the continent.

There was on the one hand the white man's genocidal assault upon the Indian, accompanied by the importation of black slaves from Africa to a continent that was later to be textualized in chaste Enlightenment rhetoric as a new nation conceived in liberty. The violence of its hundred years of Indian wars and its convulsive effort to free itself from slavery has left it more and more the master of freedom in a "free" country—a country freed of Indians and slaves yet estranged from a landscape haunted by the ghosts of Indians and consternated by a society at once racially maddened and paralytically guilty in the face of blacks.

Fiedler has seen, almost from the beginning of his career— from, let us say, his superb article on Huck and Jim in 1948— how this charged racial and sexual field is the mythic ground of the American identity, and he has never doubted it. While it may be possible to doubt some of his particular emphases or interpretations, his recognition of this central field seems to me utterly sound—a true measure of his critical imagination and judgment. It makes him a central critic of American literature and culture, just as it has freed him to move from "high" literature to popular literature on into movies and television—for his mythic ground extends right through the whole spectrum of our imaginative and fictive experience.

This freedom of movement is for me the very soul of Fiedler's criticism. It is first of all a democratic freedom, making the whole range of literature equally accessible to the force of his critical intelligence without the usual influx of condescension or self-gratulatory liberal sentiment. Of all false charges that might be levelled against him, the worst, I think, would be that as his field of literature expands his standards were weakened. Anyone who reads his work knows that aesthetic judgment is never asleep but always operating all along the lines of his sentences in such a way as to be part of the very tension of his prose. It is never some abstract formula or inert value to be applied to a book. If he knows the evasive moves that all writers, whether "great" or popular, can and do make, he also knows that the kind of exclusive standards deployed to separate high from popular literature act to protect rather than to penetrate ignorance. Thus he is able to give genuine critical attention to *Uncle Tom's Cabin, Gone With the Wind,* and Thomas Dixon's *The Clansman* (as well as *The Birth of a Nation*) without crumpling into a mere thematic or weak sociological survey. He knows that the kind of power all these books have had poses a real problem for anyone claiming to be a literary or cultural critic, just as he knows that his lifelong preoccupation with the racial myth so central to both American classic and popular literature provides a far different perspective from that of a social or a literary historian.

Not only has Fiedler succeeded in making literature a more inclusive term, thereby putting egalitarian pressure on the inevitable aesthetic hierarchies that flourish under systems of classification and exclusion; he has in the process achieved a moral freedom as well as a freedom from morality—the stifling morality that pervades so much that passes for criticism in the academy as well as in book reviews. Fiedler is wonderfully *uninhibited* in his response to literature because he is in touch with a power of image and narrative that is indeed beneath the ideational content of narration and representation—a power that has to do with primordial desire. That is why Fiedler can truly look at *The Clansman* and wonder at the power in it that Griffith could see and translate into *The Birth of a Nation*. It is also why Fiedler was able to move into issues of race and gender long before black and feminist literature became "fields" sustained by political constituencies.

The fate of adherents to such constituencies is that their work imagines itself as revolutionary yet relies on a whole substratum of attitudes that are not only conventional but are conventionally approved. (It is the approval that, after all, sustains the field in the first place.) This delusion results in a sentimentality far more depressing than the sentimentality of sentimental novels. It has been labelled "political correctness" by those long in power, who, equally deluded, suddenly convert themselves into an imaginary minority and produce a reactionary criticism equally depressing. The end result of this "discourse"—to adopt the term now in vogue—is true depression. Fiedler's work has never been depressing. It is refreshing—as refreshing reading it now in my retirement as it was when I first encountered it forty years ago. It is true American criticism by a true American.

Leslie Fiedler: a Tribute

R. W. B. LEWIS

When I first came to know Leslie Fiedler in Princeton in the 1950s, he was a young professor from the University of Montana. But he was away so often from his home base, as a visiting academic in the American East or in Europe, that he became referred to as the Professor from Montana. Then, as always, he tended to be all over the place, both mentally and physically.

At Princeton, I listened absorbedly to the discourses of Leslie Fiedler that led in the early 1960s to *Love and Death in the American Novel*. I reviewed the work, finding it, as well I should, an absolutely major contribution to the still rather new field of American literary studies. I was taken aback by the author detecting a homoerotic attraction between Dimmesdale and Chillingworth in *The Scarlet Letter*, and I regretted Leslie's skeptical view of Henry James. But my main feeling was that Leslie Fiedler, as a cultural analyst, was here twisting American culture into some very strange new shape, like a pretzel. Only slowly did I realize that this was in fact the true, the real shape of American culture over a century and a half, and that Leslie was in effect twisting it back into its proper shape after it had been distorted by the then contemporary pundits.

Indeed, surveying Leslie Fiedler's career from the present perspective, what strikes us most is not only the extraordinary verve and energy and sassiness of his writing, the electrifying brilliance of some of his *aperçus* and his holdings-forth. It is even more the way that, from the start, he ran measureless miles ahead of the successive waves of cultural fashion. Over these decades we have seen the intensifying (and altogether valid) concern with American black culture, with the status and achievement of women, with gay and lesbian interests and values. Leslie Fiedler has been taking these matters for granted as crucial elements in our national makeup at least since the essay "Come Back to the Raft Ag'in, Huck Honey" in 1948. In what has become the most acclaimed

153

and influential critical essay of its time, Leslie Fiedler drew our attention to the remarkable prevalence of what is now called male bonding in classical American literature—between young black and young white, between Indian and white, between Polynesian and white.

It may be that even Leslie Fiedler did not, for a while anyhow, fully comprehend the revolutionary novelty of his theses. The original essay, along with *An End to Innocence,* the volume that contained it, with *Love and Death* and *Waiting for the End* (one of my personal favorites)—all these were published over the name Leslie A. Fiedler. By the time of *What Was Literature? Mass Culture and Mass Society* in 1984, the initial A has been dropped, and the opening chapter of that book—which I recommend to one and all—is a sort of autobiographical musing called "Who Was Leslie A. Fiedler?" Here Leslie returns to "Come Back to the Raft" and reviews—with a kind of wonder at that old self of his—his deepening involvement with those phases of our culture that have since been so obsessively emphasized. He does so, it can be noted, even while once again showing the way in cultural alertness—that is, by stressing and illustrating the historic and present importance of *popular* culture. If the study of that phenomenon has become so pronounced in the American academy in recent years, it is in good part the consequence of *What Was Literature?*

What is so gratifying is that Leslie never abandons hard-headed literary values and standards—the way so many academics are doing today—in some self-serving pursuit of some fashionable line. I sat next to Leslie at a recent two-day conference in New York, a planning session for a PBS series on the American novel in the twentieth century. I was positively distracted by the way Leslie would listen silently to the buzz and whirl of conversation from the other twenty-five participants—many of them with their own special interests and agendas, and their different ways of leading the discussion astray; and then would quietly interject a remark that would turn the entire session around, or upside down, back to where it ought to be. And where it ought to be was not some issue-strewn political arena, but the world of literature: the most important American novelists and novels since 1900, the nature of fiction and of novel-making, the special nature of language in fiction, why we read novels, what it means to hold a novel in your hands and turn the pages.

In the course of about fourteen hours of talk, Leslie Fiedler saved the day—quietly, crisply, with just a phrase or two and a quick wry smile—half a dozen times. He was never more like Henry James, who used to say that there was no substitute for liking a novel or not liking it. Saving the day is what Leslie has been doing these many years, and will of course, happily for us, continue to do.

Fiedler on the Roof

David R. Slavitt

A joke title, of course, but as with many jokes, there's a truth to it. I remember a lecture Fiedler gave once—I can't remember where or when, exactly, but it must have been more than thirty years ago. It was about the Jews of Newark, like Philip Roth and like him.

I have no idea what his thesis was, but I remember vividly his explanation of how the Jews settled there. Baltimore, it seems, was a major port of entry for immigrant ships. And these Jews would get on the train, as they had been instructed to do, and would buy a ticket for New York. But at a certain point, a conductor would go through the train announcing that the next station stop was, "Newark, Newark," which sounds, if you know only Yiddish and Polish and Russian, like "New York, New York." So they got out and settled. And lived there for a generation or so before they realized that there was this unused part of the ticket and that they'd made a mistake.

* * *

So there he is, in that city that is not New York, maybe looking out at night at the glow from the real metropolis, maybe up there on a hot summer's night on what they used to call "Tar Beach" trying to catch what Roth describes so vividly in *Goodbye, Columbus*—a cool breeze as welcome as the promise of an afterlife. Hot, stewing, yearning, a Fiedler on the roof.

* * *

Is this enough to explain him? His sense of being an Auslander, his distance from what he takes to be the cultural epicenter (epicenter, *epes?*) is from that. Think of Manhattan in the middle, and these two Jews looking toward it with ambition and an almost hopeless yearning. Alfred Kazin in Brooklyn, and in Newark, Fiedler.

156

But Brooklyn had the Dodgers, and Sheepshead Bay, and Walt Whitman. Newark? Nothing! A place, indeed, that seems to aspire to nothingness. One sees, from time to time, in disquisitions on urban decay, pictures of some corner in Newark, where, every ten years, some photographer has come with his camera and his Schadenfreude to record moments in the deterioration. The buildings are occupied. Then abandoned. Then, like the teeth of some derelict, disappearing irregularly. At last, nothing but rubble and emptiness. All it needs is grass growing there and it could be Nebraska.

*   *   *

Outré, I guess is the word. Out of it. Fiedler's book on freaks makes it clear that you don't have to be different. You only have to feel different. And if you don't, you're not. "Once in a great while, to be sure," he writes, "there will appear among the onlookers someone who, though he has not yet learned to think of himself as a Giant, will realize that he is taller than the fabulous creature he has come to see. So Jack Earle once wandered into the Barnum and Bailey Circus in El Paso, Texas, to gawk at Jim Tarver ['the tallest man in the world'] who was in fact three or four inches shorter than he."

New York is normal. Newark is eccentric, "something else," or, in his word, freakish. As Jews are, in a sense, freakish. (Otherwise, we aren't "chosen," are we?) Fiedler, then, is the world's largest Dwarf, the world's shortest Giant. Why? Because he feels himself to be. His attitudes have been constructed upon that basis, and his odd and sometimes unwelcome truths come from that singularity of vision.

*   *   *

Figure he crosses the river with those wonderful Hudson tubes. He gets out to find that the streets of Manhattan are filthy and the people who walk the sidewalks a fairly unappetizing lot (except for Fifth Avenue from maybe Fiftieth to Fifty-Seventh, which *is* freakish). This is not big news to someone who grew up there, but to a young man who dreamed of New York, who aspired to it, who was tantalized and challenged by it, it had to have been something of a disappointment.

*   *   *

And where does he wind up? Buffalo? Beau fleuve? Freaky-
deaky! O. J. played there. And McKinley was shot there. And . . .
and that's it.

SUNY Buffalo!

Which suggests that maybe Yale and Harvard and those toney
places haven't got their priorities right. Can't tell excellence when
it bites them in the ass. Worse, these sophisticated centers of self-
congratulation are immune to the feelings of wonder and awe
that are the freaks' real stock in trade, the marvelous and the
phenomenal being, among other things, unclubbable.

But, of course, that's true.

* * *

Hard to remember, but back then, Jews were. Freaks on campuses.
Paul Weiss, one of my teachers at Yale, had been at Bryn Mawr
where, as a philosopher, he had been an interested and amused
observer of the discussions his colleagues in the English department were having—this is in the late forties—about whether "a
Hebrew" could teach English literature. Is it possible, without having that tradition "in the blood" as it were, to impart it to young
students?

Weiss, when he came to Yale, was the first Jew to hold a tenured
position in the humanities. (There had been a couple in the sci-
ences and in medicine.) There was a big problem about whether
he had to be offered membership in the Faculty Club. How could
they? (But how could they not?) At length, after much awkward-
ness, they made him a member. He went once, to have dinner
there, to celebrate having won this battle, and never set foot in
the place again.

How did that feel?

Fiedler points out that "the hideous Dwarf Abe Kusich, in *Day
of the Locust*" is "one of the few characters whom [Nathanael] West
labeled, as he did not like to label himself, a Jew."

* * *

Fiedler did not aspire to be a freak. On the contrary, as he says
with characteristic candor, in *Being Busted:* "With the B. A., M.A.,
Ph.D., I told myself, I would have a louder voice, more access to
the centers of power, a better fulcrum and greater leverage with
which to heave over the whole rotten mess out of which I had
been trying in vain to crawl."

To get out of Newark? Anything. There was admiration in the
neighborhood for making it any way one could—even for the

fellow who'd arrived at Number Fourteen on the FBI's Most Wanted List. Fiedler read Marx at thirteen and became, not surprisingly, a leftist, which was, in this country, a kind of intellectual freakishness.

* * *

This aberrance allowed him to see most of what he has seen, to understand that pop culture is interesting (it's a whole industry now, which is a way of demonstrating that it has become a cliché, but Fiedler was one of those who invented it).

Jews are no longer strangers in English departments. Yiddish is a badge of honor now, a way of signalling that some cultural fragments are valuable and ought to be preserved. Yiddish phrases are now the equivalent of allusions to Spenser. Or Latin tags. But this is a relatively recent development.

* * *

Freaks can't afford illusions. They know the cruelty and hypocrisy of the clubbable types in Manhattan, and they say "No! In Thunder . . ." which is what comfortable tweedy guys at Yale and Harvard are least disposed to say, because they have a lot to lose.

The weird thing about these freaks is not only that they are different but that they are on to us. Fiedler cites Carson McCullers' spooky observation. "'She was afraid of all the freaks,' Mrs. McCullers says of Frankie, 'for it seemed to her that they had looked at her in a secret way and tried to connect their eyes with hers, as though to say: *we know you. We are you!*'"

In that way, Fiedler has known us and been us all along, and in a much more intimate way than he could have done if his forebears had stayed on that train another fifteen minutes or so.

Leslie Fiedler: Enfant Terrible, American Jewish Critic, and the Other Side of Lionel Trilling

DANIEL WALDEN

It was 22 April 1985, during a visit to Penn State University—during which he gave two public talks, took part in three classroom discussions, and attended several lunches and dinners—that I asked Leslie Fiedler what he thought of the current state of American Jewish literature. In no uncertain terms, Fiedler stated: "I was there at the beginning and now I'm seeing the end of it. American Jewish literature is finished." Although Leslie Fiedler has predicted the end of the novel in *Waiting for the End* and in "The Death and Rebirth of the Novel," it was at this point that he put his prediction about American Jewish literature into the air. When I then rather provocatively asked him if he'd defend his position at the next MLA convention he readily agreed.

The next December, in New York, the Grand Ballroom was packed, close to thousand people were there to see Fiedler and to hear him engage in a discussion on the subject of the end of the American Jewish novel with Bonnie Lyons, Les Field, Keith Opdahl, and Daniel Walden. However, about ten days before, Fiedler called me and declared that he wouldn't be able to make it; he said he was ill. I called Cynthia Ozick, in a panic, explained the situation and asked her if she'd appear in Fiedler's place. She assented. Thus, at the convention, when I announced that Leslie Fiedler would not appear, there were a few groans and a bit of rustling; but when I said that Cynthia Ozick was to join the discussion there was a loud sigh of warmth and appreciation.

What took place that day was an example of the chances Fiedler constantly took. Because he was ill, he missed a splendid chance to argue his convictions that the American Jewish novel was dead. That Cynthia Ozick was there, and took part in a lively discussion, was proof—argued again and again by all of us so passionately devoted to the appreciation of the genre—that the American Jewish novel was alive and well, but changing, even as each of the many genres in the canon and coming into the canon were.

Fiedler, as should be well known, is a man of many parts, and many changing views. Starting from a fascination with "innocence"—"It's the original chaos, the unorganized, the intuitive, the impulsive," he said in an interview[1]; he added later, "I think of innocence as being at the heart of the thing." The stated conviction that he began crying "No, in Thunder," at the age of sixteen seems to indicate that he has been an "ambiguous rebel" all his life.[2]

Fiedler is a noted literary critic but he does not readily take to theorizing. He launched a formal attack on the New Criticism, in "Archetype and Signature" in his *No! In Thunder* (1960) and told Patricia Ward Biederman "I want to write as differently as possible from structualist, post-structuralist, deconstructionist critics who write a private jargon, a secret language, a hermetic code that's only available to the initiated."[3] At the same time he has not hesitated to borrow the insights of Marx and Freud when he needed them. Like most important critics, Fiedler is capable of creative eclecticism. The fact is that the formalist critic, the critic who is interested chiefly in the structure and language of the text and believes that a work of art is autonomous, has to explain away somehow the stereotypes of Jews produced by Hemingway, Fitzgerald, Eliot, and Pound, to name only a few. Fiedler is a critic who sees literature as evidence to support a sociological or cultural thesis, as he put it in his *Fiedler on the Roof,* and as L. S. Dembo explains cogently, and major and minor works are given importance in the perspective of this thesis, rather than in terms of their inherent literary quality.

To many of us, Fiedler is a first-rate literary critic and a well-known American Jewish critic. As far back as 1955 his essays on the Rosenbergs, the Hiss Case, and Joe McCarthy, included in *An End to Innocence* (1955), still stand tall and strong. The Jewish pieces in *Collected Essays,* especially those grouped under the heading "To the Gentiles," are a significant contribution to American Jewish literature. Similarly, his tour de force, *Love and Death in the American Novel,* and so many other books and essays attest to his literary standing. True, some may find his methods and conclusions to be questionable, which often means controversial. He shares at least two basic assumptions, however, with virtually all critics; he believes that literature is of central importance to life and he believes that by shedding light on literature the critic can help to clarify that importance for his readers. As a full-time professor (now Emeritus) and critic he has published his way into the consciousness of the literati, academic and nonacademic. Like Alfred Kazin, Lionel Trilling, and Irving Howe, he has become a celebrity at the level of high culture. Fiedler has also been a player on the level of popular culture, one of the very few to cross the lines. He is a public intellectual in the best sense of the word.

Fiedler has often been quoted, clearly, on his likes and dislikes. He admires I. B. Singer enormously. Lionel Trilling is a disappointment. As a fictionist, even as a secular Jew, one suspects, according to Fiedler, Trilling doesn't quite make it. As Fiedler put it in *The Jew in the American Novel* (1959), Trilling attempted in *The Middle of the Journey* what few writers can achieve: the story of the allure of Communism and the disillusion with it. Norman Mailer has tried his hand at it, without having quite lived through the experience; Isaac Rosenfeld has explored it a little obliquely in one short story; Fiedler circled around it in his shorter fiction. Only Trilling made the full-scale attempt; but is perhaps a bit too studied in his approach; there is a sense of his having reached this item on a list of important things that mars his book.

Lionel Trilling is the very model of the American scholar. Fiedler has been identified as a critic, or an American Jewish critic, for decades. Trilling looks tall, cool, the WASP image in a Jew who was acceptable to Columbia University at a time when Jewish intellectuals were rare in the academy. Fiedler has always been the pugnacious ex-pugilist-cum-intellectual Jew who served his time in Missoula, Montana, before making it in the big time in Buffalo. Trilling was never known as an American Jewish critic; at most he dipped his little toe gingerly in the water. Fiedler for many years has had an affair with the genre, tempered by interminable disquisitions. After pointing out in *Waiting for the End* (1964) that not until the emergence of the Jewish novelists of the fifties and sixties were the literary stereotypes of the Jews created by the twenties and preceding generations of writers dispelled, he explained that "the very notion of a Jewish American literature represents a dream of assimilation, and the process it envisages is bound to move toward a triumph (in terms of personal success) which is also a defeat (in terms of a meaningful Jewish survival)." His point was that Jewish American writers, writing the comedy of Jewish dissolution in the midst of prosperity (instead of writing about the persistence in the midst of persecution) were telling the truth "about a world which neither they nor their forerunners considered themselves guiltless of desiring."[4]

It seems clear that Fiedler did not desire such a world, one in which Jews would no longer function as the morality-bearers of the culture. Fiedler could not have written Trilling's *Middle of the Journey,* a novel about an intellectual among intellectuals in a world without Jews, "interested in the psychological and philosophic relations among fellow-travelling liberals, their response to the defection of a Party member who had heretofore held sway over them, and their interaction with the people of a New England town."[5] Unlike Fiedler, who has taken chances and put himself on record, (as have most American Jewish writers), the disaffecting Party member (whom the others believe has gone mad) accuses the protagonist and the group: "Like any bourgeois intellectual, you want to make the best of every possible world and every possible view. Anything to avoid a commitment, anything not to have to take a risk."[6]

Trilling, an admirable man in so many ways, known to these days as the author of *The Liberal Imagination,* was a distinguished critic, for a time the so-called Dean of Critics. Perhaps he wrote his convictions. Perhaps he felt he had to accommodate himself to the prevailing mores; after all, it was only a few years before, in 1906, that Ludwig Lewisohn, on the brink of a Ph.D. in English, was told not to go forward, that Jews would never be hired in a major American university. Fiedler, on the other hand, a few decades later, continued to write "from a Jewish point of view, *as* a Jew," though he was honest enough to admit, he had "abandoned all the traditional religion, almost completely lost the traditional culture and no longer speak the languages traditionally associated with Jewishness. I am consequently . . . a Jew only in retrospect, in memory; a memory that persists not in my heart or in my head but in my blood."[7] Trilling, to his credit, has been remembered in a paean to *Partisan Review's* evolution, by indirection, for ideological and classical consistency. As Fiedler put it in 1956, "From Edmund Wilson to Lionel Trilling, the most characteristic critical voice of *PR* has attempted to assert the sociological thesis against an evergrowing tendency toward intrinsic or 'pure' textual criticism, and has sought to defend it against its profanation by the Stalinist or liberaloid theory that art must embody 'progressive' ideas."[8] In turn, Trilling was described as an influential and regular contributor in most ways not untypical of the Columbia University group: "Jewish, a New Yorker who refuses to leave that city, an exploiter of the themes of anguish and alienation, a naturalist searching for tragedy. But in him the ordinarily annoying pose is mitigated by a soft-spoken style which is modesty itself—

and combined with the stance of a nineteenth-century English gentleman-dissenter to produce a version of the *PR* writer as a belated Matthew Arnold."[9]

Trilling, as Fiedler sees him, has argued that every great writer for the last two centuries has been on the side of the self against culture. But Trilling, in *Freud and the Crisis of Our Culture*, sets up an "opposing self" and calls into question the (liberal) idea of the absolute nature of culture as a criterion for judging the individual. He sees Freud's biological determinism in a way that suggests that "there is a residue of human quality beyond the reach of cultural control, and that this residue of human quality, elemental as it may be, serves to bring culture itself under criticism and keeps it from being absolute."[10] What is so impressive is Trilling's controlled dialect: in "Of This Time of That Place" (1944) he has the "liberal," academic poet, Joseph Howe, commit himself simultaneously to the system that he accepts and admires (culture, civilization), and presumably obey his impulse to recognize and preserve the unknowable (the "unconditioned" spirit, the opposing self), a tragedy of labels." The real issue in the end is psychological, not political. Nancy Crooms, a firm liberal, cannot utter the word *death* in *The Middle of the Journey;* E. M. Forster, in *The Longest Journey,* as Trilling perceived it, brilliantly wrote the scene, in which Rickie forced Agnes to "mind" [that is, take notice of] the death of Gerald, as a criticism of the British fear of emotion but also of liberalism's incompetence before tragedy.[12] In short, afraid of the word *death,* the liberal prefers the word *mad* to describe things he doesn't understand, thus, a disaffecting CP member fearing for his life, and a "mad" student given to writing in a brilliant but unique fashion.[13]

Significantly, Leslie Fiedler not only does not shrink from such words or images but actually relishes them. "I'm very fond of words like *death* of the novel," he noted in an interview, "or an *end* to innocence; it's as if I feel better when I look back than when I look forward."[14] At one point, he proclaimed that the novel "is dead as a single genre." Perhaps by way of explanation, Fiedler explained that he was convinced that one of the gifts of a great writer of fiction is the gift of being possessed by hallucinations that he then translates in such a way that the reader accepts them as his/her hallucinations.[15] Then again, there is the possibility that he is the victim of a kind of conflict between his two selves. "The critic, just like the writer of fiction, after a while creates a fictional self who tends to take over his own writing from him; after you've written your first critical work, you're in exactly the same sort of plight as the novelist or the story writer is after he's written his first thing. He becomes the victim of the first fiction which he creates of himself—as a critic, as a novelist, as a short story writer. All my life, I keep fighting to get back to find my own full, natural human voice so that I can be responding to those books as whatever that indefinable thing is that I really am instead of the Leslie Fiedler which I've already created in my earlier work."[16]

Leslie Fiedler's first book was *An End to Innocence.* He is still, in his eighties, writing. As a critic he has been an *enfant terrible* given to extraliterary generalizations, and he calls himself a "literary anthropologist." Having lived and written for more than five decades, with a career as varied as Fiedler's, it could be asked "which is the real Leslie fiedler?" One answer lies in the impressive body of insights and criticism that mark his work. Another answer is in his occasionally wrong-headed but provocative pronouncements, i.e., the novel is dead, or the Jewish American novel is history. But perhaps the best answer is in Emerson's insight, that "the integrity of impression made by manifold natural objects . . . distinguishes the stick timber of the woodcutter from the tree of the poet."

NOTES

1. In Geoffrey Green, "Reestablishing Innocence: A Conversation with Leslie Fiedler," *Genre* 14, no. 1 (1981): 136, 148.

2. L. S. Dembo, "Dissent and Dissent: A Look at Fiedler and Trilling," in *Contemporary Jewish Literature: Critical Essays,* ed. Irving Malin (Bloomington: Indiana University Press), 136.

3. In Patricia Ward Biederman, "Leslie Fiedler: The Critic as Outlaw," *Buffalo Courier-Express,* March 7, 1982, pp. 9–11, 13–15.

4. Fiedler, *Waiting for the End* (New York: Stein and Day, 1964), 70.

5. Dembo, "Dissent and Dissent," 146.

6. Trilling, *The Middle of the Journey* (New York: Viking, 1947), 301.

7. Fiedler, *Fiedler on the Roof* (Boston: Godine, 1991), xv, xvii.

8. Fiedler, "Partisan Review . . .," in *Collected Essays* (New York: Stein and Day, 1971), 2:49.

9. Ibid., 2:54.

10. Trilling, *Freud and the Crises of Our Culture* (Boston: Beacon, 1955), 48.

11. Dembo, "Dissent and Dissent," 149–50.

12. Trilling, *E. M. Forster* (New York: New Directions, 1964), 23.

13. Dembo, "Dissent and Dissent," 150–52.

14. Green, "Reestablishing Innocence," 135.

15. Ibid., 140.

16. Ibid., 134.

A Fiedler Brood

Susan Gubar

Of course, you might say, "But he *has* literal children of his own flesh, this one in film, that one in banking" or again you might exclaim, "But he did *not* have offspring, on such grounds, for these reasons, and haven't you read *those* essays?" I cannot tell which objection to anticipate since I haven't read every word Leslie Fiedler has written. Nor do I write personally about Leslie Fiedler, having only met him briefly at one or two conferences, at a party during an MLA convention, a reception starting a regional lecture series, where he was inevitably accompanied by a wife so solicitous, so genuinely unaffected and warm that I instantly thought, why can't I have one like that? In any case, though, I don't want to resort to the paternal metaphor, don't wish to see Leslie Fiedler as "the father of us all." I need another, more subversive, less authoritarian image to describe the ways in which the work of this extraordinary individual anticipated and played out so many of the most exciting ventures of literary criticism at the turn of the twentieth century because what made possible the books and essays was precisely Fiedler's rejection of staid, traditional, (dare I use an outdated word?) patriarchal business as usual.

Despite some of his gibes at feminists, I can picture the bad boy who got busted and then revelled in telling the tale as a sort of big brother and in particular a kinsman of the feminist critics beginning to write during the late seventies, at the time Sandra Gilbert and I published *The Madwoman in the Attic.* Quickly cognizant of the same postwar forces of dissent (the beats, civil rights activism, militant protests against Vietnam, the sexual revolution) that eventually readied the stage for the women's movement outside the academy as well as feminist criticism inside it, Fiedler embarked on a series of projects that may not have set out to do so, but nevertheless ended up offering an analysis of women's function in American fiction almost two decades before I and my peer group of feminist critics in American Studies—Judith

166

Fetterley, Annette Kolodny, Myra Jehlen, and Jane Tompkins—produced comparable contributions.

Fear of women and of sex, Fiedler demonstrated, inundates the classic canonical texts, motivating their heroes to band together as they determine to light out for the territories. So many classic American texts can be found in the children's department of public libraries because of their authors' trepidations about mature, heterosexual relationships, or so he argued. One of the earliest theorists of misogyny, Fiedler traced its complex, often contradictory manifestations in literature that would sometimes link women to civilization, a corrupt literary marketplace, the stifling conventions of petty urban pieties and properties, but sometimes to the savagery or silence of a natural, virgin landscape in need of penetration. Before it was fashionable to do so, *Love and Death in the American Novel* uncovered not only a ubiquitous but also an aesthetically generative anxiety among the canonical authors of American letters that love of women spelled death for men.

If Fiedler adumbrated the first stage of feminist criticism—the phase Elaine Showalter called "critique" in which resisting readers criticized the reification of female images in books written by men—he also participated importantly in the second step that Showalter less happily, more medically named "gyno-criticism"; that is, the period of recovery where texts that had been neglected or devalued because composed by women received new interpretive appreciation. Not simply a line on his vita, *Opening Up the Canon* remained a passion for Fiedler, whose treatment of *Uncle Tom's Cabin* helped put Harriet Beecher Stowe's name back into the principal position in twentieth-century literary history that reflects her centrality in the nineteenth-century literary scene. Fiedler insisted on studying minor as well as major, popular as well as elite texts, all the while questioning the categories "minor" and "major," "mass" and "elite." As he demonstrated his sensitivity to the connections between gender and genre as well as to the sex-antagonism at work in the economy that produces publishing houses, reviews, bestsellers, and reputations, his work contributed to the intellectual climate in which Sandra Gilbert and I completed our three-volume appraisal of the literary interaction between the sexes in the modern period, *No Man's Land,* as well as the first edition of our *Norton Anthology of Literature by Women.*

That at times in his publications Fiedler seemed to promulgate precisely the misogynist strains he uncovered, that at other times he reinvented gendered stereotypes for the women writers he reclaimed; that Fiedler sometimes ignored, baited, or teased the feminists who followed him: don't these phenomena simply accord with the role of older brothers who rarely allow their regard for their siblings to deter their heckling or harassing them?

With what ambivalent feelings was this big brother watching another sibling growing up in the brood, an addition to the family born later enough in time to regard Fiedler more as a kind of uncle? Whether or not they disavow him as homophobic, such queer theorists as Joseph Boone, Wayne Koestenbaum, Gail Reuben, and Eve Kosofsky Sedgwick remain indebted to Fiedler's perspicacity about white male fantasies of a dark male beloved whose embrace will make well all manner of evils that have accrued from white supremacy. Fiedler's often anthologized, often quoted "Come Back to the Raft Ag'in, Huck Honey!" presages the emphasis in gay studies on the feminine functioning in sexual and textual contexts as an object of exchange, serving primarily as the glue bonding man to man. Although Fiedler termed that bonding "homoerotic," whereas queer theorists now use the phrase "homosocial," he intuited the complex spectrum of amorously passionate feelings of white men attracted toward African American masculinity and not simply prompted by a shared dread of women but also motivated by the dynamics of racial guilt over white privilege.

Perhaps this is why I turned to Fiedler when I embarked on a project in which I attempted to engender racial categories that were paradoxically as unstable as they were recalcitrant. Especially in my last book, *Racechanges: White Skin, Black Face in American Culture,* chiefly in the chapter on white artists fascinated by hypersexualized stereotypes of a black "penis-not-a-phallus," I found myself quoting passages in which Fiedler demonstrates his understanding of the importance in American psychology and literature of cross-racial and homosexual desire. After all, he had placed the white man–black man couple at the very center of America's imagination.

"Born theoretically white, we are permitted to pass our childhood as imaginary Indians, our adolescence as imaginary Negroes, and only then are expected to settle down to being what we really are: white once more": this intuition in *Waiting for the End* brings me to the last, but perhaps most multiply inflected critical stance anticipated by Fiedler throughout his numerous essays. From the very beginning of his professional career, he has engaged ethnic, racial, religious, regional, and national manifestations of what are today called "subject positionalities" or "cultural identifications," refusing to let his knowledge of the sensitivity of these topics inhibit his intellectual absorption in them.

Yet probably many of the practitioners in these fields would not feel the need to name Fiedler as a progenitor or adopt him as a precursor. In fact, his views about Simone Weil or about "terminal Jews" could outrage Jewish Studies proponents no less than the assumption that "we" are "really white" might offend blacks and Jews alike. Neither an older brother nor an uncle in the venue of Ethnic Studies and deeply committed to an understanding of the mutability of racial identity, Fiedler is not perceived as a partisan of Jewish Studies or a spokesman for African American Studies, Native American Studies, or the newly emerging field of White Studies (and, I should hasten to add, certainly all these area studies had very different histories within the institution of the academy, in large part after he published most of his writing). Would Fiedler seem to these professionals a vaguely embarrassing because unpredictable, irreverent, irascible second cousin twice removed?

Thinking along those lines, I have to admit that most feminist critics would resist considering Fiedler part of their intellectual genealogy, as would the majority of queer theorists. Perhaps even the non-patriarchal family metaphors break down as analogues of Fiedler's influential prominence in twentieth-century criticism because he remains what the abiding figure in his work has always been, the single trope that sustains even the most polychromatic of his investigations. Add to the themes and issues I have already described Fiedler's extensive writings on science fiction and the alien, on the freakshow and the monster, and on the stranger on stage and screen. The composite figure emerging from this dauntingly variegated set of subjects appears to be none other than the Other: an eccentric, even a renegade, the Other might be the female or the freak, the black or the Jew, the homosexual or the Native American or, of course, the critic himself.

A maverick, not a maven, Fiedler could be relied upon to throw political correctness to the winds, to trample on many people's most cherished convictions of rectitude. To the usual categories by which one labels members of English departments, Fielder has issued a categorical, *No, In Thunder,* though his work has stimulated many who have manufactured those brands. Gleefully provocative, he defiantly played out many of his most subversive maneuvers not in the name of feminism or queer theory or Jewish or Black Studies but under the banner of a visionary form of what today we would call Cultural Studies, but a Cultural Studies different from today's to the extent that its practitioners would

eschew not only any narrowly political set of preordained assumptions but also the jargon and the pretentiousness of academese.

In an essay composed in 1970 and entitled "Cross the Border—
Close the Gap," Fiedler called for "a New New Criticism, a Post-
Modernist criticism" that would be "contextual rather than textual." Employing "not words-on-the-page but words-in-the-
world," the "New New Criticism" would be "comical, irreverent,
vulgar" in its efforts to lead us "out of the Eliotic church" with
its elitist dismissal of "low" or "popular" art as well as its widening
of the gap between professional critic or artist, on the one hand,
amateur audience or reader, on the other. Musing on Fiedler's
eclectic brood, brooding on Fielder as a cantankerous muse, we
might remember that the literary critics who lessened the gap
between popular and elite art, between artist and public, represent such an infinite variety of congruent and incongruous alli-
ances that contemporary criticism can never be imagined as
simply a family concern. Though we contentiously continue our
debates quite definitively outside "the Eliotic church"—not in
small measure because of the vigorously eccentric part Fielder
has played in American criticism—we still need to learn from him
how to make our words comic, irreverent, and vulgar enough to
come alive in the world, as his so robustly have.

Thinking About Leslie Fiedler

ROBERT BOYERS

For a man never apt to be mistaken for any other, Leslie Fiedler has always been a bit of a puzzle. As a writer he seemed to do everything well, and he took on a dizzying variety of assignments and ideas. Of course he will always be associated with *Love and Death In The American Novel,* which ought to be required reading—a quaint concept, that—in English departments, where not so long ago the bright Americanists could recite from memory their favorite Fiedlerian passages. But many of us first discovered Fiedler in the magazines, where he taught us how to think freshly about Alger Hiss and Whittaker Chambers, about Italian writers and Jewish writers, about the near past and the distant past. Fiedler knew his Shakespeare and his Dante, his Chaucer and Pavese, like the learned literary man he never ceased, through his manifold incarnations, to be. But he knew also many things academic people rarely bothered to learn, and he could talk about politics and popular culture without holding his nose or striking superior postures. He could ask embarrassing and important questions without inviting us to congratulate him for his candor or his daring. He couldn't help being candid. He was bound, some of the time, to be offensive. Susceptible, more than a little, to the siren call of the Dionysian and the vatic, the subversive and the countercultural, he could generally be counted upon to keep his feet firmly planted and to tell the difference between a genuine idea and a specious concoction.

Fiedler's voice, stance, and preoccupations are instantly recognizable in his many essays. Even when his subject is not explicitly the mythical he tends always to talk about a culture's sense of itself, the way we respond to events, persons, books, and ideas by drawing on our deepest notions of who we are, where we come from, and what we are supposed to be. These notions, as he deals with them, often contain equal parts wishful thinking, delusion and reality. Long before they became commonplace, Fiedler was comfortable with designations like "patriarchal" and "matriar-

171

chal" to describe cultural structures and assumptions, and he routinely identified the "mood" or "sentiment" that underlay a common practice we had not thought to examine, so much a part of ordinary unconscious life was the practice. For all of his tendency to categorize—no other literary man has given us so many amusing and suggestive terms with which to define and organize our experience—he has tried to explain how seemingly incompatible formations (the "magical, mechanical, psychological," the ego and the id, the heterosexual and the homosexual) are complexly related. The goal is to emerge from our reading, as from our encounter with persons and events, "with a confirmed sense of the ambiguity of life," a sense we can sustain only if we abide with "many readings," learn "to endure them all," without supposing that one reading is interchangeable with another, or one practice reducible to another.

Of course the tolerance of ambiguity and the enthusiasm for many readings have nothing to do with a blithe embrace of the patently delusional or simplistic. Fiedler is often a harsh critic of readings that seem to him dumb, misleading, or vicious. He readily resorts to terms of derogation like "philistine," "middlebrow," "pious," "pretentious," "genteel," and "solemn." There is much that Fiedler dislikes, much that seems to him to armor us unduly against the shock of the new or disturbing. Attitudes, like pacifism, that might seem noble or otherwise admirable can seem to Fiedler ridiculous or unworthy because, in the present state of the culture, they are safe, predictable, or "compulsory." Persons engaged in what might once have seemed respectable academic work are, in the state of things, charged with "status seeking" and with a prim respectability that diligently avoids dirtying its hands with merely popular or ephemeral material. Those who make a fetish of their openness to ostensibly "advanced" work are similarly susceptible to criticism—Fiedler is as likely to accuse a writer of being "arty" as of being "prematurely middle-aged." Enthusiastic about candor and about the reader-critic's willingness to explain where he is coming from, he nonetheless derides tendencies to "confession" and "peep-show," and he laments the shift of psychoanalysis from "theory of the mind" to "weltanschauung," where it exerts undue influence on persons too fond of "mechanical" readings of everything under the sun.

Like other first-rate critics, Fiedler is very much a man of his time, which is to say that, even when he is writing about Dante or Shakespeare, he reflects the preoccupations of his own moment. His sense of the mythic is a 1950s construction. He is no more "dated" as a critic than Matthew Arnold or Roland Barthes, but there is no doubt that his essays of the 1950s—or 1970s—could have been written only in those decades. This is most obvious in essays devoted to topical matters, where Fiedler is assiduous to chart recent shifts in the way his contemporaries behave and think about burning issues.

The essay on "Negro and Jew: Encounter in America," origi-nally a review of James Baldwin's book *Notes of a Native Son,* has good reason to seem interesting to us principally as a historical document, the sort of thing we'd look up principally to discover what American intellectuals were saying on this subject forty years ago. But the essay seems to me still a work of compelling vitality, and if it is occasionally wrong-headed or dubious in several re-spects, well, that is generally what we always felt about the work of this great American original. We take him as he is, embracing what is all of a wonderful piece, the fresh and penetrating insight alongside the novel idea pushed just a bit too far or made to seem adequate where it can be at best suggestive.

"Negro and Jew," which was included in Fiedler's book *No! In Thunder,* considers the shifting relations of two American "minor-ity" populations. Those relations, Fiedler writes, have been exacer-bated by the fact that Negroes and Jews have been "so alike and so different." How alike? At least "in the complicated fear we stir in the hearts of our neighbors," and in the "restrictions" others have devised to deal with both groups—restrictions as to "what clubs and fraternities they can join" and as to "whom they can marry." The two groups have been alike as well in existing always "for the Western world . . . as archetypes, symbolic figures . . . projecting aspects of the white, Christian mind itself."

But, says Fiedler, the differences between the two groups had long come to seem more important than the similarities. Jews had prospered in the United States, most Negroes had not. Jews usually had the option of assimilating and, as it were, disap-pearing, while most Negroes had no such prospect. When Fiedler wrote his essay a rising generation of radical black leaders and a good many black writers were readying to take aim at American Jews, including liberal sponsors of civil rights causes, and to make of difference itself a rallying cry. Whatever Jews had thought to make of the common minority status they shared with Negroes, whatever the strong participation of Jewish liberals in organiza-tions like the NAACP and in the civil rights movement of the 1960s, there had long been Negro resentment against Jewish store owners in predominantly Negro neighborhoods. Many Jews were puzzled by the poverty in which many Negroes continued to live, and feared contamination by dissolute Negroes in their communities. So Fiedler contends, and so others sometimes said.

Fiedler accounts for the origin of the troubled relationship in a way that may well have seemed doubtful even to early readers of his essay. "The Jew is, by and large," he writes, "a late-comer in the United States" and therefore does not share in "the guilts and repressions" of the native population—guilts, moreover, that often bear on American treatment of black people. By contrast, he goes on, "the Negro arrives without a past, out of nowhere . . ., out of a world he is afraid to remember" and is involved in this country in a unique way, helping—whether by desire or circumstance—to "forge the conscience of the country." These facts, Fiedler argues, have much to do with the fate of the two populations, and it ought not to surprise us that "the Negro boasts grimly that he has helped shape with terror the American spirit," while Jews "admit shamefacedly that we have profited by its generosity."

It is easy to say that Fiedler got it all wrong when he contended that blacks arrived here without a past. And it is easy to say that many American Jews were in flight from their own dark Eastern European or German past, and thus closer to the Negro and to other immigrant groups in wanting rapidly to become a part of America. No doubt Fiedler was aware of efforts, on the part of many black intellectuals, to remember their African past at a time when Africa seemed to everyone else an undifferentiated heart of darkness. He would have done well to reflect on these efforts in developing his thesis. But Fiedler was not mistaken when he suggested that most American blacks before the 1960s were not much concerned with their African roots, and even today he would have grounds for arguing that the turn to Africa has cost young blacks a great deal in the last twenty-five years, distracting them from the task of rebuilding their communities and addressing the rising tide of black nihilism. That would be another argument, to be sure, and it would take Fiedler in directions he chooses not to follow. But the basis for such an argument is present in the essay Fiedler gives us.

Fiedler may well have underestimated the degree to which American Jews assumed the guilts and, later, the resentments to which other white Americans were susceptible. Though, as he says, Jews were not responsible for the institution of American slavery or for subsequent oppressive regimes directed against blacks, they profited from the system in ways that set them apart from most black people and often made them wonder what they might have done to close the gap between themselves and the less fortunate. Is it accurate to say that the Jew has always known that "he has not helped to force the conscience of the country"? American liberalism, in its twentieth-century version, is at least in part the creation of American Jews, who have known it and taken credit for it. Fiedler's view of the thing follows rather too schematically from the originary opposition he sets up for the essay—Jews as outsiders, Negroes in the American grain—and it is fair to say that the schematicism often gets in the way when Fiedler addresses political and social issues.

Of course Fiedler is not a sitting duck for this or any other kind of criticism. Later in his essay, returning on his own argument in a characteristically graceful way, he concedes that "yet it is not true that the Jew feels no guilt toward the Negro; he merely believes that he *should* feel none." In other words, earlier formulations in the essay are to be, not quite discarded, but refined, though readers are not to think in terms of contradiction or logical error or, even, the habit of changing one's mind in midstream. Rather, contradiction is to be allowed, embraced, welcomed, as a matter of course, as the inevitable price one pays for continuous refinement, expansion, self-correction. Fiedler is to be permitted to keep on moving as the spirit of the inquiry demands, and to deliver as he goes the resonantly categorical formulations around which he organizes his local observations. No wonder he once said of himself, in a panel discussion I chaired in 1980, "often wrong, but never in doubt."

The best thing about Fiedler's essay is not the categorical element, however much it permits him to establish long perspectives and to frame his more immediate observations. Here, as in many other instances, we value most Fiedler's way of speaking candidly on a subject bounded by taboos. This feature of Fiedler's writing often allows him to ground his more eccentric contentions and to move from experience to ideas with a brio that is frequently exhilarating to behold. Recalling his adolescent friendship with a Negro porter who spoke to him gravely about sex and who, in retrospect, he believes he related to as a type, not a person, he goes on to recall a Negro maid and other Negro customers who frequented his father's pharmacy. These recollections, not entirely innocent, lend a certain authority to characterizations that might come under the heading: What "the Jew sees in the Negro." Items include "a care-free and improvident life-style" (which the Jew is said to envy, at least a little), a tendency "to laugh overloud and drink overmuch . . ., to buy spangles at the expense of food, to despise thrift and sobriety and to be so utterly a fool that one is *forced* into taking financial advantage of him." This Negro, Fiedler concludes, is either "real or legendary," but either way, the Jew, who thinks of him in this way, "knows that somehow he has failed an obligation," and Fiedler knows that as an adult he has always been exasperated by what follows from all of this.

Why, Fiedler asks, have we been unable "to treat the Negroes as more than instances of their color"? Not because we are racists, or not only, or primarily, or always. Those who feel that they have failed an obligation are perpetually afraid to do further injury, to make conditions worse than they are by stirring up hostilities. Meanwhile, those who feel that they have been abused and under-estimated and feared are naturally sensitive to every criticism, which is likely to seem unjust, directed at them though not at others, malicious in intent. And so the parties to the conflict, Negro and Jew, learn not to speak truthfully to one another, not to listen to one another even when the situation behooves them to listen.

And so, Fiedler describes as "unendurable" what must as-suredly seem unendurable to an intellectual, if not to others, what was impossible to miss when there were relations to speak of be-tween blacks and Jews. In radical circles, often dominated by Jews, "girls chose Negroes as boy friends *because* they were Negroes." Negro officials were appointed *because* of their color. Much worse, "one could not call a sonofabitch a sonofabitch if he happened to be black," and "a comrade who was sullen, uncooperative and undependable was immune to blame because he was colored." These complaints are not offered as a way of defining what is most important in the situation of black people in America. Fiedler's is not the lament of a man who carries a grievance so large that it obliterates for him the brutal realities with which most black peo-ple contend. But it does speak to Fiedler's sense that relations between Jews and Negroes are contaminated and corrupted by the conditions presently obtaining in our society. If Negroes and Jews cannot speak truthfully to one another they cannot expect to sustain a relationship worthy the name.

Would anyone contend that circumstances have changed for the better in the many years since Fiedler wrote his essay? That they have changed no one will deny. Some blacks are a good deal better off than they were forty years ago. Many others, by far a greater number, live in a destitution far worse than most white Americans thought possible in the 1950s and '60s. No doubt, too, some American Jews continue to be engaged with black people in efforts to rebuild the black community. But in the main, quite as Fiedler's essay would seem to have predicted, American Jews do not much speak to black people. Their interests seem less and less to coincide, and they do not much think it worth their while to struggle with one another, to hear one another out and to try to get past their troubling resentments, guilts and inhibitions. Fiedler's essay, complicated and tendentious, speculative and occasionally wrong-headed, compassionate and provoking, has much to tell us not only about his characteristic ways of getting inside an issue, but about enduring features of American culture.

The Once and Future Fiedler

GEOFFREY GREEN

I first met Leslie Fiedler twenty-seven years ago, in November 1969, at Brown University's Forum on Fiction. I was a freshman, and Leslie Fiedler was, like some medieval knight, jousting with a score of feisty competitors before a packed arena: with one arm he held his antagonists at bay and with the other, he questioned, probed, and challenged the critical assumptions of the forum. He attacked the platitude that writers were either realist or anti-realist and presented his vision of the writer as "magician, a dealer in illusions." Writers, he insisted, are beholden to audiences whose favor they must court by communicating their shared dreams and visions. With a prescience that is astonishing, he warned that "there are a lot of people who call themselves revolutionaries who are the reactionaries of tomorrow." At a party after the symposium I told Leslie that he had rocked the house. He responded: "I've never talked down to anyone in my life. I never will."

This first encounter contains for me the essential components of Leslie Fiedler's greatness—as a writer, literary critic, teacher, friend, and human being: have no fear; always be honest and candid; question the prevailing order; communicate your ideas in plain language to general audiences; empathize with everyone, especially the downtrodden, the voiceless, and the marginalized; be true to yourself and to your art; fuck 'em if they can't take a joke!

Five years later, I arrived at Buffalo as a doctoral student. As English Department chair, Leslie was very busy, but he remembered our meeting and agreed to direct my dissertation. We would meet two, three, sometimes four times a week—it was a Fiedlerian form of psychoanalysis. Our discussions would take place anywhere: twice a week at Leslie's university office, but also at Leslie's study at home, the front stoop of his house, by his pool, waiting in line at the grocery or deli, playing poker, both of us leaning over a grand piano while Anthony Burgess improvised, backstage at the Toronto Convention Center with Bob Dylan, Allen Ginsberg, and O. J. Simpson. We would devote ourselves to our literary projects, our creative writing, the state of the world and of writing. Along with extensive readings in fiction, drama, film, and popular culture, we engaged in mutual *shmoozing*, the most essential activity to Fiedlerian learning. From my meetings with Leslie Fiedler, I derived the broadest possible engagement with the world of cultural activity, an engagement that reflects the best sense of humanism: no boundaries; no high or low; nothing is forbidden.

Of the many invaluable contributions Fiedler made to my doctoral dissertation, I cherish most the advice he gave me early on: write in the first person, be yourself. Speak to the reader directly and don't duck the big questions. Despite Fiedler's emphasis on mass culture and the contemporary, we repeatedly journeyed back to the distant past to chart motifs, influences, mythic resonances, historical patterns. I insist, to this day, that my students strive for just such a compendium of present and past, of trend and tradition.

During my years in L.A., I saw a good deal of Leslie Fiedler. He was there for several months, acting in a movie; he returned at another point to address a science fiction conference. His diversity of interests may be gleaned from where we went (the movie studio; the movie location; the Clark Library; the Huntington Library; a deli on Fairfax Avenue; the Olympic Auditorium for a boxing match; a blues club; a magic club; a variety of parties) and whom we encountered (professors; actors; dwarfs; magicians; circus folk; gypsies; washed-up vaudevillians; pugilists; writers; directors; confidence men and women): in all of this, Leslie Fiedler was absolutely comfortable and at home. He specialized in the melding of categories, in life as well as art: when introduced to my friend, a professor of Renaissance drama, Leslie arranged for him to act in the movie. On another occasion, we (Leslie and Sally, Marcia and I) drove straight from an academic conference at UC Riverside to the Malibu home of Carroll O'Connor, yet another of Leslie's students and friends, to watch *Archie Bunker's Place* on TV.

Leslie Fiedler agreed to be interviewed by me in what is his most expansive formal interview. In that interview, he mused that he was fascinated by "terminal boundaries: beginnings and ends, and the fading of ends into beginnings. Maybe it's the ambiguity of the negative that interests me more than anything: the yes that's under the no, the beginning that's under the end. In a funny way, I think of myself as a secret affirmative writer pretending to be a nihilist. I know that someplace there are absolute categories, I equally know that we never perceive them."

Nineteen years after our first meeting, Leslie Fiedler and I returned to Brown University for the sequel to the conference at which we first had met—this time, both of us were panelists. But I am moved by how pervasively Leslie Fiedler's participation at this "Celebration of Iconoclastic American Fiction" reaffirmed all those heroic intellectual traits that had excited me initially so many years before. First of all, Fiedler seized upon the irony encompassed by the notion of "iconoclastic fiction": implicating himself in the process, Fiedler labeled the conference participants as "iconoclasts with tenure," thus holding up to critical question the prized integrity of the panelists' iconoclasm. Then, naturally aware that these postmodern writers thought about writing as an act of High Modernistic solitary pleasure, Fiedler reminded them that he had invented the term postmodernism and challenged them by inquiring: "for whom do you write?" He "disavow[ed]" his own invented term, alluded to modernism and postmodernism as merely two "forms of romanticism" committed to the "myth . . . of the alienated artist" and reminded one and all that "the separation between the elite audience and the popular audience . . . institutionalized by modernism" was as much a part of our intellectual life as ever before. Fiedler's comments—incisive and provocative—were a veritable roadmap to the central territories of Cultural Studies: once again, I witnessed him in the fray, jousting with characteristic temerity, accuracy, and unfailing aim.

Leslie Fiedler's contribution to American and international intellectual life has been enormous: he invented the first-person critical voice in American letters; he originated what we now call cultural criticism and queer theory; he was an early champion of multiculturalism; he singlehandedly assaulted the elitist literary canon; he established the field of American studies in Europe; he pioneered efforts to understand art in terms of popular and mass culture, society, race, religion, psychology, and our own shared human dreams. Fiedler's life work is now emerging ineluctably into its full degree of radiance and immanence, as is appropriate to his colossal contribution.

On a personal level, Leslie Fiedler convinced me that all of us share a dream where, in his words, "the contradictions are all resolved"; at the same time, the "myth of oneself that one creates is just as real as anything else, so he might as well speak from wherever he is at the moment." He inspired me to be the best

Geoffrey Green I could possibly be since the best we are ever able to achieve is the chronicling of our own personal *farblondjet* reality.

Leslie Fiedler is a supreme Mensch, a writer of deep passion and overflowing personality: the once and future Fiedler. We are—all of us—in his debt for the writing he has given us and continues to give us and for his inimitable presence. His example sets new standards to which we all aspire: he is a true *tzaddik,* a righteous man.

NOTES

The Fiedler quotations in this piece derive from four sources. The quotations I used from the 1969 Brown University symposium are taken from Roger Henkle's symposium report, "Wrestling (American Style) with Proteus," in *Novel* 3 : 3 (Spring 1970): 197–207. My interview with Fiedler, "Reestablishing Innocence: A Conversation with Leslie Fiedler," is in *Novel vs. Fiction: The Contemporary Reformation,* ed. Jackson Cope and Geoffrey Green (Norman, OK: Pilgrim Books, 1981), 133–49. I used the 1988 Brown University symposium Fiedler quotations from the conference proceedings, "'Nothing but Darkness and Talk?': Writers' Symposium on Traditional Values and Iconoclastic Fiction," as they appeared in *Critique* 31 : 4 (Summer 1990): 233–55. All other quotations are reconstructed from memory and verified with Fiedler.

Leslie Fiedler, Freak

Sanford Pinsker

In roughly the same playful spirit that Benjamin Franklin wrote himself down as "Benjamin Franklin, Printer" or that William Faulkner insisted he was "William Faulkner, Farmer," my title means to suggest that the single word Fielder, at the ripe age of eighty, might affix to his name is *freak*. This, of course, was not always the case. In *An End to Innocence* (1955), Fiedler's first collection (and his first book), he made no bones about the fact that the essays contained within would tell the truth "about my world and myself as a liberal, intellectual, writer, American, and Jew." And good as his word, the essays did precisely that, unpacking painful truths about a generation of liberal intellectuals who simply could not bring themselves to believe that Alger Hiss had lied or that Ethel and Julius Rosenberg were traitors. After all, these were people of good will, people on the Left, people, in short, like them. Hiss and the Rosenbergs *couldn't* be guilty as charged because if they were, then so too were they. Even the prospect that this just might be true was enough to cause many liberal intellectuals to close ranks and to engineer distinctions between the Larger Good (to which Hiss and the Rosenbergs were presumably devoted) and what they characterized as small legal infractions.

The sobering news Fiedler delivered was that a generation found itself on trial along with Hiss, and "not, it must be noted, for having struggled toward a better world, but for having substituted sentimentality for intelligence in that struggle, for having failed to understand the moral conditions that must determine the outcome." Thus, Fiedler early on declared himself as one who was persuaded, however reluctantly, to put away ideological certainty for a more complicated movement from a "liberalism of innocence to a liberalism of responsibility." Not surprisingly, the word "controversial" was quickly attached to Fiedler's name and it has hung securely around his neck—as an albatross, a noose, or defining adjective—ever since. Equally unsurprising is Fiedler's mild amusement at this turn of events, although one suspects that on certain afternoons he realizes full well that he has been the architect of his flamboyant, "controversial" public reputation.

Take, for example, what must surely be his most anthologized essay, "Come Back to the Raft Ag'in, Huck Honey!" (1948), an exercise in myth-making that seeks to uncover the deepest rhythms of our American classic. The article gave (and continues to give) many students fits, for it projects an image of male bonding and homoeroticism that forces them to see Huck and Jim in new, often disturbing ways. And like all criticism of real consequence, ridding *Adventures of Huckleberry Finn* of its Fiedlerian stamp proved difficult, if not impossible. No matter that Fiedler's proudest boast was that he had effectively added a line to Twain's classic (as careful readers discover, Jim never utters the words of Fiedler's title), or that responsible Twain scholars felt his chutzpah was the very essence of irresponsibility; the essay took hold.

Love and Death in the American Novel (1960) expanded Fiedler's central thesis about the primal dream of a white male and his dark companion who flee home, hearth, and most of all, domesticity (read: fatherhood) to find freedom over the next hill, in the deepest reaches of the forest, or below the decks of ocean-going ships. Fiedler's brilliant, albeit quirky reading of American archetypes not only explained why our literature is, at best, one boy's book after another, but also that "the failure of the American fictionist to deal with adult heterosexual love and his consequent obsession with death, incest, and innocent homosexuality" had a reach well beyond the printed page. Indeed, it affected daily life and eventually came to influence "the writers in whom the consciousness of our plight is given clarity and form."

These, in short, are the writers who truly matter, and the characters who find a home in our collective unconscious: Natty Bumppo and Rip Van Winkle; the *Pequod's* multicultural sailors; virtually any Poe protagonist; Jim, Huck, and the raft. Later, Fiedler would come clean about his sentimental side, publicly declaring his long-standing affection for Charles Dickens and three-hanky novels such as *Uncle Tom's Cabin,* just as, during the 1970s, he would come out of the sci-fi closet to make extraordinary claims for what most critics dismissed as a minor subgenre.

But that is to get ahead of our story. Fiedler began his long career as a serious scholar-critic (his dissertation was on John Donne), one rightly respected for possessing a first-rate intelligence. Perhaps a single example—drawn from the notebooks of

Lionel Trilling—will suffice. Portions of an entry dated "September 1948" read as follows:

> Read my paper on the novel ["Art and Fortune"] to the English Institute, the response seemed very warm, hearty and prolonged applause.... The effort of reading 7500 words in 50 minutes enormous—to keep up the rhythm and intensity—I did it well, but ended hoarse and exhausted—wanted desperately to be praised by [Mark] Schorer and Fiedler.

Given the mantle of moral gravitas and magisterial authority that would descend on Trilling's shoulders only a few years later (his enormously influential *The Liberal Imagination* would be published in 1950), it seems odd—at least in retrospect—to learn how much Trilling would have valued Fiedler's regard. Two more different personality types could hardly be imagined—Trilling, famous (or perhaps infamous) for his Anglophilism and high-minded cultural pronouncements; Fiedler, rambunctious, free-wheeling, every inch the rebel. Nonetheless, Trilling's self-doubt remained a considerable part of his private life (see Diana Trilling's *The Beginning of the Journey*), partly because he never developed into the novelist he had hoped to be, and partly because Trilling was a very different person away from the lectern or writing desk. Fiedler, by contrast, always wore his self-assurance easily. What you saw was what you got—and this merely increased as the years added girth to his middle and gray to his hair and beard. Indeed, the young critic who often seemed to specialize in unpacking outrageous sexual myths came more and more to look like a satyr from some classical text.

Love and Death in the American Novel may have rigged the canonical deck (when writers such as Nathaniel Hawthorne or Henry James did not especially fit Fiedler's thesis, he tended to sacrifice nuance for overall unity, complexity for emphasis), but its impact was enormous. Undergraduate teachers sometimes acknowledged Fiedler's influence, but most of the time they simply cribbed their lectures from its pages. And undergraduates fortunate enough to lay their hands on the book itself (I number myself among them) figured that they were highlighting paragraphs delivered from no less than the Delphic oracle. The relentless tension between eros and thanatos explained, well, *everything*—or so it seemed at a time when most literary critics were dutifully churning out New Critical readings heavy on paradox, irony, and ambivalence.

And when Fiedler's long sojourn (exile?) in the West finally came to an end (with the exception of two years doing postgraduate study at Harvard, he had taught at the University of Montana from 1941 to 1964), he was fully prepared to move from influential literary presence to cultural guru. SUNY–Buffalo was then the Hot Center, and in an English department that had collected the likes of Charles Olsen, Robert Creeley, and John Barth, Fiedler—Samuel Clemens Professor of English—seemed the very personification of the cat's meow. What many forget, however, is that the same Fiedler who enjoyed nothing more than "holding court" at Modern Language Association meetings (during the days when they were genuinely exciting) was also the Fiedler who came to the office early—and who stayed late—poring over novels and assorted critical tomes. Granted, he generally tried not to let his readers see him sweat (although this is not to say he couldn't fire off a fiercely pedantic aside when the occasion required it), but what caused those aping his style to fall on their collective faces was precisely that which kept Fiedler looking fresh and provocative in the best sense. I am referring, of course, to intelligence, the one commodity that T. S. Eliot felt was essential to any sound literary criticism. Fiedler had this in abundance.

Perhaps a personal anecdote will help to explain just how central Fiedler was during the days when his paragraphs threw off insights with the happy abandon of a wet puppy saturating a living room rug, and young would-be academics hung on his every word. He provided measures of aid-and-comfort not easily found in other corners of the academy. Not surprisingly, it was his reflections on Jewish-American literature that most intrigued me, not only because the much-celebrated Jewish-American renaissance was in high gear during the mid-sixties, but also because I was then pecking away on a dissertation about Sholem Aleichem, I. B. Singer, Bernard Malamud, and Saul Bellow. To be sure, there were other critical voices in my head—Alfred Kazin, Irvin Howe, Robert Alter, Ted Solotaroff—But Fiedler's mattered most. No doubt this accounts for that recurrent dream I kept having as I pushed my chapters up the long hill leading to a Ph.D. It was always late at night—very late—and in the dream I would be working in what made do for a study. Suddenly the phone rings and I paddle off to answer it.

"Hello," a voice exclaims. "Is this Sanford Pinsker?"

"Yes, it is," I reply, dong my best to imitate the seriousness appropriate to a real writer. "And to whom am I speaking?"

"This is Leslie Feidler, calling from SUNY–Buffalo."

In a shot all my efforts on behalf of the "cool" vanished. "Professor Fiedler, what can I do for you?" I replied in a voice equally divided between excitement and nervousness.

"Well, what I wanted to know is this: Are you the Sanford Pinsker who's writing a dissertation on the schlemiel?"

"Yes, it is. I mean, that's me!"

"Well, screw off. That territory's mine." With that the phone goes dead and I awake from a dream turned nightmare, the very thing that Fiedler had made his specialty.

I should add, by the way, that Fiedler much enjoyed my moment of graduate school angst when he heard the story during my first visit to Buffalo in 1967. Granted, it reveals much more about me than it does about Fiedler, but I offer it now as an indication of how centrally important Fiedler was in the those days. What happened in the decades that followed—when Fiedler moved from guru to "freak"—is a sadder, more sobering story, and one I relate with some reluctance. For Fiedler meant much—probably *too* much—to me at a certain point in my development; and while I certainly don't want to sound ungrateful, it is equally true that I no longer wish to be his disciple.

The change did not occur during the period when Fiedler, an outspoken advocate for the legalization of marijuana, found himself in hot water with the local gendarmes. *Being Busted* (1969), Fiedler's account of how the overly long arm of the law poked itself into his house (he was accused of "maintaining a premise" where pot was inhaled), added yet another moniker to his list— namely, *martyr.* Much of the brouhaha surrounding that time, that place now seems terribly dated (politicians regularly fess up to youthful indiscretions, and life, including one's political life, goes on without so much as missing a beat. Not so when the full force of the System—as it was known in those days—singled somebody out for special attention. Fiedler's countercultural bravado made him an accident waiting to happen; and when it did, he turned a very bad patch (financially and otherwise) into a piece of New Journalism that could hold its own with the best practitioners of nonfiction's latest wrinkle.

More important perhaps was the way that the book generated sympathy—not only for Fiedler's embattled circumstances, but also for a more enlightened, less up-tight response to where the country itself was headed. For a brief, psychedelic moment, the Age of Aquarius, with its tie-dyes and bell bottoms, its love beads and uninhibited sex, seemed to loom just around the corner. Not surprisingly, Fiedler began spreading the good news, arguing that we needed to *Cross the Border—Close the Gap* (1972) and in general embrace whatever traveled under the wide umbrella of what he called "the New Mutants." At the time even Fiedler did not know—at least not consciously—that he was headed toward the moment when he would discover in "freaks" the ultimate Other he had been looking for since the salad days when he specialized in blacks and Jews, homosexuals and Indians.

In short, Fiedler's obsession with the marginalized had a long pedigree. All blacks are Jews, he was fond of declaring, and under the skin, both are Indians. The confusion among identities—racial, ethnic, sexual—often grew so pronounced that even Fiedler's closest friends didn't know if he was *davening* or doing a rain dance. Perhaps it didn't matter, for in the end what Fiedler celebrates is his version of the national myth, one in which the disabling role of cultural guilt can only be overturned by the liberating dream.

Unfortunately, what sounded bracing, if a bit giddy, during the early seventies began to seem dated, even dusty, just a few years later. And when Fiedler came clear about his disaffections with traditional criticism and responsible teaching, the die, as they say, was cast. *What Was Literature?* (1982) is an extended *apologia* for the life Fiedler has been leading since the heyday of the mid-sixties, full of sound and fury and not a few *mea culpas*. If a perennial innocent such as Holden Caulfield sees life as a pitched battle between the "phonies" and the Uncorrupted Youth, Fiedler divided academe into the dryasdusts and himself. And as with Holden, the generous measures of self-congratulation take their toll. Granted, Fiedler has more "voices" at his command (the playful, the ironic, the insightful, the learned), but he shares with Holden, with Huck Finn, with all true-blue American outlaws the same resistance to "required" *anything* and the same wide, subversive streak. No doubt ol' Holden would object to reading and writing about Tarzan, *Uncle Tom's Cabin, Gone with The Wind,* or other Fiedler favorites, and no doubt one of Fiedler's unsympathetic critics has already pointed this out. For, like it or not, Fiedler is part of the literary establishment, however much he prefers to think of himself as a "barbarian *within* the gates." After all, he makes out syllabi, holds forth at appointed hours, sets examination questions, gives grades, and not least of all, picks up a healthy paycheck. Real barbarians—within the gates or beyond them—do none of these things. More important, however, is the fact that no matter how with-it Fiedler imagines his assignments and lectures are, the bald truth of the matter is that students are likely to plow enormous amounts of extracurricular energy into projects they insist on defining for themselves, thank you very much—everything from complicated geographies of Tolkien's Middle Earth or trivia about *Star Trek* to (probably more commonplace) how Luke and Laura are doing on *General Hospital.*

The rub, alas, is that Fiedler desperately sought their approval and, worse, their adulation:

> To confess openly the passionate interest in pop which I have long shared with . . . students, but have lied about to myself as well as to them, would not just ease a classroom situation which I have come to feel intolerable, but help join together the sundered larger community, by making the university a place where we are not further separated from each other. Like all else entertained on the level of full consciousness, religion, for instance, and political ideology, what used to be "literature" divides us against ourselves; while what used to be called "trash," rooted like our dreams and nightmares in shared myth and fantasy, touches us all at a place where we have never been psychically sundered each from each.

Fiedler's vision is unashamedly utopian. It posits a university that bridges all gaps—teachers and students, fathers and sons, literatures both High and low, cultures both majority and minority—and teaches the wider world to do likewise.

Fiedler is, of course, hardly alone in exiting from the closets of popular culture (where those who had been taught better secretly binged on sci-fi or comic books), but he burst forth with more pizzaz than most. Even his "shame" had a priggish smack to it, as if he knew all along that High Culture was a lot of hooey. And if this upsets the fuddy-duddies at staid Harvard or Structuralist Yale, so much the better. Behind their smug, starchy indignation lies a vast reservoir of fear. They are afraid of myth, of story, of song—indeed, of anything primordial, inarticulate, unstructured, and genuinely *moving.* Besides, *Freaks* (1978) had given Fiedler a taste of mass cult popularity, and he hankered for more. But in much the same way that the sixties—with its communes and countercultural consciousness—slipped down the memory hole only to be replaced, and exploited, by exercises in choreographed nostalgia (the recent effort to reestablish Woodstock Nation springs to mind as a sad, predictable example), *Freaks* was more curiosity than agent of psychic change. Nonetheless, Fiedler kept his reserved seat on the popular culture bandwagon, hoping against hope that the youth revolution would make a comeback and that he could be its pied piper even as he entered his eighth decade.

Fiedler's latest book, *Tyranny of the Normal* (his twenty-fifth), is a collection of nine essays that began their life as talks delivered to a wide variety of nonliterary audiences: a World Conference of Theologians, the inaugural ceremonies for the Year of the Disabled held at the United Nations headquarters in New York City, a meeting of physicians. Fiedler has *always* been a restless academic, someone who much prefers a lively give-and-take with nonspecialists than boring conversations about the literary niceties with his English department colleagues, just as he has, for nearly fifty years, found ever-newer ways to generate both controversy and attention. Given his lifelong interest in myth-making and what has come to be known as "cultural studies," it is hardly surprising that Fiedler would be drawn to ruminating about theology and biomedical ethics—for these are the places in contemporary culture where his readings of Shakespeare and Dickens, American literature and science fiction, now seem most applicable. Throughout his long career, Fiedler tells us, he has been

> obsessed with the image of the Stranger, the Outsider, but chiefly as it is embodied in fictional portrayals of the ethnic Other. I have concentrated, that is to say, on the myths of the Negro, the Jew, and the Indian in novel and poems written by—and primarily for—WASP Americans. More recently, however, it occurred to me that for all of us able to think of ourselves as "normal," there is a more ultimate Other. That is, of course, the Freak, the Monster, the congenital malformation: a fellow-human born too larger or too small, with too many or too few limbs, hair in the wrong places or ambiguous sexual organs.

The result of these ruminations was *Freaks,* the book that propelled him from academic stardom to show-biz fame. It represents the point at which Fiedler no longer seemed much captivated by Jewish-American fiction or, indeed, by the bulk of Jewish-American experience. The golden age of that ethnicity is now over, largely because assimilation has so taken its toll that Jewish Americans seem now entirely like everybody else. This being so— at least for Fiedler—he quickly found other candidates to embrace or to vilify: the New Mutants (his term) who emerged from the Cultural Revolution of the late 1960s and set New Age religion into motion; politically correct euphemisms such as "physically challenged"; organ donation and how it is that most people reject the idea; and perhaps most of all, the ways in which our pervasive "tyranny of the normal" may ultimately lead to what Fiedler warns is a dangerous Cult of the Eternally Young and Fabulously Slim. Add to all this Fiedler's candor about "love and death" as he himself approaches eighty and the result is a collection packed with intriguing insights at one point, errant foolishness at another, and, always, marvelously engaged writing.

Take, for example, what he says about the New Church of "actual Visionaries and Saints." Originally published in 1973, "The Rebirth of God and the Death of Man" is premised on an ongoing Revolution of the young who stay perpetually young—by abandoning bourgeois Amerika (spelt with a *k* to emphasize its links to fascism), establishing communes, and blissing out on drugs. Granted, Fielder worries a bit about the shivery implications of a movement that regards health itself as bourgeois (hygiene, as he rightly points out, was never a strong suit with hippies), but, in general, he writes about the counterculture with large measures of enthusiasm. The rub, of course, is that none of Fiedler's giddy predictions came true. Thus, when one reads, in 1996, about the mass of disaffected young who have turned *The Whole Earth Catalogue* into a secular bible, the result seems more history lesson than an exercise in contemporary analysis. Put another way, Fiedler (alas) seems stuck in a time warp of his own making. As a pop culture maven, he would be better off watching selected episodes of *Friends, Seinfeld,* or even *Beverly Hills 90210.* That's where, my students tell me, the *real* action is.

One the other hand, I have more than a little sympathy with Fiedler's assessment of social engineering efforts such as the much-ballyhooed "Year of the Disabled" (he finds the emphasis on new, politically correct nomenclature well-meaning, but ultimately deluded, if not downright hypocritical). Roughly the same thing is true of our new obsession with "child abuse," as we not only forget how entangled in myth generational conflicts always were, but also how downright irritating—if not altogether nasty—children can be. Does that mean that Fiedler condones abuse per se? Hardly. Rather, it is that we need, as he puts it, "to mediate as best we can our psychic dilemma: the ever more intolerable discrepancy between what all of us secretly suspect children are and what a few of us still feel obliged to pretend them to be; as well as that between the child-rearing behavior we advocate and what we secretly wish we had never enough to practice even if we do not actually practice it."

Fiedler's RX—to the theologians, doctors, and social workers he now addressed with some frequency—is the vicarious release of literature. At times this makes for a hard sell, as doctors, for example, do not especially want to be lumped into the same category as Dr. Frankenstein, Dr. Jekyll, and Dr. Moreau. Myth, along with the literature that most deeply addresses it, makes for night sweats. And when the topic turns to freaks, the ante only goes up. But Fiedler insists that it is "especially important for us to realize that *there are no normals,* at a moment when we are striving desperately to eliminate freaks, to normalize the world."

A "normal" world—this was never Fiedler's dream, even in the days when he defined himself as a "liberal, intellectual, writer, American, and Jew." But his affinity with "freaks"—in what often has the scary look of psychological doubling—is another matter, sensationalist on one hand, small-r romantic on the other. I cannot help feeling that there are worthier subjects for intellectuals to tackle. But this is itself an old story, one dating back to my differences with Fiedler about pop culture and the college classroom. At his worst, he reminds me of the burnt-out English professor (beautifully played by Donald Sutherland) in *Animal House* who tells his students that he doesn't much care for Milton either. Such confessions cannot fail to garner laughs and probably great teaching evaluations; and in the context of an escapist comedy, one out to detail the triumph of the young over their authoritarian elders, the line makes perfect sense. But I, for one, take Fiedler at his word when he sprinkles dirt on the grave of capital-L Literature, and find myself unamused. There are times when we are enjoined to put away childish things, and times, however difficult, when we should do precisely that. Fiedler became one of those things, even though I confess to reading each of his subsequent books with interest and even large swathes of delight. But the old magic just wasn't there. The graduate student I was when Fiedler played a prominent role in my dream life was gradually replaced by an older, probably no wiser incarnation. In the 1980s I no longer seemed intellectually tethered to the Fiedler in his seventies.

Still, at a time when critical debates are no longer conducted in plain English and when most expressions of "theory" are as tedious as they are impenetrable, I think some kind words about Fiedler are in order. It is not just that he wrote with brio and brilliance, or even that he often fails to get full credit for pioneering aspects of feminist criticism, culture studies, or queer theory, but, rather, that his passion for what the imagination might tell us about life stayed the course. His career needs no special pleading, much less apology. The books are enough, and they always were.

Poem

LEONARD COHEN

You have kept it in your face
the love of women
the love of choirs
leaning over the Talmudic tablecloth
leaning over the American moonlight
        like the shyest gargoyle
who will not become angry or old

Contributors

Novelist and Professor Emeritus in the Johns Hopkins Writing Seminars, JOHN BARTH was a colleague of Leslie Fiedler's at SUNY–Buffalo from 1965 through 1973.

ROBERT BOYERS edits *Salmagundi* and is Tisch Professor of Arts and Letters at Skidmore College. His books include *Atrocity and Amnesia: The Political Novel Since 1945* and *After the Avant-Garde: Essays on Art and Culture.*

Singer and songwriter LEONARD COHEN is also the author of the novel *Beautiful Losers.*

JAMES M. COX is Professor Emeritus of English at Dartmouth College and the author of *Mark Twain: The Fate of Humor* and *Recovering Literature's Lost Ground: Essays in American Autobiography.*

JOSEPH DEWEY teaches English at the University of Pittsburgh and is the author of *In a Dark Time: The Apocalyptic Temper in the American Novel of the Nuclear Age* as well as essays on William Goyen, George Garrett, and Richard Powers.

Editor of *The Hollins Critic,* R. H. W. DILLARD is director of the creative writing program at Hollins College. He is the author of *Omniphobia, Understanding George Garrett,* and *After Borges.*

IRVING FELDMAN is Professor of English at SUNY–Buffalo and a MacArthur Fellow. His poetry collections include *All of Us Here* and *The Life and Letters.*

GEOFFREY GREEN is Professor of English at San Francisco State University and co-editor of *Critique.* His books include *Freud and Nabokov* and *Literary Criticism and the Structures of History.*

SUSAN GUBAR is Distinguished Professor of English at Indiana University. She is author of *Racechanges,* co-author of *The Madwoman in the Attic,* and co-editor of *The Norton Anthology of Literature by Women.*

Professor of English at the University of Delaware, JAY L. HALIO is the author or editor of more than twenty books, including editions of *The Merchant of Venice* and *King Lear.*

BROOKE HORVATH is author of *Consolation at Ground Zero* and an editor with *The Review of Contemporary Fiction.*

STEVEN G. KELLMAN is Ashbel Smith Professor of Comparative Literature at The University of Texas at San Antonio, author of *The Self-Begetting Novel*, and co-editor of *Into the Tunnel: Essays on William Gass's Novel*.

DAVID KETTERER is Professor of English at Concordia University and author of *Canadian Science Fiction and Fantasy, New Worlds for Old: The Apocalyptic Imagination, Science Fiction, and American Literature*, and *Imprisoned in a Tesseract: The Life and Work of James Blish*.

R. W. B. LEWIS's books include *The American Adam, Edith Wharton: A Biography, The Picaresque Saint*, and *The Jameses: A Family Narrative*.

IRVING MALIN is the author of *William Faulkner: An Interpretation, New American Gothic*, and *Jews and Americans* and co-editor of *Into the Tunnel: Essays on William Gass's Novel*.

SANFORD PINSKER is Shadek Professor of Humanities at Franklin and Marshall College and editor of *Academic Questions*. His books include *The Schlemiel as Metaphor* and *Bearing the Bad News: Contemporary American Literature and Culture*.

HAROLD SCHECHTER teaches English at Queens College and is the author of *The A-Z Encyclopedia of Serial Killers, The Bosom Serpent: Folklore and Popular Art*, and *Original Sin: The Visionary Art of Joe Coleman*.

DANIEL SCHWARZ is Professor of English at Cornell University. His books include *The Transformation of the English Novel, 1890–1930, Reading Joyce's Ulysses*, and, most recently, *Reconfiguring Modernism: Explorations in the Relationship Between Modern Art and Modern Literature*.

DAVID R. SLAVITT is a novelist (*The Cliff*), poet (*Epic and Epigram*), and translator (*The Oresteia*).

DANIEL WALDEN is Professor of American Studies, English, and Comparative Literature at Pennsylvania State University and editor of *Studies in American Jewish Literature*. His books include *On Being Jewish, On Being Black*, and *Twentieth Century American Jewish Fiction Writers*.

MARK ROYDEN WINCHELL teaches English at Clemson University and is working on a biography of Leslie Fiedler.

Index